THE ORIENTAL INSTITUTE OF THE UNIVERSITY OF CHICAGO

STUDIES IN ANCIENT ORIENTAL CIVILIZATION · NO. 35

John A. Wilson

STUDIES IN HONOR OF JOHN A. WILSON

SEPTEMBER 12, 1969

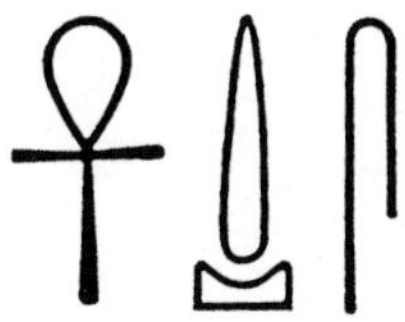

THE ORIENTAL INSTITUTE OF THE UNIVERSITY OF CHICAGO

STUDIES IN ANCIENT ORIENTAL CIVILIZATION · NO. 35

THE UNIVERSITY OF CHICAGO PRESS · CHICAGO · ILLINOIS

Library of Congress Catalog Card Number: 76-81081

THE UNIVERSITY OF CHICAGO PRESS, CHICAGO 60637
The University of Chicago Press, Ltd., London, W.C. 1

FOR JOHN A. WILSON ON HIS SEVENTIETH BIRTHDAY SEPTEMBER 12, 1969

A man's impact on his fellows may be keenly felt, but it is not easily measured against some absolute scale. Nonetheless, if the impact is at all significant, it is fit that those who have profited by it should take public note of the fact, acknowledge their debt, and offer their appreciation. That a community of scholars—his students and colleagues at the Oriental Institute—should select a man's seventieth birthday as the appropriate time for such acknowledgments is, of course, arbitrary and conventional, for this is not a time for a grand summation but rather only a pause to take a subtotal. And so the contributors to this volume take the occasion of John A. Wilson's seventieth birthday as an opportunity to offer to him these tokens of their esteem for the many contributions he has made.

One of the contributors, when only a beginning student, asked Professor Wilson to characterize his scholarly self. The reply was that he thought of himself as a grammarian. It is the transcendence of such narrow confines which has introduced his name into an arena seldom entered by members of the Egyptological community. It may be true that Professor Wilson began as a grammarian—he has always emphasized the comprehension of and sensitivity to the surviving Egyptian texts—but he has gone much further. He has sought to clarify some problems for his colleagues and has made important contributions to the specialized literature. But *The Burden of Egypt* has brought to student and layman alike an insightful and clearly composed attempt to explain the nature of ancient Egyptian civilization. *Signs and Wonders upon Pharaoh* has conveyed to a wide audience the romance of America's role in the rediscovery of Egyptian antiquity. In his writing, in his teaching, and in public lectures, John A. Wilson has sought to make ancient Egypt intelligible and meaningful to the modern world.

Nor are his labors conducted exclusively in the library or at the desk, for he is also a doer, an activist. He has served in the field in Egypt as an epigrapher and as field director. He has been Director of the Oriental Institute, a demanding job. When the needs of a new Egypt threatened the relics of the old, he gave exhaustingly of his time and energy.

John Wilson is more than grammarian or philologist or epigrapher. He is a cultural historian in the broadest possible sense and a gifted teacher in a classroom far larger than that in which several of the contributors sat. It is not at all mean praise to say of John A. Wilson that he cares.

In the words of the ancient texts, we say: "May he live, prosper, and be healthy like Re forever and ever."

GERALD E. KADISH

HARPUR COLLEGE
STATE UNIVERSITY OF NEW YORK AT BINGHAMTON
January 1969

TABLE OF CONTENTS

LIST OF TEXT FIGURES

ZUR ÜBERSETZUNG DER PRÄPOSITIONEN UND KONJUNKTIONEN *m* UND *ḏr*

RUDOLF ANTHES

Die Übersetzung von Präpositionen in unsicherem Kontext ist problematisch. Wir sind wohl alle versucht, die uns gerade passende Bedeutung in die Präposition hineinzulegen, und dieser bequeme Weg wird dem Anfänger besonders nahegelegt, wenn verschiedene Übersetzungen in lexikalischer Form zur Auswahl angeboten werden. Vermutlich bin ich nicht der einzige, der bei seinen Schülern und sich selbst darauf dringt, daß man im Zweifelsfall zunächst auf die mutmaßliche Grundbedeutung der Präposition sich besinnt und prüft, ob die im jeweils vorliegenden Text vermutete Bedeutung in Einklang mit ihr steht. Ist solcher Einklang nicht erkennbar, so ist das ein Warnzeichen. Diese Methode hat ihre Gefahren: es ist eine Rechnung mit zwei Unbekannten, nämlich der Grundbedeutung und der jeweils vermuteten Bedeutung; sie darf nicht schematisch angewandt werden, weil mannigfache Faktoren des Sprachgebrauchs, der Sprachentwicklung maßgebend beitragen können zur Verwendung dieser oder jener Präposition; auch mag es von vornherein debattierbar sein, ob wir eine Grundbedeutung bei jeder Präposition annehmen dürfen; und sicher gehören Überlegung und Erfahrung zu dem Urteil darüber, wieweit wir den Einklang zwischen Grundbedeutung und jeweiliger Bedeutung pressen dürfen. Aber es lohnt sich doch wohl, die genannte Methode zu exemplifizieren wenigstens an *m* und *ḏr*, die sich mir für diesen Zweck zunächst angeboten haben.[1]

Für *m* hat mir seit langem die Annahme sich bewährt, daß es die Grundbedeutung "in" hat auch im Sinne der Gleichsetzung des (wie ich hier sagen darf) Gefäßes mit seinem Inhalt. Die Ursprünglichkeit dieser identifizierenden Funktion des *m* wird m.E. beispielhaft nahegelegt durch den Ausdruck *ḫpr m*. Das ist für den Ägypter offensichtlich zunächst ein einheitlicher Begriff, während wir ihn je nachdem mit "entstehen aus" oder "werden zu" übersetzen müssen.[2] Wenn aber für diese Phrase auch die naheliegende Deutung herange-

[1] Ursprünglich zielte diese Untersuchung auf das schwierige *n*, aber *m* und *ḏr*, die als methodologische Beispiele vorangestellt werden sollten, haben den verfügbaren Raum und die gesetzte Frist reichlich ausgefüllt: die komplexe Situation der Übersetzungen von *ḏr* wurde mir nur schrittweise klar.

[2] Demonstriert an Memphitische Theologie, Zl. 35 f., in *JNES* XVIII 196, n. 38. Totb. Nav. 17, 28, *ỉnk pwy ḫpr ỉm.ṯn*, mag verschiedenartig übersetzt werden können, aber für den Ägypter bedeutete es gewiß "ich bin es, der aus euch (scil. den Vorfahren, *ỉmyw bꜣḥ*) entstan-

zogen werden mag, daß *m* analog zu anderen Präpositionen nicht nur das Verharren "in" sondern auch die Bewegungen "hinein in" und "heraus aus" bezeichnen könnte, so reicht das nicht aus für das Verständnis von z.B. *Pyr.* § 1652 c, *iššn.k m Šw* "du hast ausgespieen in Schu"; es bedeutet, daß der Speichel zu Schu geworden ist, aber in der Ausdrucksform liegt die Identifizierung des Atum mit seinem Speichel, dieses Speichels mit Schu und folgerichtig die mythologische Identifizierung des Erzeugers mit dem Erzeugten, die auch in *ḫpr m* liegt.

Diese identifizierende Eigenart von *m*, die übrigens vielleicht auch im deutschen und englischen "in" ursprünglich liegt,[3] ist in allen bei Gardiner, *Eg. Grammar* (3. Auflage) § 162, Abs. 1–7a, gegebenen Bedeutungen und Zitaten erkennbar. Das *m* "of instrument" (*ibid.* Abs. 7) kann aus dem räumlichen "in" nicht verständlich werden, wohl aber aus dem identifizierenden "in" auf dem Wege über den Begriff, daß Kleidung und Werkzeug Ergänzungen und damit Bestandteile des Lebenden sind, und daß z.B. *sḫrw* "Plan", "Rat" verwirklicht ist durch das Geschehen. Das sog. *m* "of concomitance" (Abs. 7a) kann m.E. in allen von Smither und Gunn (*JEA* XXV 166 ff.) genannten Beispielen aus dem A.R. und M.R. als das *m* "of instrument" verstanden werden im Sinne von "versehen sein mit", z.B. "mit 300 Eseln", "mit einem Heeresgefolge".[4] Zum *m* "of separation" (Abs. 8) vgl. oben die Bemerkung zu *ḫpr m*. *Šw m* "leer, frei von" ist nicht nur sprachlich, sondern wohl auch sachlich in Analogie zu *mḥ m*, *ᶜpr m* "gefüllt, versehen mit" verständlich, also im Sinne der Gleichsetzung von der Leerheit der

---

den ist, und der nun wieder eines wird mit euch". Vgl. *JNES* XVIII 211 für die dem *ḫpr* ähnliche Lage bei *prì m* "herauskommen aus", das in der alten Sprache auch "herauskommen in etw. hinein" (*Pyr.* § 632 c) heißt, und anscheinend auch "herauskommen als" (*Pyr.* §§ 199 a, 1875 a–b; s. auch § 2206 c).

[3] Z.B. "in Bronze gießen", "in Bargeld zahlen", "im Urtext lesen" identifizieren das Gießen, Zahlen, Lesen und ihr Objekt mit dem durch "in" bezeichneten Nomen. Vgl. weiter z.B. "ähnlich im Aussehen", "siehst Helena in jedem Weibe". In Merriam-Webster, *Dictionary*, ist die Bedeutung von "in" vielfältig aufgezählt wie die von *m* in Gardiner, *Eg. Grammar* (3. Auflage) § 162, und in weitgehender Übereinstimmung zwischen "in" und *m*.

[4] Ein gutes Beispiel zusätzlich zu den von Gunn *JEA* XXV 158, Nr. 1, genannten Zitaten ist *prì.f m ḥḏ Gb* "er tritt hervor mit der Keule des Geb" (Osirishymnus des Amenmose im Louvre, Zl. 6 und 18–19), das ich schon *ZÄS* LXXXVI 85 über das *m instrumentalis* erklärt habe. Der Unterschied zwischen dem *m* "of concomitance" und *ḥnᶜ*, den Smither, Gunn und Gardiner verschieden bewertet haben, erscheint deutlich bei Verwendung der groben Übersetzungen "*m* = versehen mit", "*ḥnᶜ* = gesellt, gepaart mit". Ist das richtig, so erscheint mir Smithers Übersetzung seines Zitates Nr. 5 (Zweiter Hekanecht-Brief, Zl. 5) im Sinne von "ich habe den heutigen Tag erreicht *ìm.ṯn ḥr sᶜnḫ.ṯn* (belastet) mit euch in der Fürsorge für eueren Unterhalt" passender als die des Herausgebers der Papyri, James, der "among you" statt "with you" setzt: der Vater spricht als Versorger und Oberhaupt der Familie, nicht als irgendeiner von ihnen. NB! zu dem von James hier herangezogenen Totb. Nav. 17, 28 s.o. Anm. 2.

Schale mit dem in ihr erwarteten Kern. Sogar in allen idiomatischen Verbindungen (Abs. 9)[5] glaube ich den Grundgedanken des "eine Einheit herstellen mit" zu finden, so auch bei *ỉnỉ m* im Sinne von "sich verlassen auf".[6] Bei *m* als Konjunktion (Abs. 10–12)[5] ist der Ausdruck der Einheit m.E. offensichtlich.

Zwei von Gardiner § 162 genannte auffallende idiomatische Redewendungen verlangen aber ausdrückliche Klärung. *Mdw m* "speak against" (Abs. 9) ist von Edel, *Altäg. Grammatik*, § 758 k, unter einer Rubrik "*m* = feindlich gegen" zusammengefaßt mit einem einzigen anderen Beispiel, nämlich *wdỉ m* "feindlich Hand legen an" nach *Urk.* I 102, Zl. 12. Aber ich kann das dort und auch in *Urk.* I 106, Zl. 5, sich findende *wdỉ* (ohne Objekt) *m śnw.f* nur verstehen als "in seinen Gleichgestellten (und mit ihm identifizierend) das hineinlegen, was man hineinlegen will oder kann",[7] dem Zusammenhange nach im Sinne von Kompetenzstreitigkeiten, "Übergriffe machen in den Zuständigkeitsbereich des Kollegen".[8] So bleibt m.E. auch bei Edel nur *mdw m* als Beispiel für scheinbares "*m* = gegen". Soweit es sich dabei um eine Sache handelt, also z.B. "gegen ein Schriftstück sprechen", so dürfen wir es vielleicht verstehen analog den deutschen gleichartigen Phrasen "hineinreden in etw.", "Einspruch erheben in (gegen) etw.", wobei ägyptisch wie deutsch das *m* "in" aus seiner

[5] Je ein Fall von Abs. 9 und 11c ist im folgenden besprochen.

[6] Gunn in *Recueil de travaux* XXXIX 105 zitiert für *ỉnỉ m* "have recourse to" Lebensm. Zl. 116 ff., 123 ff.; Ptahh. 231, 348–49; Ichernofret, Zl. 6. *ᵓInỉ r dmỉ* heißt nicht "holen von oder aus der Stadt". Also dürfen wir Ptahh. 348 L2, 𓂜 *ỉntw ḥtp m ḏrḏrỉ*, wegen der Prisse-Var., 𓂜 *ỉntw ḥtpt r dmỉ*, gewiß nicht verstehen als "one does not obtain satisfaction from a stranger" (Gunn, ähnlich Žába mit "obtenir"), und "Frieden bringen (vgl. *Wb.* III 193, 2) zur Stadt, in den Fremden" würde anscheinend nicht in den Kontext passen. *ᵓInỉ ḥtp*(*t*) wird vielmehr bedeuten, absolut gebraucht in Totb. Nav. 110 Einl. 8 Aa: "Einverständnis herbeiführen", und hier "zum Einverständnis gelangen mit (*m* der Person, *r* der kollectivischen Sache)". Das objektlose *ỉnỉ m* (Ptahh. 349 L2) muß nach dem Textzusammenhang ungefähr das Gleiche bedeuten, bringt vielleicht eine Steigerung: "(348) Man findet kein Einverständnis mit einem Fremden, (349) aber man verläßt sich auf den Freund im Elend". Zum objektlosen Gebrauch von *ỉnỉ* "das herbeiführen, was man herbeiführen will oder muß" vgl. denselben bei *ỉrỉ* "tun" und *rdỉ* "geben" im A.R. nach *JEA* LIV 31 ff.

[7] Zum objektlosen *wdỉ* s. den Hinweis in Anm. 6.

[8] Ich übersetze die Una-Stellen mit dem in Einzelheiten nötigen Vorbehalt: "Ich war derjenige, der die Anweisungen für sie traf, während mein Amt das des *ỉmy-rꜣ-ḫnty-š* war, auf Grund der Richtigkeit meiner Stellung, damit nicht einer von ihnen (scil. den Beamten und Hauptleuten) übergriff in die Zuständigkeit seines Kollegen" (*Urk.* I 102) und "ich versah den Dienst des Vorstehers von Oberägypten für ihn (scil. den König), damit alles reibungslos verlief, und damit ich als solcher(?) nicht übergreifen mußte in die Zuständigkeit eines (? seines, d.h. des Vorstehers?) Kollegen" (*Urk.* I 106). Professor Baer verweist mich hierzu freundlichst auf Ptahh. Dévaud-Žába 125, *bwt kꜣ pw wdt* (Var. *ḏꜣt*) *ỉm.f*, für das ich nun die Übersetzung wage "der Ka liebt es garnicht, wenn man in seine Sphäre sich einmischt (Var. sich ihm in den Weg stellt)", im Sinne von "man soll bekanntlich die Leute nicht beim Essen stören"; das ist also eine Zwischen-Sentenz, die die Beziehung des Suffixes *-f* des folgenden Satzes auf den vorher genannten Gastgeber nicht aufhebt. Eine einfachere, aber blassere Übersetzung von *wdỉ m* würde sein: "jmd. in seiner Tätigkeit behindern".

identifizierenden Bedeutung besser verstanden werden kann als aus der räumlichen. Als "sprechen gegen jmd." kommt bloßes *mdw m* nach *Wb.* II 179, 17–18 erst in der Zeit des Neuägyptischen vor. In den älteren Texten lautet die Phrase entweder *mdw.f m rn.ỉ ḏw* oder *mdw.f ỉm.ỉ ḏw*[9] "er nennt mich (er spricht von mir) indem es böse ist". Damit ist also eine böse, gehässige Identifizierung der Rede mit dem Namen, der Person des Anderen gemeint, und aus dieser Phrase ist das spätere Idiom *mdw m* "Böses reden gegen jmd." unmittelbar verständlich. Die Konjunktion "*m* = though" (Abs. 11c) findet sich anscheinend nur in *m mšḏḏ ỉb.f* und ähnlichem. Aber wörtlich übersetzt heißt, als Beispiel für alle, *Urk.* IV 969, Zl. 2–3 "(ich sorge dafür, daß auch der Freche dem Gesetze folgt) *m mšḏḏ ỉb.f* indem sein Herz unwillig ist". In unserer Ausdrucksweise mit "obgleich", wie wir "though" hier übersetzen würden, sehen wir den Gegensatz zwischen Tun und Wollen, aber der Ägypter sieht die Gemeinsamkeit ihrer Wurzel im Menschen und bezeichnet diese durch identifizierendes *m*.

Unter dem Gesichtspunkt der Pädagogik, die in Grammatik- und Wörterbüchern berücksichtigt werden muß, vermeiden wir also möglichst, dem ägyptischen *m* die Bedeutungen "gegen" und "obwohl" zuzuschreiben ohne die Einmaligkeit des idiomatischen Gebrauchs klarzumachen; sie widersprechen der Grundbedeutung von *m*. Dieses Ergebnis unserer Prüfungsmethode ist zwar sehr geringfügig, aber die Diskussion auf dieser Grundlage berechtigt uns wohl, sie bei *ḏr* weiterzuführen.

Zunächst sei daran erinnert, daß die Präpositionen *r* "an" (Erman, *Ägypt. Grammatik*, § 446, genauer: "außen an"), *ḥr* "auf", *ḫr* "bei" und andere anscheinend ursprünglich sowohl die unbewegte Lage, als auch die Bewegungen hin zu dieser Lage und eigenartigerweise auch von ihr weg bezeichnen können. Die Grundbedeutungen dieser Präpositionen liegen also vermutlich nicht in einem dieser Bedeutungsaspekte,[10] sondern in den oben angegebenen räumlichen Beziehungen. Die Existenz des Nomens *ḏrw* "Grenze" berechtigt uns nun, auch bei der Präposition *ḏr* von der lokalen Bedeutung auszugehen, die nur sehr früh belegt, später durch die temporale Bedeutung vollständig verdrängt worden ist. Nehmen wir aber folgerichtig an, daß, wie die vorher genannten Präpositionen, auch *ḏr* die verschiedenen Aspekte der Richtung in sich schließt,[11] so müssen wir einen Unterschied beachten. Während nämlich *r*, *ḥr* u.a. das Subjekt der Bewegung in die Beziehungen "an", "auf" u.a. von außen her zu einem Zentrum hin setzen, muß doch wohl *ḏr* die lokale Beziehung

[9] Dies letztere in A. de Buck, *The Egyptian Coffin Texts* I 173 g, nach Edel a.a.O.

[10] Gardiner § 163 versteht allerdings "in the direction of" als "original signification" von *r*, nicht aber das Entsprechende bei den anderen Präpositionen.

[11] Die Übersetzung "an dem Orte, wo(?)" (*Wb.* V 592, 11) ist von Junker, *Die politische Lehre von Memphis*, S. 24 f., mit Recht abgelehnt worden.

des Geschehens vom Zentrum her nach außen hin enthalten. "Hin zur Grenze", "fort von der Grenze" müßte also eine Bewegung sein, die beiderseits begrenzt zwischen dem Standpunkt etwa des Redenden oder Angeredeten und der Grenze verläuft, nicht etwa außerhalb der Grenze. *Ḏr bw* könnte also je nach dem Zusammenhang "von dem (entfernten) Orte her" oder "nach dem (entfernten) Orte hin" übersetzt werden, und in beiden Fällen müßte es bedeuten "zwischen hier oder dort und dem entfernten Orte (an dem du geboren bist, an dem Osiris im Wasser dahintreibt, an dem oder den du gegangen bist), aber nicht über diesen Grenzpunkt hinaus", und dementsprechend sonst.[12]

Ist diese Deutung des lokal gebrauchten *ḏr* richtig, so dürfen wir auch bei dem temporalen *ḏr* annehmen, daß es nur den Zeitraum zwischen der relativen oder absoluten Gegenwart und einem zeitlichen Grenzpunkt bezeichnen kann, der nach der Theorie in der Vergangenheit oder in der Zukunft liegen könnte. Das ergibt ein "seit (jenem Zeitpunkt bis zur Gegenwart)" oder ein "(von der Gegenwart an) bis (zu jenem Zeitpunkt)", also "seit" oder "bis" für die Präposition, "seitdem" oder "bis" für die Konjunktion. Dagegen könnten die Übersetzungen "vor oder nach (jenem Zeitpunkt)" resp. "bevor oder nachdem" nicht zutreffen, weil mit diesen Präpositionen und Konjunktionen jener entfernte Zeitpunkt nicht als Grenze, sondern als Zentrum begriffen wird. Die hiermit logisch, doch nur theoretisch erschlossene Alternative für das zeitliche *ḏr* als "seit" oder "bis" erledigt sich von selbst für *ḏr* als Präposition dadurch, daß es "seit", niemals aber "bis" heißt. Aber wo *ḏr* als Konjunktion gebraucht wird, sind in den letzten Jahrzehnten neben "seitdem" und "weil", auf welches letztere wir noch zurückkommen, auch die Übersetzungen "bis", "bevor", "sobald (als)" und "wenn" aufgetaucht, und zwar an autoritativen Stellen. Zunächst mit "bis", das wir als mögliche Übersetzung theoretisch erschlossen haben, und mit "bevor", das nach unserem Verständnis unvereinbar ist mit der Grundbedeutung von *ḏr*, müssen wir uns ohne Vorurteil an Hand der angeblichen Beweisstücke auseinandersetzen.

Die Bedeutung "bis" ist m.W. zuerst postuliert worden von Breasted für Pap. Edwin Smith ii 21–22 = iv 11 (s.u. Zitat 30),[13] aber seine Deutung dieser

[12] Oben übersetzt sind *Pyr.* §§ 24, 615, 766; Memphitische Theologie, Zl. 8 und 10–11. Weiter sehe ich das lokal gebrauchte *ḏr* in *Pyr.* § 1238 b *ꜣw mdw pn ḏr ḥr.k Rꜥ* "lang ist dieses Wort (d.i. weit reicht dieses Wort) von hier bis zu deinem Gesichte, Re" (anders Sethe), und in *Pyr.* § 1139 "die *ʾImtt* greift sich meinen Arm *ḏr ḫm.ś ḏr śšṯꜣ.ś* von ihrem Heiligtum, von ihrer Abschließung her"; *ḫm* und *śšṯꜣ* können, entgegen Sethes Deutung, wohl deswegen nicht Infinitive oder nomina actionis sein, weil wir dafür trotz Sethe zu *Pyr.* § 309 c, aber mit Edel § 681, 3 und *Wb.* III 281 *ḫmt* erwarten dürften. Sehr erwägenswert erscheint mir auch eine Übersetzung von *ḏr hꜣt Rꜥ* als "(von hier) bis zum Orte des Sonnenunterganges" in *Pyr.* § 1355 b, hier unten Zitat 10.

[13] "This 'when' (i.e., *ḏr*) evidently has the force of 'until' when it is preceded by a negative" (Breasted, *The Edwin Smith Surgical Papyrus* I 170, Kommentar zu ii 21–22).

Stelle ist durch von Deines-Grapow-Westendorf gewiß mit Recht korrigiert worden. Dann hat Gardiner in der zweiten und dritten Auflage seiner *Eg. Grammar*, §§ 176, 4 und 407, 1, die Bedeutung "bis" angenommen mit dem einzigen Hinweis auf die Senmut-Inschrift *Urk.* IV 405, Zl. 8 (s.u. Zitat 15). Entgegen der sonst üblichen, aber unglaubhaften Übersetzung der entscheidenden Stelle als "seit dem Tode seines Vorgängers"[14] übersetzte Gardiner § 407, 1 in der ersten Auflage "I have been (lit. am *or* was) in this land holding his command ever since death overtook him, lit. happened upon his hands", aber seit der zweiten Auflage hat er diese sachlich unbefriedigende Übersetzung unter wörtlicher Beibehaltung des Übrigen geändert durch die Worte "under his command until death overtook him". Bei dieser Übersetzung müßten wir m.E. den darauf folgenden Satz höchst unbefriedigend verstehen im Sinne von "aber wirklich gelebt habe ich nur unter der wie gesagt verstorbenen Hatschepsut, die immerdar lebt";[15] und ein weiterer Einwand gegen Gardiners Übersetzung ist der, daß sein Verständnis von "death happened upon his hands" als "death overtook him" nach meinem Urteil ganz willkürlich ist. Wollen wir an "*ḏr* = bis" festhalten, so kann ich nur übersetzen "ich bin in diesem Lande seinem Befehle (unmittelbar?) unterstellt, bis das Sterben vor ihm entsteht (d.i. bis er dem Tode ins Auge sehen muß?)". Auch dann aber bleibt der Einwand, daß ein Satz mit "bis" unvereinbar ist mit der hier Anm. 40 erwähnten Original-Korrektur von *tp-ꜥwy.f* zu vermutlich *tp-ꜥwy* "vordem". Eine Übersetzung "bis" könnte hier m.E. nur dann beibehalten werden, wenn sie anderweitig klar nachweisbar wäre.

Früher als Gardiners einmaliges Verständnis "*ḏr śḏmt.f* = bis er hörte" im N.R. entstand Junkers[16] Deutung von *ḏr śḏmt.f* im A.R. als "bevor er hört", und sie ist von Edel[17] und Gardiner[18] angenommen worden. Junker kam zu dieser Übersetzung aus der Erwägung, die auch wir hier oben angestellt

[14] "Seit eintrat der Tod seines Vorgängers" (Sethe, *Hatschepsut-Problem,* § 106). Aber *tpy-ꜥ(wy)* als ein Singular, "der Vorgänger" (*Wb.* V 283, 7), ist sehr anfechtbar, und eine angebliche Schreibung 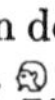 für *tpy* finde ich nur im *Wb.* V 277, 6: an der einzigen dort zitierten Stelle (*The Inscriptions of Sîuṭ and Dêr Rîfeh*, Taf. 16, Zl. 4) hat Griffith klar .

[15] Nachträglich sehe ich aber, daß Gardiner vermutlich mit Breasted, *Ancient Records of Egypt* II, § 368, Sethes alte Deutung angenommen hat, daß die Inschrift auf Thutmose III. und nicht auf Hatschepsut sich bezieht. Sethe hat diese These in *Hatschepsut-Problem,* § 106, mit geringer Überzeugungskraft wiederholt. Sie widerspricht dem Wortlaut des Textes.

[16] *Giza* III 93 f. Dazu früher Ermans "ehe(?)" nach hier Anm. 20.

[17] *Altäg. Grammatik,* § 735, unsere Zitate 1–6, 8, 10. Dem dort angenommenen "*ḏr śḏmt.f* = bevor er hört" scheint Edel allerdings selbst zu widersprechen in § 736 dadurch, daß er eine passivische Entsprechung zu *ḏr śḏmt.f* mit "seitdem", "seit" übersetzt.

[18] *Eg. Grammar* (3. Auflage) § 407, 1, unser Zitat 7. In § 176 vermerkt er, daß beide Bedeutungen, "before" und "until", ihm "strange" erscheinen.

haben, daß vermutlich in *ḏr* wie in anderen Präpositionen die beiden Richtungen "hin zu" und "von her" ausgedrückt sein können. Dabei kam er für die temporal gebrauchte Konjunktion *ḏr* auf das Richtungspaar "seitdem" und "bevor", während wir wie gesagt an dem Paar "seitdem" und "bis" festhalten müssen. Da nun der Unterschied zwischen "bevor" und "bis" sachlich nicht sehr groß ist, dürfen wir zunächst einmal versuchen, Junkers "bevor" durch "bis" zu ersetzen: "beeile dich, bis (statt 'bevor') dieser Aufseher kommt" (Zitat 1), "gib acht (auf die Herde), bis (statt 'bevor') sie ins Wasser gehen" (Zitat 5). Diese Übersetzung "bis" gibt auch bei unseren übrigen Zitaten 1–8 und 10 einigermaßen Sinn. Aber auch hier erheben sich sachliche Einwände ebenso wie wir bei Gardiners "bis" einen Einwand festhalten mußten.

Der erste Einwand bezieht sich auf unser Zitat 1. Denn wenn wir die Darstellungen auf den Grabwänden des A.R. mit Recht als Bilder des wirklichen Lebens ansehen, dann müssen hier wie in der Wirklichkeit die Arbeiter einander zum Eifer anfeuern nicht bevor der Aufseher oder Arbeitgeber kommt, aus Respekt vor ihm wie Junker a.a.O. etwas unrealistisch denkt, sondern wenn er gekommen ist und sie beobachten kann. Die allgemeine Gültigkeit dieser subalternen Einstellung ist jedem klar, der einmal als Mitglied oder Außenseiter eine ähnliche Arbeitergruppe beobachtet hat. Ein zweiter Einwurf gegen "bis" oder "bevor" in diesem Zusammenhang ergibt sich aus Zitat 5: das Bild zeigt die Herde bereits im Wasser. Drittens erweist die Totenbuchvariante unseres Zitates 6 nach Anm. 30, daß die Ägypter mit *ḏr ḥḏt tꜣ* sicher nicht sagen wollten "bevor es Tag wird".

So dürfen wir die Übersetzungen von *ḏr* als "bis" und "bevor" fallen lassen und auf die gesicherte Bedeutung "seitdem" zurückgreifen. Es ist logisch klar, daß "seitdem" sich entwickeln kann zum kausalen "weil", zumal da wir genau den gleichen Übergang noch lebendig im englischen "since" sehen, und auch das deutsche "weil" hat seine ursprüngliche Bedeutung im Sinne einer Zeitperiode, nämlich "während", etwas bewahrt in den älteren Formen "derweilen" und "dieweil". In der Tat haben wir anderweitig unbestreitbare Beispiele für *ḏr* "weil",[19] und wir folgen nur dem zuverlässigen und nüchternen Vorgang von Erman,[20] wenn wir *ḏr* in *ḏr śḏmt.f* (unten Zitate 1–9) als "weil" oder "denn" übersetzen. Dabei müssen wir in Anbetracht der ursprünglichen Bedeutung "seitdem" das darauf folgende Verbum als ein perfektisches Präsens verstehen: "weil er gekommen ist", d.h. "weil er hier ist", und das gilt in allen Fällen, in denen wir *ḏr* als "weil" übersetzen. Wir müssen die

[19] So in *ḏr ntt*. In unseren Zitaten 9, 27 und 29 übersetzt auch Edel §§ 1043, 911, 772, und in Zitat 30 auch von Deines-Grapow-Westendorf "weil".

[20] *Ägypt. Grammatik* (3. Auflage) § 453: "*ḏr* mit *śḏmt.f*: denn, weil", wobei die Übersetzung "denn" nur auf die A.R.-Zitate (hier 1–5 ff.) anwendbar ist. Aber früher, 1919, hatte Erman "ehe(?)" in diesen übersetzt; s.u. Anm. 27 und 29 zu Zitaten 3 und 5.

Frage offen lassen, ob und wieweit die kausale Bedeutung auch hineinspielen kann in *ḏr śḏmt.f*, wo es (Zitate 12–15) "seitdem er gehört hat" bedeutet.

Wir haben gesehen, daß *ḏr* wie das deutsche "seitdem" einen Zeitraum, "zwischen jetzt und dem (in der Vergangenheit liegenden) Grenzpunkt", bezeichnet, nicht aber einen Zeitpunkt. Deswegen haben wir die Übersetzungen "nachdem" und "bevor" abgelehnt. Aus dem gleichen Grunde dürfen und müssen wir, wenn keine Notwendigkeit dagegen spricht, auch die Übersetzung "sobald als" (oder "sobald") ablehnen, die Sethe[21] in den Pyramidentexten benutzt hat, und gegen die ich ebenso wie Andere bis gestern keinen Einwand hatte.[22] Weiter sahen wir, daß aus "seitdem" leicht ein kausales "weil" werden kann, und daß diese Entwicklung auch bei *ḏr* vorliegt. Nun kann ein begründendes "da" oder "weil" auch aus "sobald als" oder "nachdem" entstehen, und "sobald als" und "nachdem" können sich auch zu einem konditionalen "wenn" entwickeln. Aber kein logischer Weg führt soviel ich sehe von "seitdem" zum konditionalen "wenn", das Edel für das A.R. in unserem Zitat 28 angenommen hat, oder auch zum temporalen "when", das Breasted[23] für unsere Zitate 31–33 mit Begründung erschloß. Wir kommen leicht ohne diese Übersetzungen aus.

Nach dieser Besinnung auf die Grundbedeutung der Präposition *ḏr* und ihre Verwendung als Konjunktion stelle ich im folgenden die mir z.Z. bekannten Vorkommen der Konjunktion aus der alten und aus der klassischen Sprachstufe zusammen in einer Ordnung, die sich von selbst hier ergeben hat. Dabei zitiere ich in jedem Falle wenigstens eine Erwähnung in der ägyptologischen Literatur, gegebenenfalls mit der dort abweichenden Übersetzung—"audiatur et altera pars". Weitere grammatikalische Folgerungen sind unterblieben.

I. *ḏr* + *śḏmt.f* a) "dieweil es (geschehen) ist", "denn es ist (geschehen)", als Begründung für einen Befehl oder ein Verbot: Pyr., A.R., Totb.:

[21] *Pyr.* §§ 715, 815, 1334, 1355 (unsere Zitate 25, 8, 6, 10). In *Pyr.* § 1139 (s.o. Anm. 12) übersetzte Sethe "beim Beginn von". Mercer übersetzte in *Pyr.* §§ 815 und 1355 "as soon as", § 715 "since", § 1334 "before". Speleers in diesen vier Fällen "dès que".

[22] Gegen meine Deduktionen könnte eingewandt werden, daß ebenso wie wir "seitdem" und "sobald als" offenbar durcheinander gebracht haben, und wie aus franz. "dès" ein "dès que" gefolgt ist, auch die Ägypter beide Bedeutungen in *ḏr* gesehen haben könnten. Die hier unten mitgeteilten Zitate zeigen, daß dies bis zur 18. Dyn. anscheinend nicht der Fall war.

[23] *Edwin Smith Surgical Papyrus* I 150, Kommentar zu ii 6 (hier Zitat 31): "In view of the fact that the surgeon's examination and diagnosis have already declared the presence of the 'split' (*pšn*), it is clear that this clause refers back to the previous establishment of this fact. *Yr ḏr* must therefore mean 'now as soon as,' or 'now when,' introducing the observation already made. . . . It is decidedly an archaic use of the particle *ḏr*".

Zitate 1–9. Fraglich in anderem Zusammenhang: Pyr., 19. Dyn.: Zitate 10–11.

b) "seitdem es geschah", in der Erzählung: 18. Dyn.: Zitate 12–15.

II. *ḏr* + Infinitiv(?), besser wohl Präposition *ḏr* + nomen actionis "seit dem Geschehen": M.R., 18. Dyn.: Zitate 16–17.[24]

III. *ḏr* + *ś*ḏm.f* (nicht geminierend) "seitdem es geschah": A.R. bis 18. Dyn.: Zitate 18–24.

IV. *ḏr* + *śḏ*m.f* (geminierend) "weil es (geschehen) ist": Pyr., A.R., Pap. Edwin Smith: Zitate 25–34. Dabei als Begründung für eine Vorschrift, Pap. Edwin Smith: Zitate 31–33.

1. "Melke, mach schnell, *ḏr ỉyt ḥkꜣ* denn der Aufseher ist hier" (Steindorff, *Das Grab des Ti*, Taf. 111).[25]
2. "Bringe mir diese Antilope, *ḏr ỉyt ẖry-ḥb* denn der Vorlesepriester ist schon gekommen" (Capart, *Une rue de tombeaux à Saqqarah*, Taf. XLV).[26]
3. "Steh schnell auf, mein Genosse, bringe dieses Rippenstück aufs Haus(?), *ḏr ỉyt ẖry-ḥb r ỉrt ỉḫt* denn der Vorlesepriester ist schon zum Opfern gekommen" (*ibid.* Taf. LVI).[27]
4. "Brate, beeile dich, *ḏr ḫprt wnm tꜣ* denn (die Zeit zum?) Brotessen ist da (d.i. es ist Mittagpause?)" (*Kêmi* VI 118).[28]
5. "Hirte, gib acht auf dieses Scheusal (*šy pw*), das im Wasser ungesehen herankommt, *ḏr hꜣt.śn r mw* denn sie (scil. die Rinder) sind schon im Wasser" (Kairo Kat. 1784).[29]
6. "Schlagt den Seth, 'rächt' den Osiris, *ḏr ḥḏt tꜣ* denn der Tag ist angebrochen" (*Pyr.* § 1334).[30]
7. "Nenne mir meinen Namen, sagt der Wind, *ḏr fꜣt.k ỉm(.ỉ?)* dieweil du in mir (? ihm?) zur Fahrt aufgebrochen bist. . . . Nenne mir meinen

[24] Edel §§ 718 und 736 versteht auch Zitat 19 als Infinitiv und 20 als Infinitiv oder nomen actionis. *Wb.* V 593, 7–8 nennt als *ḏr* + inf. ("seit" resp. "als") auch unser Zitat 11 resp. die Totenbuch-Version von Zitat 6 (s. Anm. 30). Zu Sethes Verständnis von *Pyr.* § 1139 b mit *ḏr* + inf. oder nomen actionis s.o. Anm. 12 und 21.

[25] Junker, *Giza* III 93; Edel § 735 (beide "bevor").

[26] Nach Edel § 735 bb ("bevor").

[27] Wie Anm. 26. Erman, *Reden, Rufe und Lieder*, S. 15: "ehe(?)".

[28] Wie Anm. 26. Montet a.a.O. "maintenant que", sonst aber mit anderer Auffassung der Inschrift.

[29] Wie Anm. 26; s.o. im Text die Besprechung dieses Zitates. Die vorhergehende Warnung hier nach Erman, *Reden, Rufe und Lieder*, S. 30 ("ehe[?]"); *šy* ist sing. masc. nach einer *ibid.* zitierten Inschrift, trotz Pluralzeichen, kann also nicht mit *hꜣt.śn* gemeint sein.

[30] Wie Anm. 26; vgl. Sethe u.A. hier Anm. 21. Die Totenbuch-Version, Nav. 137A, 11, hat *ḏr ḥḏ tꜣ* "seit Tagesanbruch" (mit *ḥḏ* als Infinitiv oder *ś*ḏm.f*-Form); *Wb.* V 593, 8: "als (es Tag wurde oder geworden war?)".

Namen, sagt der Fluß, *ḏr ḏꜣt.k im.i* dieweil du auf mir fährst" (Pap. Nu; Brit. Mus. 10477, Bl. 21 und 22, Zl. 27–28, nach Budge, *Book of the Dead* [1898] S. 207–8).[31]

8. "Schließe nicht die Doppeltür des Himmels, wehre nicht mit seiner Wehrtür, *ḏr šdt.k kꜣ* dieweil du den Ka des NN zum Himmel entrissen hast, . . . (sondern) er soll Fürsprecher des NN sein beim Großen Gotte, er soll den NN zum Großen Gotte aufsteigen lassen" (*Pyr.* §§ 815–16).[32]
9. "Sagt ihm, dem König, nichts Böses gegen mich lügenhaft, *ḏr wnt ity rḫ* denn der Herrscher kennt meinen Charakter und meine Art" (*Urk.* I 195, Zl. 9–10, ergänzt von Edel, *Mitteilungen des Instituts für Orientforschung* I 213, Bl. 2).[33]
10. (Fraglich, ob *šḏmt.f*) "Das sind die vier Wege vor dem Grab des Horus, auf denen man das Weggehen zum Gotte vollzieht, *ḏr hꜣt Rꜥ* dieweil die Sonne untergegangen ist (? oder besser: [vom Grabe] bis zum Orte des Sonnenunterganges? s.o. Anm. 12)" (*Pyr.* § 1355).[34]
11. (Fraglich, ob *šḏmt.f*) Horus spricht, gibt dem König "mein Amt, meinen *nšt*-Sitz, meinen *št*-Thron, *ḏr rdt.i(?) m št itf* denn ich habe(?) die Einsetzung auf den väterlichen Thron vollzogen" (Abydos, Seti-Tempel).[35]
12. ". . . alles, was mir geschehen ist . . . , *ḏr prt.i* seitdem ich aus den Lenden meiner Mutter kam" (Lehre im Grab des Amenemhet, Zl. 2–3; s. *ZÄS* XLVII 92 und Taf. I).[36]
13. "Meine Soldaten marschieren wo nichts gewesen ist, beladen mit Schätzen, *ḏr ḫꜥt.i* seitdem ich als König erschien" (*Urk.* IV 386, Zl. 2).[37]
14. "Meine frühere Erscheinung hat sich erhöht, *ḏr prt.i* seitdem ich hervortrat im Schmucke des . . . , befördert zum Gottesdiener der Maat" (*Urk.* IV 1073, Zl. 9–11).[38]
15. "(Der König, d.i. Hatschepsut[39]) machte mich groß vor den beiden Ländern, er machte mich zum Obersten Mund seines Hauses, der Recht

[31] Gardiner, *Eg. Grammar* (3. Auflage) § 407, 1 ("before"). Zu *fꜣi* "sich aufmachen" s. *Wb.* I 573, 6. Wind und Wasser haben den Schiffer schon in ihrer Gewalt, erpressen also seine Antwort.

[32] Wie Anm. 26; vgl. Sethe u.A. hier Anm. 21.

[33] Edel § 1043 (*ḏr wnt* "weil").

[34] Wie Anm. 32.

[35] *Wb.* V 593, 7 (*Belegstellen* V 103) versteht *rdt.i* als Infinitiv, also wohl "seitdem ich gesetzt wurde"; die Lesung *rdt(w).i* hat die gleiche Bedeutung. Vom Inhaltlichen aus kann ich nicht entscheiden zwischen "denn ich habe gesetzt" und "seitdem ich gesetzt wurde"; vom Sprachlichen aus vgl. die Besprechung des objektlosen *rdi* im A.R. (*JEA* LIV 37).

[36] Gardiner, *Eg. Grammar* (3. Auflage) § 407, 1.

[37] Wie Anm. 36. *Wb.* V 593, 2 bezeichnet dies irrig als *šḏm.f*-Form.

[38] Wie Anm. 36.

[39] S. Anm. 15.

spricht im gesamten Lande. Ich wurde Oberhaupt der Obersten, Vorsteher der Arbeitsvorsteher, *ỉw.ỉ m tꜣ pn ẖr wḏ.f ḏr ḫprt mnỉ tp ꜥwy(.f)*[40] und so bin ich in diesem Lande (unmittelbar?) unter seinem Befehl, seitdem das Sterben ihm entgegentrat (Korrektur: seitdem vor Zeiten das Sterben geschah), und so bin ich im Leben unter der Herrin der beiden Länder, König Hatschepsut, die immerdar lebt" (*Urk.* IV 405, Zl. 6–8 = Hocker des Senmut, Berlin 2296, Zl. 6–8).[41]

16. "... für den Ka des ..., *ḥsy ḏr prt m ẖt* Gelobten von Mutterleibe an ... *Mn-ḫpr*" (*Urk.* IV 1198, Zl. 16).[42]
17. "Kein Unheil hat mich umfangen, *ḏr mś(w)t.ỉ* seit meiner Geburt" (Pap. Millingen, S. 2, Zl. 9).[43]
18. "Einen Monat hat es gedauert bis zu diesen Tagen, *ḏr wd.ỉ ꜥ.ỉ* seitdem ich meine Hand an diese Figur legte, die in meiner Hand ist" (Hassan, *Excav. Giza* II, Fig. 219).[44]
19. "Niemals bin ich (auch) in der Nacht ohne das Amtssiegel gewesen, *ḏr rdt(w.ỉ)* seitdem ich zum *śr*-Beamten gemacht wurde" (*Urk.* I 223, Zl. 9).[45]
20. "Ich bin niemals geschlagen worden vor dem Magistrat, *ḏr mśt(w.ỉ)* seitdem ich geboren wurde" (*Urk.* I 75, Zl. 14).[46]
21. "Sein Gesicht ist darauf gerichtet, *ḏr mśtw.f* seitdem er geboren wurde" (Sinuhe B 69).[47]
22. "Die Götter sind gnädig für Ägypten, *ḏr ḫꜥy.k* seitdem du als König der beiden Länder erschienst" (Inscr. dédic., Zl. 61).[48]
23. "Ich habe eine Elite von Grafen erhöht, *ḏr wn ꜥꜣmw* seitdem die Asiaten inmitten Ägyptens waren" (*Urk.* IV 390, Zl. 6–7).[49]
24. "Es hat dabei kein Unrecht gegeben, *ḏr wn ḥm.ỉ m ỉnp* seitdem meine Majestät ein Kind war" (*Urk.* IV 157, Zl. 7).[49]
25. "Die Götter freuen sich über NN, *ḏr mꜣꜣ.śn* weil sie ihn verjüngt sehen (erblickt haben)" (*Pyr.* § 715).[50]

[40] Ich konnte mich davon überzeugen, daß das Suffix *f* im Stein sorgfältig getilgt ist; so Roeder in *Ägyptische Inschriften Berlin* II 36. Die Frage, ob *tp-ꜥwy* oder, sachlich unwahrscheinlich, *tp-ꜥwy.ś* gelesen werden sollte, bleibt offen.

[41] Gardiner, *Eg. Grammar* (3. Auflage) § 407, 1 ("until"); s.o. S. 6 mit Anm. 14–15.

[42] *Wb.* V 593, 7.

[43] *Wb.* V 593, 3 liest *mśt(w).ỉ*, übersetzt "als". Die *śḏmtw.f*-Form wird aber in den vorhergehenden Textzeilen anders geschrieben.

[44] Nach Edel § 487.

[45] Edel §§ 718 und 736 liest *rdt.ỉ* als Infinitiv; s.o. Anm. 24.

[46] Edel § 736 liest *mś(w)t.ỉ*; s.o. Anm. 24. *Wb.* V 593, 3 irrtümlich "als".

[47] Gardiner § 176, n. 11. *Wb.* wie zu Anm. 46 (" ... war gerichtet, als ..."?).

[48] *Wb.* V 593, 2. Ähnlich Kubanstele, Zl. 14.

[49] Zitate 23 und 24: Gardiner § 176, n. 12.

[50] Edel § 487 ("sobald"). Vgl. Sethe u.A. hier Anm. 21.

26. "Ihr werdet ein *pr-ḫrw* zu meinen Gunsten herausnehmen aus den Einkünften dieses Gotteshauses, indem dies für mich getan wird auf Grund meiner Anordnung, und indem ihr diese eure Arbeit zu meinen Gunsten selbst verrichtet, *ḏr m33.ṯn* weil ihr meine vom König verliehenen Würden seht (erblickt habt)" (*Urk.* I 119, Zl. 7–11).[51]

27. "Sie dankten mir, *ḏr wnn.śn rḫw* weil sie (mich?) kannten (erkannt hatten; das Folgende zerstört)" (*Urk.* I 233, Zl. 17).[52]

28. "Macht mir ein *pr-ḫrw* von Brot und Bier *mỉ ỉrrtn.ỉ(?)* entsprechend dem, was ich(?) euren eigenen(?) Vätern getan habe, *ḏr wnn mr n.ṯn* weil es euch lieb ist, daß ich *sb* bin(?) auf euch in der Nekropole. Sagt euren Kindern den Tag, an dem ich abgeschieden bin (s. Edel § 672) und den Wortlaut des für mich bestimmten *pr-ḫrw*" (*Urk.* I 218, Zl. 1–4).[53]

29. (mit 3rad. Verbum) "(aus der Verhandlung über böse Nachrede bin ich in Frieden herausgekommen) *śk ḫr(.ỉ?)* indem ich fiel (? oder: *śk ḫrw*, pseudopart., indem was fallen sollte zurückgefallen ist?) auf die, die redeten, *ḏr b3ḳ.ỉ* weil ich darin geklärt worden bin, *ḏr ḏd.śn ỉś* weil sie somit mich verleumdet hatten" (*Urk.* I 223, Zl. 14–16).[54]

30. "Dies Zittern und Flattern unter deinen Fingern geschieht, *ḏr ngg 3ỉś* weil das Gehirn seines Schädels aufgebrochen ist" (Pap. Edwin Smith ii 21–22 = iv 11).[55]

31. "*ỉr ḏr gmm.k* weil du bei dem Manne gefunden hast, daß (unter den beim Befund genannten Symptomen die folgenden vorliegen) . . . , so sollst du ihn nicht verbinden (Pap. Edwin Smith ii 6); ihn in der Sitzlage halten, obgleich der Fall hoffnungslos erscheint" (*ibid.* Kol. viii 4).[56]

[51] Edel § 487 ohne Übersetzung. Für *m ỉr(y?)t n(.ỉ) n wḏ(.ỉ)* Sethe schlägt die Emendierung *m ỉrt.ṯn n(.ỉ) wḏ* vor. *ᵓIr(y?)t* kann Infinitiv oder Part. perf. pass. fem. sein. Daß *n wḏ* im Sinne von "auf Grund eines Befehles" sonst nicht bekannt zu sein scheint, spricht für Sethes Emendierung.

[52] Edel § 911 ("*ḏr wnn.śn* = weil sie . . .").

[53] Edel § 1037 b übersetzt "wenn es euch gewünscht ist, daß ich für euch in der Nekropole eintrete, so sagt euren Kindern . . .". Aber bei einem derart vorangesetzten, durch das ursprünglich temporal verstandene *ḏr* eingeführten Satz muß doch wohl ein einleitendes *ỉr* erwartet werden (s. Edel § 1032 g), wie es hier unten (Zitate 31–33) in der Tat steht. Zu der hier, *Urk.* I 217, Zl. 16–218, Zl. 4, m.E. vorliegenden Satzfolge vgl. *Urk.* I 205, Zl. 2–4 und 12–14; 218, Zl. 16–219, Zl. 1. Obgleich *sb* (*Urk.* I 218, Zl. 10 und 12) etwas Unreines zu sein scheint, muß es hier etwas Wünschenswertes sein. Jedenfalls scheint mir diese scheinbare lexikalische Diskrepanz den Vorschlag *Wb.* V 593, 12 nicht zu rechtfertigen, daß nämlich *ḏr wnn* hier hieße "oder ist es der Fall, daß . . . (?)".

[54] Edel § 772 c.

[55] Übersetzung wie von Deines-Grapow-Westendorf, *Übersetzung der medizinischen Texte,* S. 176.

[56] In Zitaten 31–33 übersetzen Edel § 1032 g und *Wb.* V 593, 10 *ỉr ḏr gmm.k*: "sobald du findest"; von Deines-Grapow-Westendorf treffender: "wenn du also findest"; zu Breasted s. hier Anm. 23. Lefèbvre, *Grammaire* § 721, der sonst an "depuis que" festhält, übersetzt in dieser Phrase "aussitôt que".

32. "*ỉr ḏr gmm.k* weil du bei dem Manne gefunden hast, daß das Band seines Unterkiefers gebunden ist (beim Befund *ibid.* Kol. iii 3 war gesagt, daß er seinen Mund schwer öffnen kann), so sollst du ihm etwas Warmes machen lassen" (*ibid.* Kol. iii 7; s.o. Anm. 56).
33. "*ỉr ḏr gmm.k šḏ pfꜣ* weil du jenen Bruch gefunden hast . . ." (*ibid.* Kol. iv 10; s.o. Anm. 56).[57]
34. (mit 3rad. Verbum) "es ist so, daß jede Wunde trocknet, die auf seiner Brust entstanden ist, *ḏr wbꜣ.f ḏś.f* weil sie sich von selbst geöffnet hat (d.h. die dadurch entstanden ist, daß sie sich von selbst geöffnet hat)" (*ibid.* Kol. xiii 9).[58]

Es ist mir eine Freude, diese kleinliche Untersuchung einer scheinbaren Kleinigkeit dem Jubilar widmen zu dürfen, weil ich vor allem seine Übersetzungen in *Ancient Near Eastern Texts Relating to the Old Testament* sehr viel benutzt und dabei stets ihre Sorgfalt auch im kleinen bewundert habe. Aber es tut mir leid, daß ich diese Untersuchung sprachlicher Probleme nicht in seiner mir lieb gewordenen Muttersprache durchführen konnte, dieweil sie aus dem Denken in deutscher Sprache entstanden ist.

[57] Die hier, in Fall 8 (iv 10–12), folgende Beschreibung hat garnichts mit dem vorher genannten Befund dieses Falles zu tun, sondern sie ist die an vier Stellen korrigierte Wiederholung des zweiten Teiles von Befund und Diagnose aus Fall 6 (ii 19–21). Offensichtlich sollte hier wie in den Zitaten 31 und 32 die Behandlung eines bestimmten Symptomes aus Fall 8 durch *ỉr ḏr gmm.k* eingeleitet werden, aber sie ist ausgefallen. Statt dessen verwechselte der Schreiber dieses *gmm.k* mit dem *gmm.k šḏ pfꜣ*, "und findest du jenen Bruch", von ii 19–20 und setzte diesen Text fort. Daß ein Durcheinander mit Fall 6 hier vorliegt, ist natürlich von allen Bearbeiten bemerkt worden, aber die Erklärung ist wohl jetzt erst ermöglicht.

[58] Von Deines-Grapow-Westendorf übersetzen "wenn sie von selbst aufgeht"; Westendorf, *Papyrus Edwin Smith: Ein medizinisches Lehrbuch aus dem alten Ägypten*, S. 76: "sobald sie sich von selbst öffnet". Beides wurde anscheinend bezogen auf "jede Wunde trocknet".

ILLUSIONISM IN EGYPTIAN ARCHITECTURE

Alexander Badawy

The study of illusionism in Egyptian architecture is but one small topic in the vast fresco of Egyptian culture to which Professor John A. Wilson contributed so brilliantly. The following pages are a small tribute to him.

Egyptian architecture, like other aspects of Egyptian art, was basically functional. Art for art's sake hardly appeared as an incentive to the Egyptian artist. Yet some architectural monuments tend to a visual effect which creates an illusion. This effect ranges from the simple reproduction of an element alien to architecture to a design aiming at an optical illusion or *trompe-l'œil*. Whereas the first type, that of the simple reproduction, is coupled more or less directly with symbolism, the second does not always aim at any abstract concept but tries to create the irreal by visual means. Both aspects of illusionism occur from the earliest dynasties on.

The archaic theriomorphic shrine that appears on labels of the 1st dynasty was built of light materials such as reeds and wickerwork and probably represented a crouching jackal.[1] It symbolized the animal sacred to Anubis, or rather it was intended to be the animal itself inside which a certain ritual was performed (Fig. 1). In the mortuary temple complex of Pharaoh Neterikhet Djeser of the 3d dynasty at Saqqara most of the dummy structures and elements imitate in limestone the earlier architecture of reeds and wood.[2] Fences, tall slender bundle columns engaged on façades or in transverse walls, doors represented ajar, façades of pavilions with columns supporting a flat vault above a lower partition wall crowned with a kheker-frieze, ribbed ceilings, all copy elements and structures built of vegetable materials. The illusion must have been still more perfect with the colors that covered the whole complex—green for leaves and reeds, red for dry reeds and wood. Its architect, Imhotep, was particular about representing details of the earlier structures in light materials because of their symbolism even though it meant such a complicated design on a large scale and arduous carving in stone. Illusionistic copying of plant elements similar to those of Neterikhet but more stylized remained a consistent component in the design of temples and funerary chapels from the 5th dynasty on.

[1] Alexandre Badawy, *Le dessin architectural chez les anciens Égyptiens* (Cairo, 1948) pp. 17–21.

[2] Alexander Badawy, *A History of Egyptian Architecture from the Earliest Times to the End of the Old Kingdom* (Cairo, 1954) pp. 71 ff.

As a matter of fact, the design of the temple as a whole and that of its elements were based on illusionism coupled with symbolism. Some parts of the mortuary temples of the Old Kingdom have been interpreted as representing the hallowed sites mentioned in the legends of the gods, such as the early palm forest at Buto, where the predynastic kings were buried,[3] or the papyrus bush where Isis hid with her infant Horus at Chemmis.[4] The hypostyle hall of the typical cult temple would have been a model of the Nile Valley:[5] tall papyrus stalks with open flower bordering the Nile along the nave and shorter lotus

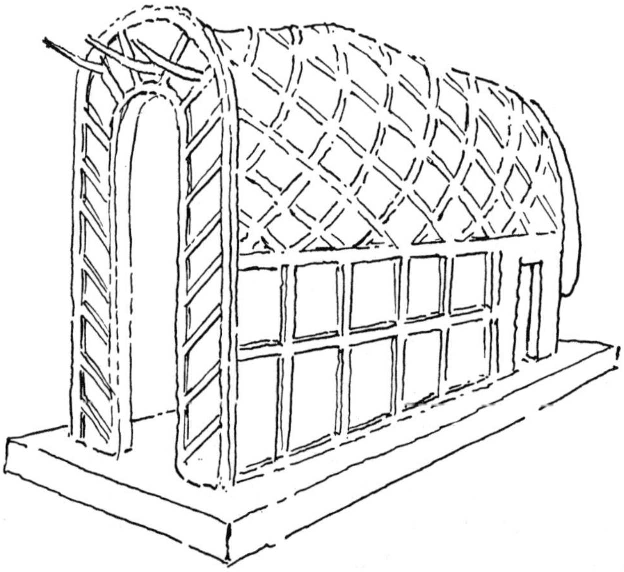

FIG. 1. RECONSTRUCTED PERSPECTIVE OF AN ARCHAIC THERIOMORPHIC SHRINE, PROBABLY THAT OF THE ANUBIS JACKAL, AFTER DESIGNS ON SEALS.

thickets represented as bundle columns beyond in the aisles. It is significant that the papyrus column has the same name (*wꜣḏ*) as the papyrus plant itself. The high ceiling was the sky (*ḥr.t*), where rows of vultures sacred to Nekhebet fluttered protectively over the pharaoh and the god when they proceeded in the nave, while thousands of golden stars twinkled in the blue above the aisles. Parts of temples might have given the illusion of being abodes in heaven, such as the "Portal of Nut" and the "Portal of Nun"[6] in the mortuary temples and

[3] H. Ricke, *Bemerkungen zur ägyptischen Baukunst des Alten Reichs* II (Cairo, 1950) 73.

[4] Alexander Badawy, "The Architectural Symbolism of the Mammisi-Chapel in Egypt," *Chronique d'Égypte* XXXVIII (Brussels, 1963) 78–90.

[5] H. H. Nelson, "The Egyptian Temple with Particular Reference to the Theban Temples of the Empire Period," *The Biblical Archaeologist* VII (1944) 44–53.

[6] Ricke, *op. cit.* pp. 46 and 62.

the naos of the cult statue as the heavenly residence of its deity.[7] To enhance this effect in the typical cult temple a gradual rise in the floors toward the rear was coupled with a gradual decrease in the height of the ceilings and in the intensity of light.

The two towers of the pylon forming the façade of the cult temple in the New Kingdom were an illusionistic representation on a reduced scale of the two mountains between which the sun rises on the luminous mountain horizon (*ꜣḫ.t*).[8] The god of the temple appeared when carried in procession through the gate or was shown to the people, as at Edfu, from the terrace above it. The term defining this appearance in glory of the god (*ḫʿỉ*) was the same as that used for the rising of the sun. In the small chapel of Reʿ-Horakhty in front of the large temple at Abu Simbel it was the sun disk itself that appeared at sunrise between the two towers of the miniature pylon. A similar theophany was probably observed in the temples and chapels at ʿAmarna. An illusionistic representation of this appearance was worked in the copper sheathing of the door leaves and gilded to shine as the sun itself. This illusion of the terrestrialized sun was achieved also in the gold sheathing of the pyramidions glittering at the tops of pyramids and obelisks. They were illusionistic counterparts of the sun in the sky, and it is in this sense that we should interpret the hieroglyph determining the name of the obelisk of the sun temples of the 5th dynasty showing the sun disk atop the pyramidion,[9] or building inscriptions describing the tall obelisks of the Empire as being "like the four pillars of heaven"[10] and as monuments which "mingle with the sky."[11] A similar concept probably was embodied in the design of the mortuary complex of Mentuhotep Nebhepetreʿ at Deir el-Bahari, where the pyramid surmounting the temple would have formed the illusionistic counterpart of the pyramid-shaped peak El-Qurn rising just above in the mountain range and worshiped as a goddess.[12]

While illusionism aimed at interpreting connections with the sun or gods in the sky, bringing them, as it were, within the range of the eye, it also sometimes connected the earth with the netherworld. The false door of the funerary chapels of the mastaba tombs in its simplest form gave the perfect illusion of a door, even to the sliding lock. Through it communication with the nether-

[7] W. Spiegelberg, "Die Auffassung des Tempels als Himmel," *Zeitschrift für ägyptische Sprache und Altertumskunde* LIII (1917) 99.

[8] T. Dombart, "Der Zweitürmige Tempel-Pylon altaegyptischer Baukunst und seine religiöse Symbolik," *Egyptian Religion* I (1933) 87–98.

[9] See Herbert Ricke, *Das Sonnenheiligtum des Königs Userkaf* I ("Beiträge zur ägyptischen Bauforschung und Altertumskunde" VII [Kairo, 1965]) 5.

[10] See J. H. Breasted, *Ancient Records of Egypt* (Chicago, 1906) III, § 545.

[11] See *ibid.* § 548.

[12] See K. Lange and M. Hirmer, *Egypt: Architecture, Sculpture, Painting in Three Thousand Years,* translated from the German by R. H. Boothroyd (London, 1956) Pl. 119.

world was established at the "going forth of the voice" (*prt-ḫrw*), when the ritual was performed to enable the deceased to partake of the offering set for him or her on the offering table. The false door was sometimes carved in high relief with an illusionistic representation of the deceased issuing forth from the sill of the door, as in the tomb of Idw, or the lintel, as in the tomb of Nebreᶜ, or walking out of the doorway, as in the tombs of Mereruka and Neferseshem-ptah. To the same category must be ascribed statues representing the deceased kneeling and presenting a slab in a niche in the east face of the pyramids built above the tomb chapels of the New Kingdom at Thebes.[13] These statues were so placed in relation to the appearance of the sun at sunrise that the deceased might be able to greet the god at his rising. A similar idea governed the design of the frieze of baboons raising their hands at the top of the façade of the temple of Reᶜ-Horakhty at Abu Simbel.[14] It was the first part of the temple to be lit at sunrise, giving the illusion of a row of baboons gesturing and uttering cries of joy as such animals are wont to do when they see the sun at dawn. Through the doorway the rays of the sun would first reach the heads of the pseudo-Osiride pillars in the hypostyle hall[15] and in turn those of three of the four seated deities in the sanctuary, bringing to life their features and then gradually their busts, torsos, and bodies to give the illusion that Ramses II, Amun, and Reᶜ-Horakhty during two periods of the year (Feb. 10–Mar. 1 and Oct. 10–20) emerged daily from the dark.[16] This architectural statuary was so designed as to give the illusion of deities brought to life by the sun, whereas Ptah, the mummiform god of the dead, remained in the shade.

An element of illusionistic statuary commonly used in architecture was the waterspout shaped as the forepart of a lion protruding at the tops of temple walls. The illusion was that of lions protecting the structures against the devastation of storms and rains,[17] whose tamed waters poured safely between the lions' paws. More symbolical though still illusionistic was the effect of colossal lion or sphinx statues flanking processional avenues—called "the way of the god"—and gateways of temples. An illusionistic effect at Medinet Habu was planned in the heads of prisoners prone on their bellies, side by side in a row, carved as brackets carrying figures of Ramses III on the eastern gate and the façade of the palace.[18] According to the concept of the Egyptian these figures were real beings, trodden under foot by Pharaoh.

[13] G. Steindorff und Walther Wolf, *Die thebanische Gräberwelt* (Glückstadt, 1936) p. 59.

[14] See Kurt Lange und Max Hirmer, *Ägypten* (4th ed.; München, 1967) Pl. 248.

[15] *Ibid.* Pl. 250.

[16] See Louis-A. Christophe, *Abou-Simbel et l'épopée de sa découverte* (Brussels, 1965) p. 201.

[17] See C. de Wit, *Le rôle et le sens du lion dans l'Égypte ancienne* (Leiden, 1951) p. 84.

[18] Uvo Hölscher, *The Excavation of Medinet Habu* III (*OIP* LIV [1941]) Fig. 18 and Pl. 3. Similar brackets were found at Saqqara, Damanhur, and Tanis. For those of Tanis, dated

Illusionism was also used in mural paintings in conjunction with architecture. We have seen how the ceilings of temples were always painted with vultures and stars on a blue ground to imitate the sky. Sometimes the elongated figure of the sky goddess Nut stretched across a funerary vault.[19] In the palace of Amenhotep III at Malqata, floors were painted to imitate ponds out of which grew tall slender columns shaped like papyrus or lotus stems. When, in the same palace, Amenhotep III was portrayed sitting in state on either side of the doorway between the harem hall and his throne room, no doubt the purpose was to give the illusion of the scene that would appear behind the closed door. Very often an illusionistic effect was intended in the composition of the murals in temples and tomb chapels. At the bottom ran a dado imitating pink granite[20] or recessed paneling[21] forming a kind of proscenium to a scenic staging. Illusionism was carried further with the expression of depth in the arrangement of the scenes in superimposed registers, the lowest depicting the nearest scenes, usually enacted on the Nile itself, and the highest representing the most distant ones in the mountain, as in the tomb of Antefoker at Thebes (12th dynasty). Though often hampered by the conventions of Egyptian graphics such as composite projection of figures, ground line, lack of scale, and heroic size, an illusionistic effect similar in many respects to that of a cavalier perspective was achieved occasionally.

The second type of illusionism is totally deprived of symbolical implication. The architect seems to have pursued some aesthetic impulse, sometimes allied to a conceptual element. For how else could we explain the arrangement of niches imitating windows or doorways set in the alignment of real openings to achieve symmetry on the inner walls of the villas at ᶜAmarna and probably in the domestic structures of other periods also, a feature copied later in the palace of Darius at Persepolis? Or the consistent use of batter in the outer faces of walls? This characteristic, which originated in the use of slippery mud in prehistoric architecture, had no symbolic connotation and could have been maintained because of tradition, but probably also because it gave the illusion that the wall was of greater height. We are encouraged in this surmise of an Egyptian pursuit of aesthetics for its own sake through the analysis of several other instances. The optical illusion for greater height is carried to its maximal

---

to Ramses II, see P. Montet, *Fouilles de Tanis*. III. *Les constructions et le tombeau de Chéchanq III à Tanis* (Paris, 1960) pp. 37–38 and Pl. XXI.

[19] E.g. in the sarcophagus chamber of Ramses VI; for an excellent photograph see F. Daumas, *La civilisation de l'Égypte pharaonique* (Paris, 1965) Fig. 123.

[20] R. Lepsius, *Denkmäler aus Aegypten und Aethiopien* (Berlin, 1849–56) Abtheilung IV, Pl. 130, tomb chapel of Khnumhotep II at Beni Hassan (12th dynasty).

[21] A. M. Blackman, *The Rock Tombs of Meir* VI (London, 1953) Pl. XXII, tomb of Ukhhotep son of Ukhhotep (12th dynasty).

effect in the faces of pyramids to give the impression that they vanish into infinity. This peculiar illusion, which impresses so strongly all who visit these structures, results from the fact that the angle of vision encompassing the face of the pyramid becomes wider as one approaches, until the line of sight becomes parallel to the face at the foot of the pyramid (Fig. 2). The faces of the pyramid express a dynamic factor, an upward surge understood from the

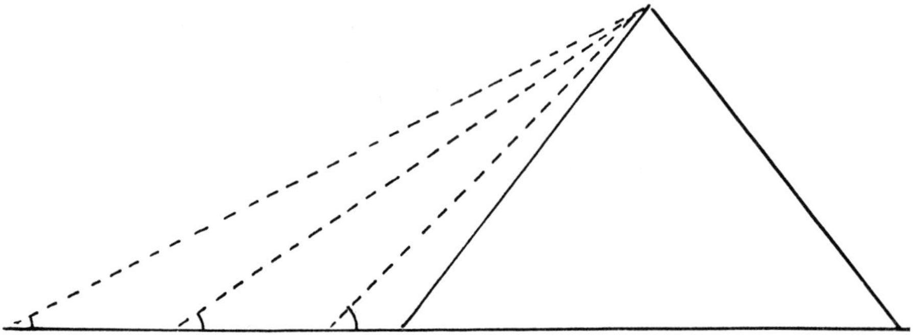

FIG. 2. DIAGRAM SHOWING GRADUAL INCREASE OF VIEWING ANGLE AS ONE APPROACHES FACE OF PYRAMID.

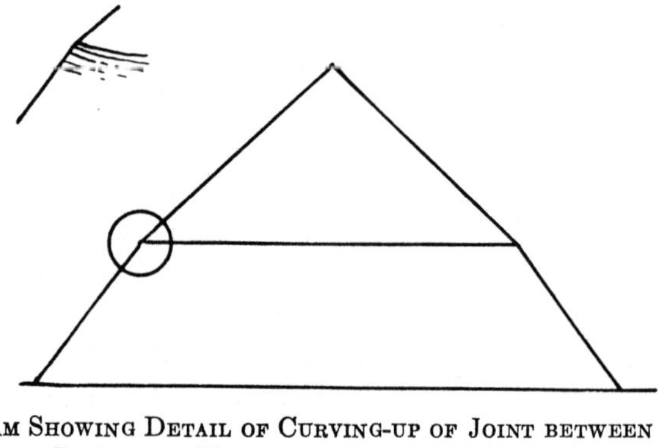

FIG. 3. DIAGRAM SHOWING DETAIL OF CURVING-UP OF JOINT BETWEEN TWO PARTS OF FACE OF RHOMBOIDAL PYRAMID AT DAHSHUR.

name of the pyramid itself, *mr*, possibly from *ʿr*, "to ascend." It may be of interest to note that the faces of the pyramids were not always plane. The two parts of each of the four faces of the Rhomboidal Pyramid at Dahshur meet along a horizontal line or arris which curves up slightly at either end (Fig. 3).[22] The fact that the casing blocks of the Great Pyramid of Kheops at Giza "shows a periodical decrease for a certain number of courses up the face" has been explained as evidence that available stone was worked out before a new supply was drawn upon;[23] or perhaps it was to decrease the weight of individual

[22] See J. Ph. Lauer, *Observations sur les pyramides* (Cairo, 1960) p. 89 and Pl. XII 2.

[23] See S. Clarke and R. Engelbach, *Ancient Egyptian Masonry* (Oxford, 1930) pp. 128–29.

blocks in the upper layers; or, again, to give an illusion of greater height to the pyramid by combining the periodical decrease in the height of the casing courses with their apparent decrease resulting from perspective.

Optical illusion per se was sought in many monuments. The avenue rising to the entrance gate in the middle of the façade of the temple of Amun built by Sheshonq I at El-Hiba was bordered by two parapets diverging toward the façade.[24] From a certain point in front of the façade, at which only their outer ends were visible, the two parapet walls would seem to be parallel and hence, though hardly seen, would emphasize the depth of the avenue and focus the view on the central part of the façade with its gateway flanked by two criosphinxes. The process was applied much later by Michelangelo on a larger scale in his design of the square of the Campidoglio in Rome.[25] The terraced approach to the tombs of the nomarchs of the Middle Kingdom at Qaw, and on a grander scale in the mortuary temple of Hatshepsut at Deir el-Bahari, created an illusionistic effect enhancing the verticality of the spatial concept of the whole complex. "What appear to us as horizontal planes are mere pauses on an eternally upward-moving path. This is expressed with great daring by embedding a finely articulated human structure within the immense verticality of this great rock amphitheater, which draws the eye up to its summits."[26] The link between the heavenly abode and the deceased personage was thus crystallized through the illusionistic design of the funerary temple well adapted to its natural environment.

A similar relationship was achieved in the ground plan of the temple of Amun at Luxor between the bark chapel of the main sanctuary and the earlier chapel of Thutmose III at the opposite end of the same axis (Fig. 4, *bottom*). As a result the forecourt added by Ramses II was planned in the shape of a parallelogram and its axis diverged from the main axis in the direction of the Great Temple of Amun at Karnak (Fig. 4, *middle left*). Two partially conceptual visual effects were thus achieved. The subtle shift in the axis and in the shape of the court is hardly discernible from the interior of the court. A similar illusionistic process occurred along a bent axis of courts and pylons connecting the Great Temple of Amun to that of Mut at Karnak (Fig. 4, *top*).

Illusionism was probably intended in the sharp entasis of the shafts of plant columns to enhance their height, or in the inverted taper of the tent-pole columns of the Festival Hall of Thutmose III at Karnak to counteract the apparent decrease in diameter toward the top resulting from perspective de-

[24] See Hermann Ranke, *Koptische Friedhöfe bei Karâra und der Amontempel Scheschonks I bei el Hibe* (Berlin und Leipzig, 1926) Fig. 79 and Plans 9–10.

[25] See S. Giedion, *Space, Time and Architecture* (Cambridge, Mass., 1956) Fig. 23 and pp. 69–70.

[26] S. Giedion, *The Beginnings of Architecture* (New York, 1964) pp. 412–34.

formation.[27] A sharp contrast between the narrow, confined space within the entrance gateway of a pylon and the vast court beyond would even be enhanced into a spatial illusion echoing the name *wsḫt* (lit. "the broad one"), "hall" or "court."

The most refined illusionistic composition was achieved in the eastern gate of the Mortuary Temple of Ramses III at Medinet Habu. The sides of the passageway between the two front towers were offset to allow for a small court, beyond which the passage narrowed so that its flanking pseudo-towers would give the illusion of a second pair of real towers.[28] At the same time, an

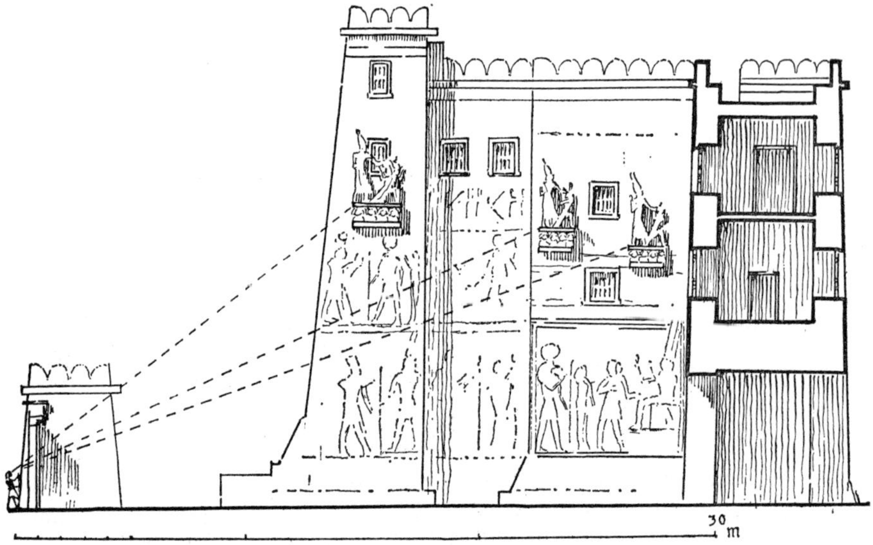

FIG. 5. NORTH SIDE OF PASSAGEWAY IN EASTERN GATE OF MORTUARY TEMPLE OF RAMSES III AT MEDINET HABU. AFTER HÖLSCHER, *The Excavation of Medinet Habu* IV, PL. 7.

impression of greater depth resulted from the narrower second stretch of the passageway. Three stela-like groups of statuary representing the triumphant Ramses III striking an enemy were applied on brackets protruding along the passageway at different heights decreasing toward the back. The decrease was calculated to enhance the illusion of depth in the passageway (Fig. 5). Optical deformation resulting from perspective could occasionally be corrected, not only in individual architectural elements such as the columns of the Festival Hall of Thutmose III but in a whole architectural composition. The four colossi of Ramses II in front of the façade of his temple to Reᶜ-Horakhty at Abu Simbel were carved so that their bases were on a slightly curved alignment, probably to counteract the effect of perspectival caving-in. This feature

[27] See Lange and Hirmer, *Egypt* (1956) Pl. 139.

[28] See Hölscher, *The Excavation of Medinet Habu* IV (*OIP* LV [1951]) Pls. 3 and 7.

occurred also in the massive inclosure walls in Egyptian temples and in the façades of Mesopotamian structures such as the one sketched on the tablet of Gudea of Lagash. The two obelisks flanking the entrance to the forecourt of Ramses II in the temple of Luxor were not of the same height, the smaller one to the west (now in the Place de la Concorde in Paris) was erected in front of the alignment of the larger one to the east. Provided with exact measurements, one could determine the original viewing point chosen by the architect so that from it the two obelisks would appear equal in height (see Fig. 4, *middle right*). It is safe enough to presume that this location was deemed important enough—perhaps at the gate of the sacred precinct—to play such a role in the layout of the approach to the temple. In the wall scenes decorating the monumental gateway of Sheshonq in the western stretch of the inclosure of the temples at Tanis the larger scenes are at the bottom, and the size of the registers decreases with the upper ones.[29] Here again planned illusionism enhanced the relative distances and hence the height of the wall.

This study shows that the Egyptian architect knew how to make use of illusionism in his designs, often coupled with symbolism. Inasmuch as symbolism was functional, most illusionistic architecture also was functional. To the ancient Egyptian a sanctuary shaped like an Anubis jackal was really Anubis, the mortuary dummy complex of Neterikhet Djeser consisted really of structures in plant stems, the hypostyle hall of the cult temple was the Nile Valley, the two pylons were the two mounts between which the sun god appeared, and the obelisk was the link connecting the sun to the earth. Illusionism established also connections with the netherworld for the benefit of the deceased. Color added a realistic touch to illusionism.

In addition to this essentially functional type of illusionism there was a second one devoid of any symbolical implication. It aimed at a visual effect coupled with a conceptual one as when it formed a link between two sanctuaries or even a spatial effect alone to prevent an impression of perspectival caving-in, to enhance verticality (batter of walls), to emphasize the depth of a passageway, or to correct an optical illusion in a way akin to that used in Greek architecture. This purely aesthetic pursuit reached its greatest achievements in the New Kingdom, when other non-utilitarian art forms such as figurines and statuettes were created for visual enjoyment only.

[29] P. Montet, *Tanis: Douze années de fouilles dans une capitale oubliée du Delta égyptien* (Paris, 1942) p. 49.

A RITUAL BALL GAME?

Carl E. DeVries

Among the features of ancient Egyptian life that have often received comment is the love of a good time. The interest in diversion and recreation took many forms, including participation in a variety of games and sports.

Since Professor Wilson has shown a keen interest in the sporting aspects of ancient Egypt, as evidenced by his article entitled "Ceremonial Games of the New Kingdom,"[1] and since in 1944 he was the first person at the Oriental Institute to encourage me to investigate pre-Greek athletics and sport, it is with pleasure that I present this short study in his honor.

The recreational activities of the Egyptians included a number of exercises or games involving the use of a ball, and the total archeological evidence indicates that the employment of a ball in play and games must have been widely known in ancient Egypt. A number of spheroids of various materials are shown in museum collections; though many of these were acquired by purchase from dealers, others were found in excavations. One may guess that often such objects were included among the grave furnishings of children, but most of the tombs known to us are of adults and most usually represent officials or so-called "nobles." Unfortunately, the tomb art does not illustrate ball games in the depiction of the play of children, but the identification of many of the objects themselves is quite certain. The manner of their use may be deduced from tomb scenes at Beni Hasan which depict various games of ball played by women. In these Middle Kingdom tombs, catching, throwing, and juggling are shown, along with one game of particular merit which has been discussed elsewhere as evidence that the Egyptians had at a comparatively early time developed a feeling for team play.[2]

One may surmise that children engaged in such activities for their own amusement, but the portrayal of women's games at Beni Hasan suggests that the women were participating for the entertainment of observers, thus indicating the existence of spectator sport. On the basis of "the appearance and especially the arrangement of the hair of these women," Samuel Birch even proposed that they were professionals.[3] If this view could be substan-

[1] *JEA* XVII (1931) 211–20.

[2] Carl E. DeVries, "Attitudes of the Ancient Egyptians toward Physical-Recreative Activities," unpublished Ph.D. dissertation (University of Chicago, 1960) pp. 361–63.

[3] See Sir J. Gardner Wilkinson, *The Manners and Customs of the Ancient Egyptians* (new ed., revised and corrected by Samuel Birch; London, 1878) II 66, n. 4. Birch gave no fur-

tiated, it would provide an argument for a sophisticated development of athletic games at the time of the Middle Kingdom.

Though it may be strange that children's ball games are not shown in the tomb reliefs and paintings, it may be quite otherwise with ball games for men, for it is possible that such games were not played by adult males. On the other hand, there are a number of representations which show a man, the king, standing with a kind of ball in his hand. Interestingly, all of these scenes, which occur only on temple walls, include the representation of some sort of stick or club, apparently for hitting the ball. Usually the scenes are accompanied by a terse label, something to the effect of "striking the ball for" the deity named. In addition to these reliefs there is an obscure statement in the Pyramid Texts which may refer to the striking of a ball as a pastime.

Since the life of the Egyptians was permeated by religion, one would expect activities of all kinds to be associated with religious art and literature and even to have a religious significance, though aspects of a performance may be essentially or completely secular. In the reliefs just mentioned it is difficult to determine exactly what the activity is. One can only examine the representations, analyze them for elements common to all of them, and seek to determine whether the evidence is sufficient to permit definite conclusions.

The passage in the Pyramid Texts, if it has been correctly interpreted, probably is the oldest reference to ball play, whether in art or literature, and the only occurrence of such a reference in all the ancient Egyptian literature so far published. Spell 254, couched in the typical enigmatic metaphors of much of this writing, seeks to obtain for the deceased victories over those who oppose him and to bring him to a place of recognition as "the bull of heaven." In finding his way to the "horizon," to the "beautiful west," the deceased king is addressed by the Enneads, who instruct him in § 279 *d* to "manipulate the rope, traverse the *msḳt*, hit the ball on the meadow of Hapi."[4] Since the first two elements appear to involve travel, probably including travel by boat, the last clause seems incongruous unless it is regarded as the goal or result of the previous actions. This may well be possible, for it is the final statement of a series and § 280 *a* introduces another speech, addressed to a different entity.

The translation "hit the ball on the meadow of Hapi" is problematical, and even if we could be sure of it we could not ascertain its precise meaning.[5] Sethe

ther reasons for his conclusion. Cf. E. Norman Gardiner, *Athletics of the Ancient World* (Oxford, 1939) p. 6.

[4] See Kurt Sethe, *Die altägyptischen Pyramidentexte* I (Leipzig, 1908) 150, and *Übersetzung und Kommentar zu den altägyptischen Pyramidentexten* I (Glückstadt, 1935) 298. Cf. Samuel A. B. Mercer, *The Pyramid Texts in Translation and Commentary* I (New York, 1952) 78.

[5] Was this really a game? If so, how was it played? What equipment was used? These are typical of our unanswered questions.

unhesitatingly produced the translation and described the activity as appearing to be "ein Zeitvertreib der seligen Toten am Himmel."[6] If his interpretation is correct, the text refers not to a religious rite but to a form of recreation and one may expect that the entertainments of the beatified Egyptian would reflect the practices and aspirations of the living. Aside from the possible reference to hitting a ball, this text has nothing in common with the later depictions on the temple walls, to which we now turn.

The earliest, and in many respects the most intriguing and the most instructive, of these reliefs is in the temple of Hatshepsut at Deir el-Bahri, in the shrine of Hathor, on the east wall of the columned hall or anteroom, immediately to one's right as he passes through the doorway of that hall.[7] In this scene Thutmose III is shown performing a ceremony before the goddess Hathor. The king, wearing the *ꜣtf*-crown, broad collar, and elaborate kilt with royal tail, stands at the viewer's right, facing the goddess. He holds a ball in his left hand and has in his right hand a long stick of strange undulating form. Before him is an inscription which reads *sḳr ḥmꜣ n Ḥwt-Ḥr ḥrt tp Wꜣst*, "striking the ball for Hathor, who has authority over Thebes." Between the king and Hathor and facing the king are two prophets, shown on a smaller scale than the two more prominent characters. Each of these men has a ball between his upraised hands, as if catching it or handing it to the king. The prophets' part in the ceremony will be discussed below, along with the translation of the legend which appears above them.

One may note in passing that the translations of such words as *ḥmꜣ*, "ball,"[8] and *bḏ*, "ball(?),"[9] though generally accepted, involve some interpretation. Both the writing of hieroglyphs and their artistic representation in relief and painting suffer from being restricted to two dimensions, so that the portrayal of a round object may signify a sphere, a disk, or the end of a cylinder.[10] In many in-

[6] Sethe, *Übersetzung und Kommentar* I 315–16. Cf. Mercer, *op. cit.* II 131.

[7] Edouard Naville, *The Temple of Deir el Bahari* IV (London, 1901) Pl. C (musicologists should not be misled by the misprinted caption "playing bells"); Metropolitan Museum of Art photograph 2320. Bertha Porter and Rosalind L. B. Moss, *Topographical Bibliography of Ancient Egyptian Hieroglyphic Texts, Reliefs, and Paintings* II (Oxford, 1929) 121, location 46; Harold H. Nelson, *Key Plans Showing Locations of Theban Temple Decorations* ("Oriental Institute Publications" LVI [Chicago, 1941]) Pl. XXXV, location 97.

[8] *Wb.* III 93, 10–11. Cf. Raymond O. Faulkner, *A Concise Dictionary of Middle Egyptian* (Oxford, 1962) p. 170.

[9] *Wb.* I 488, 8.

[10] For example, Gayet describes as follows the actions of the king in a scene of striking a ball: "de la main gauche il tient un disque qu'il touche de la main droite avec une baguette"; see Al. Gayet, *Le temple de Louxor* ("Mémoires publiés par les membres de la Mission archéologique française au Caire" XV [Paris, 1894]) p. 109.

stances the identification of an object may be self-evident, but in certain cases it may be very complex.[11]

In point of time and in terms of geographic proximity, the next representations which may show the striking of a ball appear in the Luxor temple. In the Mut chamber, similar scenes of the king before Mut are found on the east and west walls, just opposite each other.[12] In both, Amenhotep III is dressed in the pointed kilt and wears the royal tail, the broad collar, and the *ꜣtf*-crown. He has a ball in his left hand and grasps the end of a long, straight stick with his right hand. On the east wall, before the king, is the title of the scene: *sḳr ḥmꜣt ỉr.f dỉ ꜥnḫ*, "striking the ball that he may achieve a 'given-life.' " On the opposite wall there is an identical inscription and also the explanation: *sꜣw ỉb n ḳmꜣt nfrw.f*, "rejoicing the heart of the one who created his goodness." This seems to indicate that the purpose of the ceremony was to bring pleasure to the goddess Mut, who observes the proceedings from her stony point of vantage.

A third representation of this ritual in the Luxor temple is in the so-called "Birth Room," at the east end of the north wall, in the second register.[13] It may be remarked that here the king is wearing not the *ꜣtf*-crown but the *šwty*-headdress, with its two tall plumes. Amenhotep III again has in his hands a ball and a long, straight stick, but his right hand is awkwardly situated near the middle of the stick. Though the stick appears to be in contact with the ball, this representation may indicate not the actual striking of the ball but a preliminary position. The title, somewhat longer and with a few orthographical variants, reads *sḳr ḥmt ỉr.f dỉ ꜥnḫ mỉ Rꜥ*, "hitting the ball that he may achieve a 'given-life' like Re."

It may be more than coincidence that in the room which borrows the theme of the divine birth from the temple of Deir el-Bahri there also appears this other scene which occurs in that earlier temple. It seems that Amenhotep III deliberately copied some of the motifs of the Deir el-Bahri temple decoration, but it is not clear why he should have done so. The presentation of the

[11] Interpretation also may be uncertain; we cannot, for example, be sure whether the Egyptians conceived of the sun and moon as spheres or disks, though I am inclined to judge that they had the latter conception.

[12] The scenes are neither numbered nor mentioned in Porter and Moss, *Topographical Bibliography*. See Nelson, *Key Plans*, Pl. XXIII, Section D, Room II, locations 206 (west) and 218 (east). To my knowledge, these scenes have not been published, but I hope to publish them soon.

[13] Room G of Gayet; see Gayet, *op. cit.* p. 109 and Pl. LXVIII, Fig. 196 (Pl. LXXIV, Fig. 213). Oriental Institute photograph 9198. See also Colin Campbell, *The Miraculous Birth of King Amon-hotep III* (London, 1912) pp. 71–72, with comment: "It is difficult to understand it." Porter and Moss, *Topographical Bibliography* II, plan on p. 98, location 104; Nelson, *Key Plans*, Pl. XXIII, Section G, Room XIII, location 298.

dogma of the divine birth may have had political implications, but no logical basis presents itself for a triple rendering of the scene of striking a ball.

As one may well expect in temple art, the majority of such ritual scenes date from later periods, for the later temples are in the best state of preservation and are more completely devoted to ritual and mythological scenes than are many of the earlier temples. Unfortunately, by Ptolemaic and Roman times much of the meaning of the earlier religious ceremony had been lost, but the people of those periods were closer to the more ancient Egyptians than we are and the late temples provide information for our understanding of the earlier periods.

The Edfu temple has two examples of the scene under discussion. The earlier of these dates to the time of Ptolemy IV Philopator and is found on the west exterior wall of the sanctuary itself. This wall has three registers, each with seven offering scenes; the pertinent representation is in the uppermost register, the sixth scene from the left.[14] The king stands at the right, facing left toward the goddess Hathor, who is seated on a throne. He wears the double crown above a pair of horns and holds a club in his right hand and a ball in his left. The title of the scene is written before the king, and additional inscriptions accompany the relief.

The second Edfu example is in the library, in the lower register on the north wall, just to the east of the doorway.[15] Here the king, Ptolemy VII Euergetes II, is shown striking a ball before Hathor. Ptolemy is at the left, facing the goddess, who stands at the right. He wears the double crown and other regalia of his office; in his right hand is a clublike stick and in his left is a ball. The title of the scene is given between the two figures: *sḳr ḥmꜣ n mwt.f Wsrt*, "hitting the ball for his mother, Usert (i.e., Hathor)."

The Hathor temple at Denderah has a similar scene in the eastern crypt, on the east wall of Room B.[16] Ptolemy XIII Neos Dionysus, shown with

[14] Porter and Moss, *Topographical Bibliography* VI (1939) 146, locations 219–20 (plan on p. 130). The scene is published by the Marquis de Rochemonteix, *Le temple d'Edfou* I ("Mémoires publiés par . . . la Mission archéologique française au Caire" X [Paris, 1892]) Pl. XVI, text on p. 62.

[15] Porter and Moss, *Topographical Bibliography* VI 135, location 97 *i* (plan on p. 130). A drawing of the scene appears in Émile Chassinat, *Le temple d'Edfou* III ("Mémoires publiés par . . . la Mission archéologique française au Caire" XX [Le Caire, 1928]) Pl. LXXXII, text on p. 348.

[16] Porter and Moss, *Topographical Bibliography* VI 84, location 41 (plan on p. 82). The scene was first published in line drawing in Auguste Mariette, *Dendérah: Description générale du grande temple de cette ville* III (Paris, 1871) Pl. 22 *c′*; in Vol. VI (1875) 241, Mariette commented "scène difficile à comprendre" and made no attempt to describe or interpret the representation. A photograph of the scene is published in Chassinat, *Le temple de Dendara* V (Le Caire, 1947–52) Pl. CCCLXXII (cf. Pl. CCCLXX), text in hieroglyphic font on pp.

ꜣtf-crown and other insignia of his position, is depicted with the usual ball and stick. At the right stand Hathor and Harsomtus, before whom the ritual is performed.

The final scenes with this theme are in the temples of Philae. The second register on the exterior of the east wall of the temple of Isis has nine scenes of offerings made by Augustus. The eighth scene from the left shows the ruler striking a ball before Sekhmet, who is seated on a throne at the right.[17] The king wears the double crown above horns, as in the first Edfu relief described above. Again he holds the ball in his left hand, while in his right he holds a stick which is more accurately described as a club or bat since it is considerably thicker at the striking end than at the handle (cf. second Edfu example). The position of the arms and the grasping of the club are more realistic than in the earlier representations.

The temple of Hathor at Philae has on the façade a comparable scene of Augustus, but the goddess shown here is Tefnut.[18] Augustus again wears the double crown, but the horns are lacking. The stick does not appear to be as clublike as that on the temple of Isis, but the position of the hands is again very naturalistic. The left hand, holding the ball, is somewhat higher than the right, which holds the stick near one end, a position most practical for striking the ball.

The nine scenes described above have in common the representation of the king, dressed in royal accouterments, standing in the presence of a deity, and holding in his hands a ball and a stick. In several cases the legend states that the purpose of this ceremony is "to make a 'given-life.'" In the Mut chamber at Luxor it is also indicated that the performance is intended to bring joy to the heart of the deity. These limited statements are sufficient to account for the presence of the scenes with other ritual representations, but they do little to tell us what actually is being done. Beyond the general religious content and the mutual sense of offering there seems to be no common element that binds these scenes to those in whose context they appear.

66–67. A hand-copy of the text may be found in Johannes Dümchen, *Resultate der . . . 1868 . . . archäologisch-photographischen Expedition* (Berlin, 1869) Pl. XLVI.

According to Porter and Moss, *Topographical Bibliography* VI 76, there is another scene of this genre on the east exterior wall of this temple, but its exact position is not known. The texts have been published by Heinrich Brugsch, *Thesaurus Inscriptionum Aegyptiacarum* VI (1891) 1397–98, but he refers to the location as the south exterior wall.

[17] Porter and Moss, *Topographical Bibliography* VI 246, locations 382–83 (plan on p. 230). Georges Bénédite, *Le temple de Philae* ("Mémoires publiés par . . . la Mission archéologique française au Caire" XIII [Paris, 1893–95]) Pl. XXIX, text on p. 81 (Tableau X). Berlin photograph 329.

[18] Porter and Moss, *Topographical Bibliography* VI 251, location 19 (plan on p. 248). Berlin photograph 95.

Since the Deir el-Bahri scene is the oldest and also has some unique elements, it may well provide a starting point for analysis of the activity depicted. Naville's description and interpretation afford an interesting basis for discussion:

Here we have a rare representation, a symbolical ceremony the sense of which is not easy to understand. It is a game of ball. Thotmes III., Menkheperkara, holds a stick of wavy form, which from other texts we know to be made of olive wood, and strikes with it balls, the substance of which we do not know. The ceremony is called: "to strike the ball to (in honour of) Hathor the protectress of Thebes." Brugsch quotes an instance from Edfoo, in which it is said that the king strikes a ball in honour of his mother. It seems from the text which accompanies the ceremony at Dendereh, that the throwing of balls was a kind of emblem of victory, "the enemies are struck before them." There must have been several of them, since we see that the prophets hand them to Thotmes III., or perhaps make the catches.[19]

We must examine the reliefs carefully to see whether Naville's interpretation is right, for if he has understood this scene correctly it is the earliest known example of striking a ball with a bat, preceding by several millenniums the modern games which involve a similar action but serve a somewhat different purpose.

Assuming for the sake of argument that Naville's analysis is correct, let us see whether his treatment consistently agrees with the representations. Since the king holds the ball in his left hand, we judge that he struck it with the club held in his right. We have no way of determining whether the hitting movement was made with one hand or two hands, for the scenes always show the ball in the left hand, prior to its being released for the swing of the bat. The position of the right hand on the stick varies in the different representations; from them one could argue for either a one-handed or a two-handed blow, but the majority of cases shows the right hand so near the end of the stick that it is nearly certain that a one-handed swing is meant, unless one considers the unlikely suggestion that the king swung cross-handed, placing the left hand above the right on the handle of the stick.

The relative sizes of the club and the ball must also be considered. One could reason that the ball is shown larger than actuality because of its importance in the scene, but the stick plays an equally important part and therefore should also be shown in exaggerated proportions. One may assume that the objects are shown in about their true relative sizes. In most of the scenes the ball appears to be about the size of that used in the game of slow-pitch softball, which is 16 inches in circumference. The length of the stick may be estimated at somewhere between 27 and 44 inches. In terms of comparison, the bat used to hit a baseball (9 inches in circumference) is limited to a length of 42

[19] Naville, *The Temple of Deir el Bahari* IV 4.

inches and a diameter of $2\frac{3}{4}$ inches, though the length actually used falls between 32 and 36 inches. A softball bat has a barrel of smaller diameter, which accords with the principle that hitting a large object with a thin club is equal to hitting a small ball with a thick bat.

In the case of the Egyptian reliefs the bat seems to have been very small in diameter with respect to the size of the ball. This means that the king could hit the ball easily enough but could not drive it very far, though obviously relative mass and weight are involved as well as size. The stick wielded by the king in the Birth Room at Luxor seems a particularly inept implement, for it is quite thin and very long and looks more like a wand than a bat for hitting a ball. Also, the position of the king's hand on the stick is awkward, as noted above. On the other hand, the sticks shown in the library at Edfu and at Denderah are more practical equipment for striking a ball and the one depicted in the temple of Hathor at Philae also lends some authority to its user. The most impressive stick is that shown on the temple of Isis at Philae, for it is really a club, being small at the handle and considerably thicker at the striking end. Perhaps it illustrates a development of this equipment, for the stick at Deir el-Bahri is strangely wavy and quite unsuitable for hitting a ball. Possibly a reason not related to the function of striking a ball may account for the wavy form. The stick shown may indicate the humble beginnings of this activity, for even the name of the traditional sophisticated British game of cricket is said to be derived from a Saxon word meaning a crooked stick, such as the crude bats used in the early days of that game.[20]

At Edfu and Denderah the club is referred to as a stick of olive wood. The reason for this specification is not apparent, and the identification as olive wood is uncertain.[21]

Before leaving our discussion of implements used for striking a ball, we should call attention to the fact that in baseball a longer, thinner bat is used in batting practice for hitting long fly balls for the fielders and pitchers to catch. This fungo-stick, as it is called, corresponds in purpose to the Egyptian club, if Naville's interpretation is correct.

[20] See H. D. Altham, "Cricket," *Encylopaedia Britannica* (14th ed.; London, 1929) VI 691; H. Archie Richardson, "Cricket," *Collier's Encyclopedia* (1963) VII 433.

[21] There is no mention of the wood of the olive tree in Alfred Lucas, *Ancient Egyptian Materials and Industries* (4th ed., revised and enlarged by J. R. Harris; London, 1962); it is pointed out (p. 333) that the word for olive does not appear before the 19th dynasty, though part of an olive tree is represented in a mural painting at Amarna (see *The Mural Painting of el-ʿAmarneh*, ed. H. Frankfort [London, 1929] Pl. IX *C*). The caution concerning translating *bꜣk* as "olive" must be considered, but the substitution of "moringa tree" does not seem suitable in an instance which refers to wood rather than to oil. Possibly the Ptolemaic use of the word does refer to the olive tree, for by the time of the Ptolemies some olive trees were grown; perhaps the rare use of the wood accounts for its mention in these ritual scenes of Ptolemaic date.

The ball is the only other piece of equipment in evidence and may be the critical element for our interpretation of these scenes. Naville comments that the material of which the balls are made is not known. In listing these scenes, Porter and Moss usually describe them as showing the king striking a "clay-ball."[22] The text accompanying the scene in the sanctuary of the Edfu temple refers to a clay ball and explains the ritual as the smiting of enemies. A clay ball would afford a dramatic symbol of destruction of adversaries. If the king hit a ball of clay, he would pulverize it while holding it in his hand or would scatter the pieces about with a hard blow, either result strikingly epitomizing victory over enemies. This may explain the ritual of Ptolemaic times, but, as we shall see below, the scene at Deir el-Bahri rules out such an interpretation for the earlier period.

The balls found in excavations are ordinarily made of leather, stuffed with straw or similar substances, and sewed together with string. Usually the leather was cut into sections and assembled to form a spheroid. Those found at Thebes are said to be about 3 inches in diameter,[23] approximately the size of a baseball (9 inches in circumference) and much smaller than the balls shown in these ritual scenes.

The key argument for the kind of activity involved in these scenes is based on the role of the priests in the Deir el-Bahri relief. The two prophets are shown facing the king, and each one has both hands upraised and grasping a ball. Naville surmises that this representation indicates that possibly more than one ball was used, since three are shown, but if the depiction is particularly graphic it is more likely that only one ball was employed and that each of the participants is shown with a ball in order to describe most clearly his role in this unusual ritual. Naville suggests that the prophets either hand the ball to the king or catch the ball after it is hit. The position of their hands indicates almost certainly that the men are catching the ball, but it is likely that they immediately returned it to the king, either by throwing it to him or by carrying it to him and handing it to him in more formal fashion.

What appears to be conclusive is the short legend above the prophets. No mention of this inscription is made by Naville, though it is reproduced accurately in his publication. One can safely assume that it tells what the prophets are doing, and possibly it says more than that. Lexicographers who have worked since the time of Naville unquestioningly affirm that the word *ḫnp* here means

[22] *Topographical Bibliography* VI 84, 135, 146, 246; the reference to the Hathor temple at Philae (p. 251) does not mention a ball. The ball is not referred to in the Deir el-Bahri description (*ibid.* II 121), and the scenes in the Luxor temple are not listed.

[23] Wilkinson, *The Manners and Customs of the Ancient Egyptians* (new ed.) II 68. Other references are given in DeVries, *op. cit.* pp. 350–54.

"to catch,"[24] and thus the prophets are catching the ball which the king hits.

The inscription is unusual in the direction of its writing, for part of it faces to the right and part to the left. By coincidence, between the signs whose orientation is certain are three signs (*ḫ*, *n*, and *p*) which can be read in either direction, but if the sign to the right of this group is regarded as its determinative the group must be read from left to right. In any interpretation of this inscription the orientation of the signs must be explained as a device for associating parts of the legend with persons depicted to the right and left.

The simplest and most straightforward explanation of the text is based on taking the sign to the left of the *ḫnp*-group as the determinative of *ḫnp*, though the usual determinative of that word is the forearm with a stick and the sign carved here appears to represent a club or throwstick, neither of which is an appropriate determinative for a word meaning "to catch." Reading from right to left, however, presents even greater obstacles, for this choice leaves *ḫnp* without a determinative and the clublike sign as an abbreviated writing in a text whose words are otherwise fully written. The uncertain reading of this lone sign would be an additional and unnecessary complication of the text.

Taking *ḫnp* as written from left to right, we have two possibilities for reading the text: *ỉn ḥm-nṯr ḫnp n.f s(y)*, "it is the prophet who catches it for him,"[25] or *ḫnp n.f s(y) ỉn ḥm-nṯr*, "catching it for him by (i.e., on the part of) the prophet."[26]

Both the relief and the inscription identify the action of the scene; there can be little doubt that Naville was correct in interpreting it as representing the hitting and catching of a ball. It appears doubtful that this should be called a game, for it is clear from the persons involved and from the manner of their representation that it is some sort of ritual performance. It may be that the ceremony reflects a practice that otherwise was performed as a game or recreation, but there is no evidence for this.

The later scenes do not consistently reflect the earlier ritual, and it is likely that by Ptolemaic times the ceremony was carried out in a manner different from that of the reign of Thutmose III. As early as the time of Amenhotep III

[24] Cf. *Wb.* III 290, 12, "(den Ball mit der Hand) auffangen"; Faulkner, *op. cit.* p. 192. A writing of *ḫnp* in the Pyramid Texts has a determinative consisting of the head, shoulders, and bent arms of a man holding in one hand a round object which resembles a ball (Spell 667, § 1939 *b*), but the context shows that the word here has to do with eating and not with playing ball.

[25] With emphasis on the subject, "prophet." *ʾIn* plus noun plus imperfective active participle; see Sir Alan Gardiner, *Egyptian Grammar* (3d ed.; London, 1957) §§ 227, 3, and 373, 2.

[26] Emphasizing the action, "catching." Infinitive plus *ỉn* and noun; see *ibid.* §§ 168 and 300.

there appear to have been divergences from the practice shown at Deir el-Bahri.

Although the action of the Deir el-Bahri scene is clear, its meaning in terms of religious symbolism still escapes us. Of the nine ritual scenes described above, five are associated with Hathor (including one scene in which Harsomtus also is shown), two with Mut, and one each with Tefnut and Sekhmet. Obviously, most of the scenes relate to a goddess of joy and festivity, so that the hint of a game may not be incorrect, while with one of the two scenes in the Mut chamber of the Luxor temple there is the inscription which states that the king is bringing joy to the heart of Mut, a concept similarly related to happy well-being. The later reliefs are typically more concerned with protection against Apophis and other enemies. It is not clear that this element is reflected in the earliest representation, which seems to have a more positive note of joyful participation in a formal kind of fun, namely the hitting of a ball which was fielded by several prophets, in which the king was the officiant and the deity was both the spectator and the immediate beneficiary of the ritual act.

FOREIGN GODS IN ANCIENT EGYPT

Siegfried H. Horn

It is a well-known fact that a number of foreign gods found entrance into the pantheon of ancient Egypt. In the Old Kingdom the Egyptians occasionally became acquainted with certain foreign gods, such as *Ḫʿy-tꜣw* of Byblos, through trading and military activities. But there is no evidence that Asiatic gods entered the Egyptian pantheon in that early period. Later, the Egyptians became so active in certain foreign localities that they considered them almost as parts of their own country and then identified local deities with Egyptian gods. This happened, for example, in Byblos, where the local Baʿalat was identified with Hathor. The same thing was done also to the local goddess of the mining area of Sinai.

But a real intrusion of foreign gods did not occur until the Hyksos period, when together with other deities the powerful Asiatic Baʿal was brought into Egypt. He was identified with Seth, the Egyptian desert god, who from that time on became quite prominent. The process of adopting foreign gods was accelerated during the New Kingdom, because the building of an empire brought the Egyptians more than ever before into contact with foreign countries and nations. Egyptian nationals who lived or traveled outside their own country usually placed themselves under the protection of local foreign gods and in some instances erected stelae or even temples to these deities in their new residence cities. On the other hand, foreigners—slaves, sailors, business men, and professionals—moved to Egypt in large numbers and brought their gods along. The new gods apparently met no hostility in Egypt. To the contrary, some of these gods seem to have been received with open arms and in the course of time were adopted and placed on the same level as national gods.

For Asiatic gods who in this way found more or less permanent homes in the Nile Valley, temples were erected in Pharaonic Egypt. Baʿal had a temple in the harbor district *Prw-nfr* at Memphis, and Resheph also seems to have had a temple at Memphis. Horan possessed a sanctuary at the Sphinx of Gizeh, and Anath had a temple in Pi-Rameses (Tanis). Astarte seems to have had temples in *Prw-nfr* and at Pi-Rameses. And, finally, Qudshu apparently played a guest role in the temple of Ptah at Memphis.[1]

[1] For the latest comprehensive treatments of the influx of Asiatic gods into Egypt see Wolfgang Helck, *Die Beziehungen Ägyptens zu Vorderasien im 3. und 2. Jahrtausend v. Chr.* (Wiesbaden, 1962) pp. 480–514, and Rainer Stadelmann, *Syrisch-palästinensische Gottheiten in Ägypten* (Leiden, 1967).

For the Persian period the Aramaic papyri from Elephantine attest the existence of a Jewish Yahu (=Yahweh) temple on that island. According to the available evidence this temple was built not later than the 26th dynasty, since the Jews claimed in their letter to Bagoas in 407 B.C. that their temple had already been built when Cambyses conquered the country in 525 and that he allowed it to remain in use although he destroyed other temples in Egypt. We know, furthermore, from the same letter that the Jewish temple was destroyed by the non-Jewish soldiers of the neighboring garrison of Syene (Aswan) in 410.[2] Although the Syene soldiers were punished for their crime, the Elephantine Jews had a hard time obtaining a permit for the rebuilding of their temple, because the prudent Persian satrap demanded that they should first secure approval from the authorities in Judah. When this was finally given after the Elephantine Jews had declared their willingness to refrain from offering bloody sacrifices in the new temple,[3] the satrap evidently issued the desired building permit. The temple was then rebuilt, as the Brooklyn Aramaic papyri indicate. However, a few years later the Egyptians rose in rebellion against Persian rule. During this rebellion the Jewish colony in Elephantine seems to have been wiped out and the Yahu temple was once more destroyed.[4]

From the Elephantine papyri it is also evident that Yahu was not the only god worshiped by the Jews on Elephantine, for the gods Bethel, Ashim, Anath, and Ḥerem also appear in their texts, not only as components of personal names but also in lists of offerings.[5] Whether there were sanctuaries on Elephantine dedicated to any of these gods cannot be ascertained from the available evidence, but it is possible that the Yahu temple was not the only sanctuary of a foreign god on that island in the 5th century B.C.

In 1931 Noël Aimé-Giron published an Aramaic text mentioning a priest of Nabu, which led him to suggest that there must have been a Nabu temple or shrine at either Syene or Memphis.[6] That such a temple existed at Syene is now confirmed by the Hermopolis Aramaic papyri found in 1944 and published recently by E. Bresciani and M. Kamil.[7]

[2] A. Cowley, *Aramaic Papyri of the Fifth Century Century B.C.* (Oxford, 1923) No. 30, pp. 108–19.

[3] *Ibid.* Nos. 32 and 33, pp. 122–26.

[4] About the history of the Yahu temple and on the probable end of the Jewish colony at Elephantine see Emil G. Kraeling, *The Brooklyn Museum Aramaic Papyri* (New Haven, Conn., 1953) pp. 100–119.

[5] Cowley, *op. cit.* No. 22, pp. 65–76; about the gods of the Elephantine papyri see the discussion of Kraeling, *op. cit.* pp. 83–91, where also the pertinent literature is listed.

[6] Noël Aimé-Giron, *Textes araméens d'Égypte* (Cairo, 1931) No. 99, pp. 98–100.

[7] E. Bresciani and M. Kamil, "Le lettere aramaiche di Hermopoli," Academia nazionale dei Lincei, *Memorie della Classe di scienze morali, storiche e filologiche*, Serie VIII, Vol. XII (1966) fasc. 5, pp. 357–428.

The eight letters of this new collection were found by Sami Gabra in one of the galleries of the Ibis cemetery of Ashmunein (Hermopolis parva). In these galleries were many jars containing the mummies of sacred ibises, but one of the jars, to everyone's surprise, contained eight Aramaic papyri. At a distance of about 5 meters from this jar was found a naos bearing an Egyptian inscription including a cartouche with the name of King Darius (II?), a general indication that this material must be dated in the Persian period. The paleography of the texts indicates that the eight letters are from the late 5th century and contemporaneous with the Elephantine papyri, but their contents show that they were not written by Jews and that they came from Lower Egypt, though they concern affairs of Syene. Six of the letters are related to one another, one deals with a different matter, and one is too poorly preserved to provide any information concerning its contents. The purpose of this brief paper is not to discuss in detail the texts or contents of the letters but merely to deal with some interesting information which they contain, namely that temples of four Asiatic gods were located in Syene. These four gods were Nabu, Banit, Bethel, and the "Queen of Heaven."[8]

This information is of more than passing interest. In the first place, it confirms Aimé-Giron's suggestion that the Babylonian god Nabu had a temple in Syene in the 5th century. Nabu was the son of Marduk in Babylonian mythology and the chief god of Borsippa, a city south of Babylon. He was especially popular during the period of the neo-Babylonian empire, as attested by the many personal names of that time of which Nabu formed a component.[9] From the Elephantine papyri we learn that Babylonians were employed as officers of the Jewish garrison on that island. Other officers of the same nationality may have been stationed at Syene and must have been responsible for the introduction of the god Nabu, in whose honor a sanctuary was built and for whose cult a priest was installed, as is known from the above-mentioned papyrus published by Aimé-Giron.

The new information also shows that the god Bethel, widely revered in Syria and Palestine, had a temple at Syene, as had been surmised by earlier scholars. That this god was worshiped by the Jews of Elephantine was known from their archive and that the Israelites also had worshiped him in their homeland in pre-exilic times is attested in the Bible.[10]

[8] Hermop. Pap. I 1, II 1 and 12, III I, 1V 1.

[9] Morris Jastrow, *Die Religion Babyloniens und Assyriens* (rev. ed.; Giessen, 1905–1912) I 117 ff. and 422 ff.

[10] On the god Bethel see Otto Eissfeldt, "Der Gott Bethel," *Kleine Schriften* (Tübingen, 1962) pp. 206–33, where the biblical evidence is discussed on pp. 208–22 and the non-biblical sources are listed and discussed on pp. 222–25. To this material must be added three personal names found on an Aramaic tablet from Sefire; see J. Starcky, "Une tablette araméenne de l'an 34 de Nabuchodonosor (AO, 21,063)," *Syria* XXXVII (1960) 104–5.

However, the existence of a temple dedicated to such an obscure goddess as Banit is difficult to explain. Banit appears in some texts as one of the many names of the Babylonian Ishtar but is otherwise rarely encountered in Akkadian texts. The name occurs mainly as a component of Akkadian personal names,[11] of which some bearers were female slaves, so that J. J. Stamm thinks that Banit was a deity of female slaves.[12] But if this minor goddess had been carried to Egypt by slaves, would they have had the means to erect a temple or shrine to her? This question is easy to ask but impossible to answer. Since temples dedicated to her are not even known to have existed in ancient Mesopotamia, where her original home must have been, it is difficult to understand that a sanctuary was erected for her in faraway Egypt.

When Kamil in 1947 first announced the discovery of the Hermopolis papyri,[13] it became known that the "Queen of Heaven" is mentioned in them as one of the deities worshiped by either the writers or the addressees of the letters. Now we learn that a temple dedicated to her actually existed in Syene. This is of great interest in view of a passage in the book of Jeremiah (44:15–19) according to which the worship of the "Queen of Heaven" was attributed to Jews who lived in Pathros. Pathros is a Hebrew transliteration of Egyptian *pꜣ-tꜣ-rśy*, "the southland," called *Paturisi* in cuneiform inscriptions. It is a designation for the southernmost part of Egypt, of which Syene was the chief city. This shows that the Jeremiah passage also must refer to the cult of this goddess at Syene who had been adopted by Jews of Upper Egypt some 150 years before the Hermopolis papyri were written and that the cult of this deity and her temple must have existed in Syene for quite a long time.

It is not easy to ascertain who this "Queen of Heaven" was. Most commentators on the Jeremiah passage referred to[14] have seen in this female deity Ishtar, who throughout the ancient Near East was worshiped as the goddess of love and fertility and who in Babylonia and Assyria was considered also to

[11] *Arad-Banītu* (Knut L. Tallqvist, *Assyrian Personal Names* [Helsingfors, 1918] p. 25); *Bānīti-ērēš, Ba-ni-tú,* ^{fd}*Ba-ni-tú, Bānītu-a-a-li,* ^{d}*Ba-ni-tú-i*(?), ^{f}*Bānītum-dan-nat* (*ibid.* p. 52); see *ibid.* p. 253 for Talqvist's interpretation of Banit.

[12] J. J. Stamm, *Die akkadische Namengebung* (Leipzig, 1939) p. 69. Stamm questions Talqvist's interpretation that Banītu has a connection with *zēr banīti*. Hermann Ranke considered the possibility that ^{m}*Ba-ni-tu* might be an Egyptian name, since it occurs as the name of a witness in a contract made by Egyptians. In that case it would have a connection with the goddess Neith (see "Keilschriftliches Material zur altägyptischen Vokalisation," *Abhandlungen der königl. preuss. Akademie der Wissenschaften*, 1910, p. 37). The existence of a temple of Banit at Syene shows that Banit was the name of a deity and not a theophorous personal name of which a component was Neith. Ranke's suggestion must therefore be given up.

[13] Kamil, "Notice on the Aramaic Papyri Discovered at Hermopolis West," *Revue de l'histoire Juive en Égypte* I (1947) 1–3.

[14] See also Jer. 7:18.

be represented by the star Venus (not by the Moon, as some older books have it). In Akkadian texts Ishtar is called *šarrat šamē*, "queen of heaven," *šarrat šamāmi u kakkabē*, "queen of heaven and the stars," and *bēlit šamē*, "mistress of heaven," a title given to her in one of the Amarna letters also.[15] Her Syro-Palestinian counterpart was Astarte, the biblical Ashtoreth, a fertility goddess known from the Bible as well as from texts of Ras Shamra, Phoenicia, and Egypt.[16] The interpretation that Ishtar is the "Queen of Heaven" is supported by the mention of offering cakes, for which the Akkadian loanword *kawwanîm* is used, in the Jeremiah passages. The same custom is mentioned in an Akkadian text which speaks of the offering of *kaman tumri*, cakes baked in ashes, for Ishtar.[17] On the other hand it must be admitted that there is no known text from Syria or Palestine which calls Ishtar "Queen of Heaven," and, furthermore, Venus, a female deity in Babylonia, was considered to be a male star in Aramaic. For this reason the "Queen of Heaven" of Jewish worshipers, whether she was Ishtar or not, could not have represented Venus and could therefore not have been an exact equivalent of the Mesopotamian Ishtar.

However, the Syro-Palestinian goddess Anat also could claim identity with the "Queen of Heaven." In the northern temple of Level V in Beth-shan was found an Egyptian stela dated in the 10th or 9th century B.C. It was dedicated by a certain Hesi-nekht to "Antit, queen of heaven, mistress of all the gods."[18] Antit is Anat, the famous sister of Baᶜal and fierce goddess of warfare, who played a great role in the religious texts of ancient Ugarit. From Egyptian texts of the 19th and 20th dynasties it is known that she also was an important goddess in the Egyptian pantheon of that time, to whom a temple was dedicated in Tanis. Her cult may have spread all over Egypt and may have reached as far as Syene, where it may have flourished as late as the 5th century B.C., if our texts really refer to her.

From the brief listing of the evidence it becomes obvious that it is impossible to say with any degree of certainty whether the "Queen of Heaven" worshiped

[15] For Akkadian references see Heinrich Zimmern in E. Schrader's *Die Keilinschriften und das Alte Testament* (3d ed.; Berlin, 1903) pp. 425–26, and J. A. Knudtzon, *Die El-Amarna-Tafeln* (Leipzig, 1915) No. 23, line 26, pp. 180–81. The present author is indebted to Samuel N. Kramer for having drawn his attention to the fact that the name Inanna, the Sumerian Ishtar, has the meaning "queen of heaven." The meaning of this name may very well have been the origin of the title "queen of heaven" for Ishtar in Akkadian texts.

[16] Stadelmann, *Syrisch-palästinensische Gottheiten in Ägypten*, pp. 96–99 and 101–10.

[17] Zimmern, *op. cit.* pp. 441–42; J. Plessis, *Études sur les textes concernant Ištar-Astarté* (Paris, 1921) pp. 202–6 and 244. On the meaning of *kaman tumri* see W. von Soden, *Akkadisches Handwörterbuch* I (Wiesbaden, 1965) 430.

[18] Alan Rowe, *The Four Canaanite Temples of Beth-shan*, Part I (Philadelphia, 1940) pp. 33–34 and Pl. LXVA 1. For the dating of Level V and its temples see Henry O. Thompson, "Tell el-Husn—Biblical Beth-shan," *The Biblical Archaeologist* XXX (1967) 116 and 130–32.

by the Jews of Jeremiah's time and by the writers or addressees of the Hermopolis letters was Ishtar, the great goddess of fertility and love, or Anat, the goddess of warfare. There is evidence which favors each of the two interpretations, but no evidence is conclusive enough to pin the identification on one or the other of the two Semitic goddesses.

The new information provided by the Hermopolis papyri with regard to cult places of foreign gods in Upper Egypt is certainly of great interest. We now know that at least five sanctuaries dedicated to Asiatic gods existed at Syene and on Elephantine in the 5th century B.C. At least two (possibly three) of the gods worshiped in these cult places were Babylonian, one (possibly two) Syro-Palestinian, and one Jewish. This evidence also gives a picture of the plurality of nationals represented among the military and civilians of these two places. Furthermore, it is an additional exhibit for the continuing religious tolerance of the Egyptians, demonstrated first in the New Kingdom and now attested for a later era. That the plurality of nationals, gods, and cults caused social stresses and occasionally led to violent eruptions is witnessed by the destruction of the Yahu temple on Elephantine in 410. The new papyri have slightly lifted the curtain of our ignorance and provided us with some new and most interesting information, but much more documentary evidence is needed before we will be able to obtain a clear picture of the religious and social conditions of the foreign communities in pre-Ptolemaic Egypt.

THE CRUEL FATHER

A DEMOTIC PAPYRUS IN THE LIBRARY OF G. MICHAELIDES

George R. Hughes

This small birthday offering is made in grateful tribute to a fine scholar who has also been for nearly forty years an equally fine teacher, mentor, colleague and friend of the offerer—as well as an admirable father to his children.

The appeal to the Ibis, Falcon, and Baboon deities which is the subject of this study is in the library of Mr. Georges Michaelides in Cairo. It is one of eight such demotic appeals, most of them to Thoth, of varying ages and types in Mr. Michaelides' collection. I am grateful to him for providing the photograph and for permitting me to publish this text as well as others.

Inasmuch as I have previously edited two other such pleas to deities[1] and in so doing have written at some length about the genre,[2] it is not necessary to do so here. However, Professor Erwin Seidl has recently devoted an article[3] to some of them from the Saite and Persian periods, and he understands them as a quite different phenomenon. Instead of seeing them as letter-like appeals to deities stemming from the older letters to the dead and still "posted" in cemeteries, Seidl associates them rather with divine oracles and the well-known brief questions submitted by suppliants in quest of an oracular decision by a divine judge or otherworldly court for use in settling disputes and obtaining rights on earth. Perhaps Seidl would not deny the possibility that the demotic pleas have some relation to the earlier letters to the dead, but he is much more impressed by the legal terminology he sees in them and the legal form in which he believes them to be cast.

Without going into detail here it seems doubtful to me that Seidl has made his case. Quite apart from what appear to me to be questionable readings and interpretations at certain places in the demotic texts which he treats, there appears to be no reason to regard the pleas as legal documents in suit of an *oracular* judgment which would be a legally valid instrument enforceable on earth. This is not to deny the importance of oracles and oaths as legal in-

[1] Pap. Or. Inst. 19422 in *JNES* XVII (1958) 1–12 and a Michaelides text on linen in *JEA* LIV (1968) 176–82.

[2] The plea published here is described briefly in *JEA* LIV 177, footnote 1.

[3] "Die Gottesentscheidungen der Saiten- und Perserzeit," *American Studies in Papyrology*. I. *Essays in Honor of C. Bradford Welles* (New Haven, 1966) pp. 59–65.

struments in the Egypt of Saite, Persian, and Ptolemaic times, but these demotic pleas are much too varied in form, too careless in such matters as dates, and too lacking in precise detail in contrast to, for example, the pleas in the Siut court case.[4] They sound instead like sometimes impassioned cries for help, prayers in extremity, which do not so much as formulate the specific solution sought. Moreover, what legal construction can one place upon a plea to Thoth for protection from an evil genius?[5]

To be sure, the text translated below will no doubt appear to strengthen Seidl's case. There are in it, for example, some words and phrases freighted with legal meaning and there are matters of civil concern such as the property rights of the children as heirs of their mother. However, there is nothing in it, to my mind, to relate it to an expected oracle to be used as a valid legal remedy. The miscreant father is expected to or may take an oath, but the children imply that even his oath would be false without the intervention of the gods.[6]

It would seem, as I have said in another place,[7] that these pleas to deities exhibit a fundamental distrust of law courts and civil authorities. They even express the assumption that the only defence of the lowly mistreated person was in a strong and influential patron and champion. Lacking such an earthly champion the inditers of the pleas turned, as they often say, to a divine patron.[8]

One may wonder, of course, how the suppliants expected to receive effective relief from their earthly mistreatment if not through something like a legally valid oracle, but then how did the writers of the more ancient letters to the dead expect to gain effective relief from their troubles? How do those who pray to their gods anywhere expect their prayers to be answered? The inditers of the demotic pleas, it would seem, implicitly leave that to the wise, just, all-powerful deities.

Be that as it may, the plea published here is a very human social document. The situation, the expulsion and abandonment of his children by a father after the death of their mother and his remarriage, is one all too familiar in Egypt until very recent years. The practice was probably normal in the villages throughout Egyptian history despite what one might be led to assume from the guarantees of the rights of children in the demotic marriage contracts.[9]

[4] Sir Herbert Thompson, *A Family Archive from Siut* (Oxford, 1934) pp. 12–19.

[5] The plea published in *JEA* LIV 176–82.

[6] See line 15 of the text and note on it.

[7] *JNES* XVII 2 and 4.

[8] See line 14 of the text and the notes on it as well as *JEA* LIV 178, lines 1 and 2.

[9] See P. Pestman, *Marriage and Matrimonial Property in Ancient Egypt* ("Papyrologica Lugduno-Batava" IX [Leiden, 1961]) pp. 117–22 and 137–39. See also line 13 of this plea.

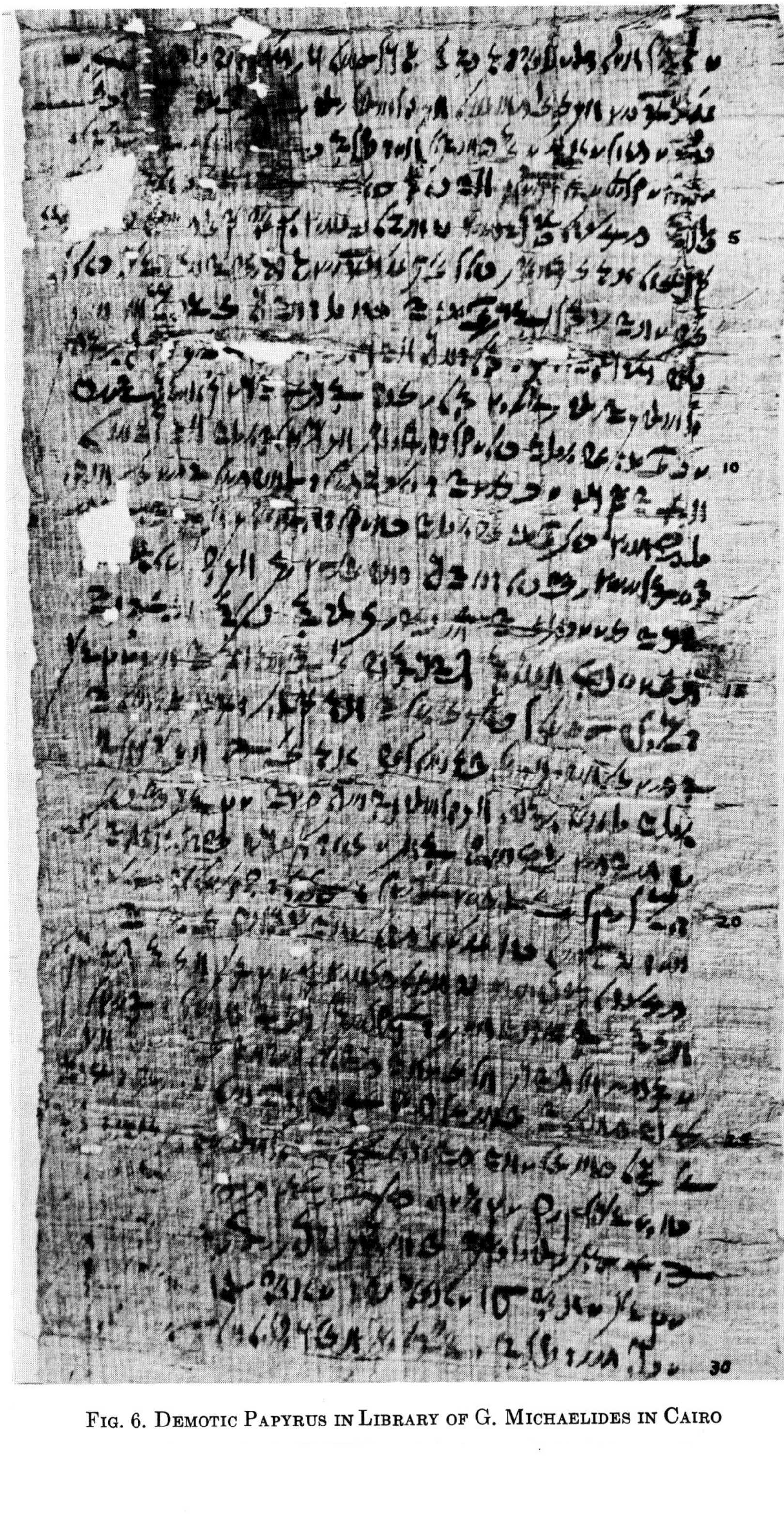

FIG. 6. DEMOTIC PAPYRUS IN LIBRARY OF G. MICHAELIDES IN CAIRO

This appeal is by far the longest and most detailed known to me. It is also one of the latest, if not the latest, in date; it is Ptolemaic and probably very late Ptolemaic. This judgment rests entirely on the paleography and certain peculiarities of orthography which are noted in the comments on the text.

There is no information as to where the papyrus was found. I have assumed in the past that all the pleas to Thoth or the Ibis came from the caverns of Hermopolis (Tuna el-Gebel),[10] but in view of W. B. Emery's discovery of an equally vast ibis and baboon cemetery at North Saqqara[11] and in consideration of certain "Bohairicisms" in the orthography of this text, it may well have come from Saqqara although it was found at least a decade ago. It is perhaps significant also that the Ibis, Falcon, and Baboon are appealed to but that the name "Thoth" does not occur in the text although the Ibis is given the epithets of Thoth in line 4.

The text is carefully written in a precise and consistent hand on a piece of papyrus 29.5 cm. high by 15 cm. wide (Fig. 6). As one would expect in the case of a letter, the writing runs at right angles to the vertical fibers of the papyrus.[12] If for no other reason, the scribe thus avoided the very long lines that would have resulted had the text been written parallel to the fibers and lengthwise on the papyrus. Demotic scribes rather consistently wrote their letters in the shortest lines possible, often crosswise on narrow strips of papyrus and not in long lines or parallel columns.[13]

The papyrus bears evidence of having been folded into a long, narrow packet. There are nine creases across the papyrus, parallel to the lines of writing. One should say, rather, that the document was rolled up and tied and eventually became flattened to produce the creases now visible. Since the creases are closer together at the bottom of the text than at the top, the papyrus must have been rolled up from the bottom leaving the beginning of the text to appear first in the unrolling as one would expect. Unlike, for example, the letter to Thoth, Pap. Or. Inst. 19422,[14] this document bears no address or notation of its nature on the verso, the outside of the roll.

TRANSLITERATION

(1) Pꜣ-šr-Ḏḥwty ỉrm wꜥt Nꜣ-nfr-ḥr nꜣ ẖm-ẖl(w) swky 2 r.ms st Ḥr-ꜥnḫ n (2) Ḥr-pn-Kmt ỉw-f ỉr why ỉw-f ḥwy-w r-bnr r.bn-[p]-f nꜥ n-w nꜣ nty ḏd (3) m-bꜣḥ pꜣ hb pꜣ bk pꜣ ꜥꜥny ỉrm nꜣ nṯrw nty ḥtp ỉrm-w (n) pꜣ ꜥwy ḥtp (4) pꜣ hb pꜣ nṯr

[10] See *JNES* XVII 1 and *JEA* LIV 176.

[11] See *JEA* LII (1966) 5 f. See also the note on lines 3 and 4 of our text.

[12] See Jaroslav Černý, *Paper and Books in Ancient Egypt* (London, 1952) pp. 17 and 21–22.

[13] See e.g. the letters in Wilhelm Spiegelberg, *Die demotischen Papyri Loeb* (München, 1931) Pls. 4–18.

[14] *JNES* XVII, Pl. I.

ʿꜣ ḥry-ỉb Ḫmnw ỉw-n mtw-tn mr[-tn n] ⸢m-bꜣḥ tꜣ ḳnbt⸣ [sḏm-tn r] (5) ḫrw-n hblꜣ grḥ ꜣyt mtre n-ḏrt wʿ why [. . .]. . . (6) wʿ sbꜣ bw-ỉr-f ỉr ḥꜣty-f mtw-w ḏd n-f Ḥr-pn-Kmt r Šr-ʿḥʿ sꜣ Wn-Mnt rn-f mtw-w (7) ḏd n-f pꜣy-n ỉt r.bn-p-f nʿ n-n nty-ỉw wꜣḥ tꜣy-n mwt ỉr rnpt ʿšꜣy ỉrm-f (8) wꜣḥ-s ms-n ⸢dỉ⸣-f n.mwt tꜣy⟨-n⟩ mwt ỉw-n sbḳ [n ms] ṯy-f kt wʿt (r) pꜣy-f ʿwy (9) ḥwy-f n r-bnr r ṯy pꜣ hrw mwt r.ỉr-s bn-p-f dỉ n-n ʿḳ ḥbs nḥe (10) pꜣ nty nʿ ḫr-r.ḥr-n mtw pꜣ nṯr mḥ n ḥꜣty-f ỉw-f nw r.ḥr-n ỉw-n ḥḳy (11) ỉw-f dỉ n-n wʿ ʿḳ pꜣ nty gm-n (n) nꜣ ʿlḳw nꜣ ḏyꜣwt ḫn pꜣ ḫry (12) ḥr rhwe mtw-f nʿ ḫr-r.ḥr-n nty-ỉw pꜣ nṯr mḥ n ḥꜣty-f ỉw-f ṯy-n (r) pꜣy-f ʿwy (13) šʿ dwe r.wn-mtw tꜣy-n mwt tꜣy-s grk(t) r.r-f ỉw-f ḥwrʿ-n [n-s] (14) bn-p-n gm pꜣ mtw-f (r) ỉr n-n tym r.r-f bnr-tn mtw-tn [nꜣ] ỉ.ỉr nḫt-n (15) ỉw-f ỉr pꜣ ʿnḫ ỉ.ỉr-ḥr-tn šn-tn s wpy-tn n ỉrm pꜣ rmṯ rn-f (16) nꜣ-ʿšꜣ-w nꜣ kmʿw mtw-f ỉr n.ỉm-w n-n ỉ.ỉr-f (*sic*) wʿ ḏrꜣ.ṯ mḫy-n (17) ḫn pꜣ ḫry ỉw-f ḏd mḫy.w st bw-ỉr-f ḏd m-ỉr ỉw-f nw (18) r.ḥr-n ḥr rꜣ (n) pꜣy-f ʿwy ỉw-f ḥwy ỉpyt m-sꜣ-n pꜣ rmṯ rn-f wn-mtw-f (19) ḥḏ prt ỉḫyw bn ỉw-f (r) pꜣ ẖʿꜣ (n) pꜣy ʿḳ ⟨r.⟩wn.nꜣw ⸢ỉr-f tꜣ ḥṯ⸣ n-n ỉn (20) nꜣ-ʿšꜣ-w r sẖ-w r bn ḏmʿ šsp-w nꜣ kw(w) nꜣ ḥwrʿw nꜣ ⸢hblꜣ(w)⸣ (21) ỉrm nꜣ ꜣnty(w) nty-ỉw Ḥr pꜣ whꜣ pꜣy-n ỉt nty ḥry ỉr n.ỉm-w n-n (22) hblꜣ grḥ ꜣyt mtre n-ḏrt pꜣ rmt rn-f ỉ.ỉr-tn (r) šn-f (23) ỉ.ỉr-tn (r) wpy-n ỉrm-f r nꜣ sꜣwtyw nꜣ wptyw nꜣ šmsw (24) (n) pꜣ ʿwy r.ỉw-w (r) šn-f ỉw-w (r) ỉr pꜣy-n hp ⸢ẖr⸣ tꜣy-n wpyt ỉrm-f (25) dỉ-n hy.n my twn⟨-n n⟩ dỉ-n ꜣnty my ⸢ḳn⸣-f dỉ-n (26) ṯy (n) ḳns my ỉr-w pꜣy-n hp dỉ-n ḥwy ⸢pꜣy ʿš [ỉ.]ỉr-ḥr nꜣ nṯrw⸣ (27) nty-ỉw nꜣy-w rnw sẖ r-ḥry pꜣ rmṯ nb (n) pꜣ tꜣ mtw-f (r) tḳ pꜣy bꜣk (n) hʿꜣ[h] ⸢r ḫb⸣-f (28) m-ỉr dỉ šm-f r-bnr ḥr ḫrw-n my ʿš-f s (n) ḥꜣt-f r pḥw-f m[y dỉ-w ʿš s] (29) pꜣ rmṯ rn-f (n) pꜣ rꜣ rsy pꜣ rꜣ mḥt pꜣ rꜣ ỉmnt pꜣ rꜣ ỉꜣbt (30) (n) pꜣ mꜣʿ r nꜣ nṯrw ḥtp n.ỉm-f ỉ.ỉr-w sḥw ⸢ỉw-w sḏm [r pꜣy] wḫꜣ⸣.

TRANSLATION

(1) Psenthotes and one Naneferho, the two minor children whom Hoankh bore to (2) Harpakême—he is cruel, casting them out without being merciful to them—, are they who say (3) to the Ibis, the Falcon, the Baboon, and the gods who rest with them in the resting place (4) of the Ibis, the great god who dwells in Hermopolis:

"We are yours. [May you] favor [us] ⸢before the Council⸣ and may you [listen to] (5) our plea:

'Misery by night, misfortune by day at the hands of a cruel one [. . .], (6) an impious one—he feels no guilt; and he is called Harpakême although his name is Sheraha son of Wenmont, and (7) he is called our father although he has not been merciful to us; with whom our mother spent many years. (8) She bore us and he ⸢caused⸣ our mother's death while we were small. He took another one into his house, (9) and he cast us out from the day on which she died.

'He has not given us food, clothing or oil. (10) He who takes pity on us, whose heart the gods fills, when he sees us hungry, (11) he gives us a meal. He who finds us in the corners of the walls in the street (12) at evening and takes pity on us, whose heart the god fills, he takes us to his house (13) until morning.

'Although there is due our mother her dowry from him, he deprives us [of it]. (14) We have not found anyone who will provide us protection from him except you; it is you who have saved us.

(15) 'If he takes the oath before you, may you interrogate him and may you judge between us and this man. (16) Many are the wrongs which he inflicts on us. If a strong man beats us (17) in the street, he says, "Beat them"; he does not say, "Do not." When he sees (18) us at the door of his house, he hurls an *oipe*-container after us. This man, he has (19) money, grain, and goods; he is not lacking in the food ⟨which⟩ ⌜he had been giving⌝ to us.

(20) 'They are too numerous to write nor would papyrus receive them: The stringencies, the deprivations, the ⌜miseries⌝ (21) and the restraints which Hor, the cruel one, our father mentioned above, inflicts on us.

(22) 'Misery by night, misfortune by day at the hands of this man! You shall interrogate him and (23) you shall judge between us and him. As for the guards, the messengers, and the servants (24) of the house, when they shall interrogate him, they shall avenge us ⌜as a result of⌝ judging between us and him.

(25) 'We have fallen, cause ⟨us⟩ to rise. We are restrained, make him ⌜cease⌝. We are (26) mistreated, cause that we be avenged.' "

We are casting ⌜this appeal before the gods⌝ (27) whose names are written above. As for anyone in the world who will set this document on fire ⌜to destroy⌝ it, (28) let him not escape from our plea, let him read it from its beginning to its end. Let (29) that man [be made to read it] at the south entrance, the north entrance, the west entrance, and the east entrance (30) of the place in which the gods rest. May they curse ⌜when they listen [to this] letter⌝.

NOTES

LINE 1. *wꜥt Nꜣ-nfr-ḥr*, "one Naneferho." The reading here and at the end of line 8 must be *wꜥt* rather than *sḥmt*, "woman," or *šrt*, "girl."

nꜣ ḫm-ẖl(w) swky, "the minor children." Basically *swky*, which is commonly written *swg* until the Roman period (Erichsen, *Dem. Glossar*, p. 417), means "incompetent, needing the care of a parent or guardian." In Petubastis (Pap. Strassburg) v 3, in a literary simile concerning the fiercely protective behavior of a wet nurse, the child in her care is called *pꜣy-s ḫm-ẖl swg*, "her minor child," "her infant," without legal connotation. The *rmṯ swg* met so frequently in the demotic wisdom texts is an incompetent person and, as an adult, a stupid person.

LINE 2. *Ḥr-pn-Kmt*, "Harpakême." The context in line 6 indicates that this was the name by which the father was known, not the name given him at birth. Unless the scribe unintentionally omitted the *pn-Kmt* in line 21, the name was further shortened to *Ḫr.* Although the name Harpakême is not known to me elsewhere, the names of his daughter and wife in line 1, Naneferho and Hoankh, are not uncommon and they happen to occur in marriage documents from Tebtynis in year 78 B.C., Pap. Cairo 30616 a 2, b 2 and a 5, b 6 respectively. These two women are not the same persons as the mother and daughter in our plea, however.

ỉw-f ỉr why . . . r.bn-[p]-f nꜥ n-w, "he is cruel . . . without being merciful to them." For a similar contrast between *why* and *nꜥ* see Insinger ii 7: *tm why n-f n nꜣy-f sww n ꜥnḫ mtw-k nꜥ [n-f ỉw-f] mwt,* "do not be cruel to him during the days of his life and merciful [to him when he] is dead." The verb *why* is used when an object of the action is expressed, but *why* is noun object of *ỉr* when no other object is expressed. The *nꜥ* here and in line 7 is construed with the dative but in lines 10 and 12 with *ḥr*. The difference in idiom is probably attributable to the fact that in the first two cases it is their father that is said not to be merciful to the children but in the latter two it is the casual passerby in the street who is said to take pity on them.

LINES 3 AND 4. *pꜣ hb . . . (n) pꜣ ꜥwy ḥtp pꜣ hb,* "the Ibis . . . in the resting place of the Ibis." The name "Thoth" does not occur in the text. Compare Pap. Brit. Museum 10230, line 4 (Reich, *Pap. jur. Inhalts,* pp. 77 ff. and Pls. XV–XVI), where there occurs in a scribe's title *pꜣ ꜥwy ḥtp pꜣ hb pꜣ bk nty ḥr tꜣ ḫꜣst Ḏm,* "the resting place of the Ibis and the Falcon which is in the necropolis of Djême." There can be no doubt that our text refers to either the vast subterranean galleries at Tuna el-Gebel (see *JEA* LIV 176) filled with mummified ibises and a few mummified falcons and baboons or the similar ibis cemetery uncovered in recent years by Emery at North Saqqara (*JEA* LII 5 f.).

LINE 4. *pꜣ nṯr ꜥꜣ ḥry-ỉb Ḫmnw,* "the great god who dwells in Hermopolis." The epithet of Thoth in demotic is usually *nb Ḫmnw,* "lord of Hermopolis," as in Pap. Or. Inst. 19422, lines 1 and 3 (*JNES* XVII, Pl. I), and in the Michaelides plea on linen, line 1 (*JEA* LIV, Pl. XXVIII). Here, however, it must contain the alternative *ḥry-ỉb* (Erichsen, *Dem. Glossar,* p. 321) despite a writing that looks like *ḥry-tb*. See what appears to be written *ḥry-tbn* for *ḥry-ỉb-n* in Pap. Rylands IX ii 14 and ꜥOnchsheshonqy ii 17. It is quite possible that the difference between "Thoth, twice great, lord of Hermopolis" in the two pleas mentioned above and "the Ibis, the great god who dwells in Hermopolis" in our text is the result of different places of origin, Hermopolis in the first instance and perhaps Saqqara in the second.

mr[-tn n] ⸢m-bꜣḥ tꜣ ḳnbt⸣, "[may you] favor [us] ⸢before the Council⸣." The traces here are confusing. The *mr* is certain, and the *m-bꜣḥ* and *tꜣ* (or *nꜣ*) are reasonably so. The reading *tꜣ ḳnbt* (or *nꜣ ḳnbwt*) is suggested by "the great Councils" in the plea on linen, line 1 (*JEA* LIV 178). The further assumption is made that the sentence began with a hortative *mr-tn* followed by another, *sḏm-tn,* at the end of the line in the manner of the hortative *sḏm-f*'s in line 15. The meaning of *mr* would then appear to be "to prefer," "to incline toward" the suppliant children.

LINE 5. *ḫrw-n,* "our plea," "our petition." See also line 28 and the note on *ḫrw* in *JNES* XVII 6–7.

hblꜣ grḥ ꜣyt mtre, "misery by night, misfortune by day." This wail is repeated in line 22, and it appears in Pap. Cairo 50110, lines 6–7. Cf. *JEA* LIV 178, note to line 1.

wꜥ why [. . .] . . . , "a cruel one [. . .] . . . ." At the end of the line there are remnants of the beginning and end of the word or phrase attributive to *why*. It is not another noun with indefinite article between *wꜥ why* and *wꜥ sbꜣ*.

LINE 6. *bw-ỉr-f ỉr ḥꜣty-f,* "he feels no guilt," ⲙⲉϥⲣ̄ϩⲧⲏϥ (Crum, *Coptic Dict.* p.

715*b*). The clause is grammatically independent and parenthetical. For the idiom compare ʿOnchsheshonqy xix 8: *ỉn-nꜣ rmt swg ỉr ḥꜣty-f ỉw-f ỉr rmṯ rḫ,* "when a stupid man feels guilt he is a wise man."

r Šr-ʿḥʿ sꜣ Wn-Mnt rn-f, lit. "whereas Sheraha son of Wenmont is his name." It would be possible to read *sꜣ Šr-ʿḥʿ r Wn-Mnt rn-f,* "son of Sheraha, whereas Wenmont is his name," but this is less likely to be correct in view of the fact that Harpakême (see note on line 2) was a nickname not apt to be followed by the patronymic. I cannot cite other examples of either name although the reading seems inescapable in each case.

LINE 7. *r-bn-p-f nʿ n-n,* ⲉⲙⲡⲉϥⲛⲁ ⲛⲁⲛ, "although he has not been merciful to us." The first person plural suffix, the first person plural dependent pronoun object, and the dative of the first person plural are all written in exactly the same way by our scribe. The verb *nʿ* is construed with the dative here and in line 2 as well as with *ḫr* in lines 10 and 12. It is not construed with the direct object (Crum, *Coptic Dict.* p. 216*b*).

nty-ỉw wꜣḥ tꜣy-n mwt ỉr rnpt ʿšꜣy ỉrm-f, "with whom our mother spent many years." The conjugation is Perfect I preceded by the relative converter, ⲛ̄ⲧⲁⲧⲉⲛⲙⲁⲁⲩⲣ̄ⲣⲟⲙⲡⲉ (cf. Spiegelberg, *Dem Gram.* § 191).

LINE 8. *wꜣḥ-s ms-n,* "she bore us." The auxiliary is clearly *wꜣḥ-* and not the Conjunctive *mtw-*. The scribe nowhere writes the *.ṯ* of the pronominal state of third weak infinitives, thus conforming to Bohairic Coptic (ⲁⲥⲙⲁⲥⲛ̄) in contrast to what is almost universally the case in demotic texts (cf. Spiegelberg, *Dem. Gram.* § 106, and note *ỉw-w šn-w* of Orakeltext ii 5 cited there). So also *gm-n* in line 11, *ṯy-n* in line 12, and *šn-f* in lines 22 and 24.

⌜*dỉ*⌝*-f n.mwt tꜣy* ⟨*-n*⟩ *mwt,* "he ⌜caused⌝ our mother to die" or "he ⌜caused⌝ our mother's death." After *ms-n* there is something much more than the expected *n-f* for "she bore us *to him.*" The suffix is too far left, and no other preposition is attested in the idiom. The *-f* must then be subject of a verb beginning the next clause, and the traces fit the only possible verb, *dỉ,* "cause." On *n.mwt* see *JEA* LIV 180 and II Khamuas v 36 and vi 28.

ỉw-n sbḳ [*n ms*], "while we were small." The restoration is necessary, for *sbḳ* is apparently not used alone in demotic to mean "young," "small" of persons; otherwise one might be led to restore *m-sꜣ nꜣy,* "thereafter," to begin the next clause.

ṯy-f kt wʿt (*r*) *pꜣy-f ʿwy,* "he took another one into his house." The remains of *ṯy* and *kt* are unmistakable. The reading must be *kt wʿt,* ⲕⲉⲟⲩⲉⲓⲉ, "another one," rather than *kt sḥmt,* "another woman," just as *wʿt* must be read in line 1. This idiom of taking a woman into the house is not known to me elsewhere as one connoting marriage (cf. Pestman, *Marriage and Matrimonial Property in Ancient Egypt,* pp. 9–10), and it is probably intentionally pejorative. The same idiom is used in line 12 of the passing stranger who takes the children into his house for the night.

LINE 9. *ḥwy-f n r-bnr,* "he cast us out." The pronoun object is the old dependent pronoun first plural found in early demotic, not the compound based on *tw->ṯ-* found in Ptolemaic texts (Spiegelberg, *Dem. Gram.* § 258).

pꜣ hrw mwt r.ỉr-s, "the day on which she died." This refers, of course, to the mother of the children, not to their father's second wife.

ʿḳ, ⲟⲉⲓⲕ, "food," "rations," "a meal." On the writing and meaning see Malinine in *JEA* XXXV (1949) 150–52. The same word occurs in line 11 with indefinite article ("a meal") and in line 19 with definite article ("the food").

LINE 10. *pꜣ nty nʿ ḫr-r.ḫr-n,* ⲡⲉⲧⲛⲁ ϩⲁⲣⲟⲛ, "he who takes pity on us." For the pronominal state of the preposition *ḫr* see *ḫr-r.ḫr-y* in I Khamuas iii 29 and 38. The verb *n*ᶜ is construed with the dative in lines 2 and 7 (see note on line 2) and again with *ḫr* in line 12.

*mtw p*ꜣ *nṯr mḥ n ḥ*ꜣ*ty-f*, "whose heart the god fills." The scribe began the same relative clause in line 12 with *nty-iw*. Also the *mtw-f ir n.im-w n-n* in line 16 is paralleled by the relative plus Present I, *nty-iw Ḥr . . . ir n.im-w n-n* in line 21. In line 14 *mtw-f ir* is written for the relative plus Future III, *nty iw-f (r) ir*, as is *mtw-f tk* in line 27 for *nty iw-f (r) tk*. The frequent indifference of demotic scribes to writing the Conjunctive and the relative plus Present I or Future III is not recognized in Spiegelberg, *Dem. Gram.* § 151, but see Thompson, *A Family Archive from Siut*, p. 106, No. 150. The idiom "to fill the heart" of a person, presumably with a good thought or impulse, is not known to me elsewhere in demotic. Even so, the writing in lines 10 and 12 appears to be *mḥ* rather than *di-s*, "put it," although the idiom *di n ḥ*ꜣ*ty* is found in ᶜOnchsheshonqy iii 13–14 and 14–15.

iw-f nw r.ḥr-n, ⲉϥⲛⲁ ⲉⲣⲟⲛ, "when he sees us." This could also be Present I, "he sees us," co-ordinate with the following Present I, *iw-f di n-n*, "he gives to us."

Line 11. *w*ᶜ ᶜ*k*, "a meal" or "a loaf." See the note on ᶜ*k* in line 9.

*p*ꜣ *nty gm-n*, "he who finds us," "whoever finds us." The pronominal state of the infinitive is the Bohairic form ϫⲙ-, not ϭⲛⲧ- (see note on *w*ꜣ*ḥ-s ms-n* in line 8), but in Coptic the durative tense would require an oblique object ⲡⲉⲧϫⲓⲙⲓ ⲙ̄ⲙⲟⲛ, *p*ꜣ *nty gm n.im-n* (Till, *Kopt. Gram.* §§ 259 and 480). That the rule does not apply in the case of these semantically undefined, nominalized relatives is amply illustrated in demotic by such examples as *p*ꜣ *nty whm-s*, "he who repeats it" (Insinger xxi 16); *p*ꜣ *nty st*ꜣ*-f*, "he who withdraws himself" (Insinger xxi 17); and *p*ꜣ *nty ir-f*, "he who makes it" (Insinger xxi 23).

(*n*) *n*ꜣ ᶜ*lkw n*ꜣ *ḏy*ꜣ*wt ḫn p*ꜣ *ḫry*, "in the corners of the walls in the street." The noun ᶜ*lk* must be the Bohairic ⲗⲁⲟⲕ, "corner," "angle" (Crum, *Coptic Dict.* p. 5*b*), but I can point to no other occurrence in demotic.

Line 12. *iw-f ty-n (r) p*ꜣ*y-f* ᶜ*wy*, "he takes us to his house." The verb appears to be *ty*, "take," rather than *in*, "bring." For a writing of *p*ꜣ*y-f* ᶜ*wy* see the end of line 8. Here again (see note on *p*ꜣ *nty gm-n* in line 11) the Present I, a durative tense, would seem to require the oblique object, *iw-f ty n.im-n*, ϥϫⲓ ⲙ̄ⲙⲟⲛ, but the tense could be Future III, *iw-f (r) ty-n*, "he will take us," thus obviating the difficulty. The pronominal state of the infinitive of *ty* is normally *ty.ṯ-* (Erichsen, *Dem. Glossar*, p. 663) and it is ϫⲓⲧ-, ϭⲓⲧ- in all the Coptic dialects including Bohairic (Crum, *Coptic Dict.* p. 747*b*), yet it is *ty-* here. See note on line 8.

Line 13. *r.wn-mtw t*ꜣ*y-n mwt t*ꜣ*y-s grk(t) r.r-f*, "although there is due our mother her dowry from him." The past tense, *r.wn-n*ꜣ*w wn-mtw t*ꜣ*y-n mwt*, "although there was due our mother," is not used probably because the property still legally belonged to her heirs.

*iw-f ḥwr*ᶜ*-n [n-s]*, "he deprives us [of it]." For the preposition after *ḥwr*ᶜ see Insinger xvii 8, *iw-f ḥwr*ᶜ *n-s*, "he is deprived of it," and xvii 17, *p*ꜣ *nty-iw iw-w ḥwr*ᶜ*-f n w*ᶜ*t n.im-w*, "he who is deprived of one of them."

Line 14. *p*ꜣ *mtw-f (r) ir n-n tym*, "anyone who will provide us protection." For another such writing of the relative plus Future III see line 27 and note on line 10. For *ir tym n-* see the Decree in Honor of Ptolemy IV, Cairo 50048, line 9, and ᶜOnchsheshonqy vi 1. The children have no human protector or patron (cf. *JNES* XVII 9, note j).

*mtw-tn [n*ꜣ*] i.ir nḥt-n*, "it is you who have saved us." There is space for the restored *n*ꜣ and it should have been present in Ptolemaic demotic although it might be absent in a pre-Ptolemaic or Roman period text (Spiegelberg, *Dem. Gram.* §§ 452 and 454).

LINE 15. *iw-f ir pꜣ ꜥnḫ i.ir-ḥr-tn*, "if (or 'when') he takes the oath before you." The *iw-f* appears to be the result of a correction. The preposition *i.ir-ḥr* instead of *m-bꜣḥ* is unexpected (cf. Kaplony-Heckel, *Die demotischen Tempeleide* I 21–22). Otherwise the phraseology, containing as it does the definite article (*pꜣ ꜥnḫ*), is precisely that which occurs in the copies of actual oaths (*ibid.* p. 32, No. 1, line 7) where it is said that if the accused takes the prescribed oath he will be proven in the right. Here, however, the gods are asked to interrogate the accused father, presumably to reveal the anticipated falsity of his oath.

šn-tn s wpy-tn n irm pꜣ rmṯ rn-f, "may you interrogate him and may you judge between us and this man." The hortative *sḏm-f* is used in addressing the deities; in lines 22 and 23 the Future III is used injunctively with the same verbs for the same purpose. On the dependent pronoun first plural object see note on line 9. The idiom for judging between persons is the ancient one, *wpy* A *ḥnꜥ* B, in which A is the plaintiff (*Wb.* I 299:5), but I cannot cite another instance of it in demotic except in lines 23 and 24 of our text.

LINE 16. *nꜣ-ꜥšꜣ-w nꜣ kmꜥw*, lit. "many are they, the wrongs." The adjective verb has the third plural suffix subject (ⲛⲁϣⲱⲟⲩ) as it has at the beginning of line 20. To my knowledge, *kmꜥ*, "wrong," verb and noun, is always written *gmꜥ* in demotic until writings like *kꜥmy*, ϭⲱⲱⲙⲉ, appear in some texts of the Roman period.

mtw-f ir n.im-w n-n, ⲉⲧϥ̄ⲉⲓⲣⲉ ⲙ̄ⲙⲟⲟⲩ ⲛⲁⲛ, "which he inflicts on us." On the writing of the relative plus Present I see note on line 10 (*mtw pꜣ nṯr mḥ*). For the word order (durative tense, oblique object, dative) see Till, *Kopt. Gram.* § 378.

i.ir-f (sic) *wꜥ ḏrꜣ.ṯ mḥy-n*, "if a strong man beats us." That the scribe wrote *i.ir-f* instead of the correct *i.ir* is shown by comparison with the *bw-ir-f* immediately below in the next line. The *ḏrꜣ.ṯ*, with a clearly written *.ṯ* following the determinative, suggests the variant Qualitative of this verb in Coptic, ϫⲣⲁⲉⲓⲧ, ϭⲣⲏⲟⲩⲧ, etc. Note the writings of *pꜣ nꜥ.ṯ*, "the merciful one," in Insinger ii 16 and *pꜣ why.ṯ*, "the cruel one," in Insinger ii 17. Probably *ḏrꜣ.ṯ* has the meaning "brute," "bully," "ruffian," at least in this context.

LINE 17. *mḥy.w st*, "beat them." The *mḥy.w* may be the imperative with a very rare ending *.w* of which I know only two examples (cited by Spiegelberg, *Dem. Gram.* § 213, and Edgerton in *Studies Presented to F. Ll. Griffith*, pp. 63–64). In Pap. Rylands IX xi 5 *tms.w*, "bury," is addressed to a group of men and might have the plural ending, but Pap. Cairo 31225, line 8, has . . . *ḏd n-y wt.w st*, " . . . said to me, 'Pay them,' " hence hardly the plural imperative. The *mḥy-w st* could be perhaps the optative *sḏm-f* with impersonal subject for the passive, "may they be beaten."

LINE 18. *ḥr rꜣ (n) pꜣy-f ꜥwy*, ϩⲓⲣⲛ̄ⲡⲉϥⲏⲓ, "at the door of his house." The compound preposition can scarcely be *ḥr tw (n)*, ϩⲓⲧⲟⲩⲛ-, "beside," because the second element, which is identical with the word that occurs four times in line 29, cannot be read *tw* in the latter places. See the note on lines 28–29.

iw-f ḥwy ipyt m-sꜣ-n, "he hurls ⸢an *oipe*-container⸣ after us." The meaning of the articleless feminine noun *ipyt* is dubious. The possibilities are limited apparently to ⲟⲓⲡⲉ, the half-bushel measure, or ⲏⲡⲉ, "number," "enumeration." There appears to be no recorded idiom corresponding to *ϩⲓⲏⲡⲉ ⲛⲥⲁ-, but if *oipe*-container is to be understood, the absence of the indefinite article *wꜥt* is puzzling.

LINE 19. *bn iw-f (r) pꜣ ḫꜥꜣ (n) pꜣy ꜥḳ . . . in*, lit. "he is not at the end of this food."

The reading of the words appears certain enough; it is the idiom *ⲛ̄ϥⲉⲡϩⲁⲉ ⲙ̄ⲡⲟⲉⲓⲕ . . . ⲁⲛ, meaning "he is not lacking in this food," that cannot be paralleled. However, in demotic *ỉr ḫꜥꜣ*, ⲣ̄ϩⲁⲉ, can mean "to be in want" as in the Decree in Honor of Ptolemy IV, Pap. Cairo 50048, line 19, as well as "to be last" as in ꜥOnchsheshonqy xx 4. Note the "evil" determinative in our text and the Cairo text.

⟨*r.*⟩ *wn.nꜣw* ⌜*ỉr-f tꜣ ḥ̱t*⌝ *n-n*, lit. "⟨which⟩ he had made the beginning for us" or "⟨which⟩ should have been first for us." There is ample space for the relative indicator *r.*, but no trace of it is present now. The traces of *ỉr-f* are ambiguous at best, but they hardly suggest *ỉw-f*. For the imperfect converter *wn-nꜣw* before the *sḏm-f*, although apparently only in texts of the Roman period, see Spiegelberg, *Dem. Gram.* § 173. For a similar writing of *ḥ̱t*, ϩⲟⲩⲉⲓⲧⲉ, "beginning," although pre-Ptolemaic, see Erichsen, *Dem. Glossar*, p. 288. However, the meaning of *ⲣ̄ⲧⲉϩⲟⲩⲉⲓⲧⲉ ⲛⲁ⸗ is far from obvious even when one notes the clear contrast intended between ⲡϩⲁⲉ and ⲧⲉϩⲟⲩⲉⲓⲧⲉ.

LINE 20. *nꜣ-ꜥšꜣ-w r sẖ-w*, lit. "they are more numerous than writing them." For a somewhat similar idiom involving the comparative see *JEA* LIV 179–80, note to line 4.

r bn ḏmꜥ šsp-w, ⲉⲙⲛ̄ⲭⲱⲱⲙⲉ ϣⲟⲡⲟⲩ, lit. "while papyrus does not receive them." For the writing of the negative as *bn* rather than the usual *mn* before Present I with undetermined subject in early and late, but not Ptolemaic, demotic texts see the examples in Spiegelberg, *Dem. Gram.* § 441 and § 475 (Pap. Rylands IX xi 21 and Pap. Rhind I ii(d) 4). So heinous were the father's crimes against his children that if one tried to write them down even the papyrus would reject them.

nꜣ kw(w), ⲛ̄ϭⲱⲟⲩ, "the stringencies, "the limitations." Presumably *kw* is a writing of the usual *gw* (Erichsen, *Dem. Glossar*, pp. 574–75). Compare *kmꜥ* for the usual *gmꜥ* in line 16.

nꜣ ⌜*hblꞽ(w)*⌝, "the miseries," is badly rubbed but would appear to be the word in the wail in lines 5 and 22.

LINE 21. *nꜣ ꜣnty(w)*, "the restraints." Cf. the infinitive written *ꜣnṯ* in Insinger xiv 5, ꜥOnchsheshonqy xxi 13 and xxiv 10, and the Qualitative in line 25 of our text. The meaning in all these instances is plausibly "to restrain." Cf. *ỉnty*, "hinder," "restrain," in *Wb.* I 102 and Faulkner, *A Concise Dictionary of Middle Egyptian*, p. 24.

nty-ỉw Ḥr . . . ỉr n.ỉm-w n-n, "which Hor . . . inflicts upon us." See the note on *mtw-f ỉr n.ỉm-w n-n* in line 16.

LINE 22. *ỉ.ỉr-tn (r) šn-f*, "you shall interrogate him." On the pronominal state of the infinitive *šnỉ* see note on line 8. The tense is not Present II used injunctively, "you are to," "may you," but rather the Future III (Boh. ⲉⲣⲉⲧⲉⲛⲉϣⲉⲛϥ) in view of the use of the pronominal state of the infinitive with suffix object rather than the absolute state with oblique object (ϣⲓⲛⲉ ⲙ̄ⲙⲟϥ). See Parker in *JNES* XX (1961) 180–87. Cf. note on line 12 above.

LINE 23. *ỉ.ỉr-tn (r) wpy-n ỉrm-f*, "you shall judge between us and him." See the preceding note and the hortative *sḏm-f*'s with the same verbs in line 15. Again probably the injunctive Future III and not a durative tense, that is, Present II.

r nꜣ sꜣwtyw nꜣ wptyw nꜣ šmsw, "as for the guards, the messengers, and the servants." For *r* < *ỉr* before an anticipated element of the following clause, see Hughes, *Saite Demotic Land Leases*, p. 59, § *s*. The only other occurrences of *sꜣwty*, "guard" (*Wb.* III 418), known to me in demotic are Magical Pap. vi 13; ꜥOnchsheshonqy ii 14, iii 9, xi 17, xxi 13; and Pap. Louvre 2414 i 4 (Volten in *Studi in memoria di I. Rosellini* II 272 and Pl. XXXIV, as read by Glanville, *Instructions of ꜥOnchsheshonqy*, p. 68, note

23). The *wpty* could be a writing of *wpy*, "judge" (Erichsen, *Dem. Glossar*, p. 87), but in the context it must be *wpwty* (*ipwty*), "messenger" (*ibid.* p. 85). The *šms*, "servant," "attendant," can scarcely be read otherwise despite the unorthodox writing. These persons or beings are said to be "of the house," but of what house is not indicated. It can scarcely be the house of the father, but perhaps "the house of rest, the resting place" of the gods (line 3) or, less likely, the "house of judgment, the court" of Osiris in the netherworld as described in II Khamuas ii 3–8.

LINE 24. *r.iw-w (r) šn-f*, "when they shall interrogate him." This is the circumstantial of the Future III. On the form see Wente in *JNES* XX 120–23. On the pronominal state of the infinitive *šni* see note on line 8 above.

iw-w (r) ir pꜣy-n hp ⌜*ḫr*⌝ *tꜣy-n wpyt irm-f*, "they shall avenge us ⌜as a result of⌝ judging between us and him." I cannot cite another example of the idiom *ir pꜣy-f* (etc.) *hp* in demotic where the possessor is a person. Nims in his study of *hp* in demotic (*JNES* VII [1948] 243–60) cited no instance in which the genitive was subjective connoting the inherent rights belonging to a person but only instances in which the genitive is objective. "Its right" always means the right to or in a piece of property or the right conveyed by a legal document, and even *hp n ḥmt*, "right of wife," means a husband's conjugal rights to or in a wife. Nims does not cite the ambiguous statement by Thoth to Rêᶜ in I Khamuas iv 6: *rḫ pꜣy-y hp tꜣy-y wpyt irm* N., "know my right and my judgment with N." The ⲉⲩⲉⲣⲡⲉⲛϩⲁⲡ in our text must, I think, be equivalent in meaning to the Coptic idiom ⲣ̄ⲡⲁϩⲁⲡ, ⲣ̄ⲡⲉϥϩⲁⲡ (ⲙⲛ̄-), "work my vengeance, work his vengeance (upon)," for which see Crum, *Coptic Dict.* p. 694*a*. The ⌜*ḫr*⌝ is damaged-but it can scarcely be *irm*. If it is ⌜*ḫr*⌝, it probably means "because of," "as a result of," "by reason of." On *tꜣy-n wpyt irm-f* see note on line 15. The *irm-f* completes the idea of *tꜣy-n wpyt* as in lines 15 and 23 and does not also necessarily complete the idea of ⲣ̄ⲡⲉⲛϩⲁⲡ as line 26 shows.

LINE 25. *di-n hy.n*, "we have fallen." This is obviously not the causative *di* with dependent *sḏm-f* although the writing of the base of the Present I pronominal compound as *di* rather than *tw* has heretofore been found only in pre-Ptolemaic and less frequently in early Ptolemaic demotic. Furthermore, one would expect the verb to be the Qualitative (ⲧⲛ̄ϩⲏⲩ, ⲧⲛ̄ϩⲓⲱⲟⲩⲧ), but if *hy.n* is a writing of the Old Perfective with the historic first plural ending (Erman, *Neuägyptische Gram.* § 334), I cannot point to another instance of it even in the earliest demotic (cf. Spiegelberg, *Dem. Gram.* §§ 96–98 and 107). The alternative would be to take the *.n* as the reflexive dative *n-n* since our scribe makes no distinction in writing between the first plural suffix alone and with the dative *n-*. However, *hꜣi*>*hy*>ϩⲉ appears never to have been used with the reflex ive dative.

my twn ⟨*-n n*⟩, "cause ⟨us⟩ to rise," "let ⟨us⟩ rise." The scribe did not write the verb *twn*, "raise," at all but wrote *tw n*, "breast of," with the flesh determinative and with the genitive *n* preceding the determinative as it frequently is written in compound prepositions such as *ḥr tw n*, ϩⲓⲧⲟⲩⲛ- (Erichsen, *Dem. Glossar*, p. 612). Having made that error he compounded it by omitting the suffix subject of *twn* and probably the dependent pronoun reflexive object as well, since the verb is almost exclusively transitive in demotic (*ibid.* pp. 614–15 and Spiegelberg, *Dem. Gram.* § 263). On the first plural dependent pronoun see note on line 9.

di-n ꜣnty my ⌜*ḳn*⌝*-f*, "we are restrained, make him ⌜cease⌝." On *ꜣnty* see the note on the noun in line 21. The faint, probably misleading, traces of the intransitive verb suggest very little, but the context suggests a verb like *ḳn*, ⲕⲏⲛ, "cease," "desist."

The suffix subject probably refers to the children's father, but possibly it refers impersonally to the restraining to which they have been subjected.

LINES 25–26. *dỉ-n ṯy (n) ḳns my ỉr-w pꜣy-n hp*, "we are mistreated, cause that we be avenged." On *ỉr pꜣy-n hp* see note on line 24. Compare with this I Khamuas v 8 (with a variant in v 5): *ỉn wn-mtw-t smy n ṯy (n) ḳns ỉw-f r dỉ ỉr-w s*, "if you have a complaint of mistreatment, he will have it taken care of."

LINE 26. *dỉ-n ḥwy* ⌜*pꜣy ꜥš [ỉ.]ỉr-ḥr nꜣ nṯrw*⌝, "we are casting ⌜this appeal before the gods⌝." The traces at the end of the line are troublesome. They force us to read *ꜥš*, "cry," "call," "appeal," for the object of *ḥwy* rather than *bꜣk*, *ḫrw*, or *wḫꜣ*, which appear in the following lines. Compare the Bohairic and Fayumic idiom ϩⲓⲱⲓϣ, ϩⲓⲗⲓϣ, "throw a cry" (Crum, *Coptic Dict.* p. 257*b*).

LINE 27. *pꜣ rmṯ nb (n) pꜣ tꜣ mtw-f (r) tk pꜣy bꜣk (n) hꜥꜣ[h]* ⌜*r ḫb*⌝*-f*, "as for anyone in the world who will set this document on fire ⌜to destroy⌝ it." The *mtw-f (r) tk* is for the relative plus Future III, ⲉⲧⲉϥⲉⲧⲱⲕ. Cf. *mtw-f (r) ỉr* in line 14. There are in this sentence two words of rare frequency in demotic, known thus far only in texts of the Roman period. They are the verb *tk*, ⲧⲱⲕ, "kindle," "burn" (Erichsen, *Dem. Glossar*, p. 659), and the noun *hꜥꜣh*, ϣⲗⲁϩ, "flame," "fire" (*ibid.* p. 281, s.v. *hh*). The noun is written in the same peculiar manner as it is in Magical Pap. verso xiii 3. At the end of the line the traces suggest only *ḫb-f* written rather large. Cf. *ḫb* in Erichsen, *Dem. Glossar*, p. 353, and *ḫbỉ* or *ḫbꜣ* in *Wb.* III 251 and 253.

LINE 28. *my ꜥš-f s (n) ḥꜣt-f r pḥw-f*, "let him read it from its beginning to its end." The same phraseology occurs in Magical Pap. xxix 17–18: *ỉ.ỉr-k ꜥš-f n ḥꜣt-f r pḥ.ṯ-f*, "you are to read it from its beginning to its end."

LINES 28–29. *m[y dỉ-w ꜥš s] pꜣ rmṯ rn-f (n) pꜣ rꜣ rsy* etc., "let that man [be made to read it] at the south entrance" etc. What is restored is a conjecture only. The reading *rꜣ*, "mouth," "door," "entrance," for the word occurring four times in line 29 and once in line 18 seems inescapable. Compare certain early and late writings shown in Erichsen, *Dem Glossar*, pp. 239–40.

LINE 30. *pꜣ mꜣꜥ r nꜣ nṯrw ḥtp n.ỉm-f*, "the place in which the gods rest." This would seem to be the necessary interpretation of the final clause even though it represents a violation of the rule that a defined antecedent must be followed by the relative *nty* and not by the circumstantial as a virtual relative (Spiegelberg, *Dem. Gram.* § 538) It is hardly likely that the clause is circumstantial to the action of the partially restored main clause preceding it or to the clause following it, that is, "while the gods rest in it."

ỉ.ỉr-w sḥw ⌜*ỉw-w sḏm [r pꜣy] wḫꜣ*⌝, "may they curse ⌜when they listen [to this] letter⌝." Instead of Present II used injunctively this may be as in lines 22 and 23 the Future III: *ỉ.ỉr-w (r) sḥw*, "they shall curse." The verb is the intransitive infinitive. The *ỉw-w sḏm* appears to be reasonably certain. Faint traces at the end of the document look like the tall signs of the early and late writings of *wḫꜣ*, "letter," "dispatch." It might be possible to read *šꜥt*, "letter," but not the *bꜣk*, "document," of line 27, or the *ḫrw*, "voice," "plea," of lines 5 and 28.

EUNUCHS IN ANCIENT EGYPT?

Gerald E. Kadish

One has only to recall the titles of two of Professor Wilson's works—*The Burden of Egypt* and *Signs and Wonders upon Pharaoh*—to recognize the influence the Old Testament has exerted on his thinking. Nor is this surprising in an intellectual heir of James Henry Breasted. It seemed, therefore, appropriate to the occasion to offer a brief discussion of a problem that links Egypt and the Bible.

Much has been written about various elements of Egyptian background in the story of Joseph as recorded in Genesis. One feature of the story which has received scant attention is the apparent assertion of the Hebrew text that Potiphar, the Egyptian to whom Joseph was sold, was a eunuch. It is a minor but intriguing matter which deserves further consideration within the context of Egyptian civilization. A number of questions arise: What is the biblical writer likely to have meant by "eunuch"? Were there eunuchs in Egypt? Is there some other notion underlying this usage?

If one were exposed only to a modern translation of Genesis, one not closely tied to the Vulgate, it would come as something of a surprise to learn that Potiphar was a eunuch, for such translations commonly render the Hebrew term by "officer of Pharaoh" or some other equally indistinct phrase. Vernacular versions of the Vulgate, however, follow St. Jerome's literal rendering of the Hebrew into Latin *eunuchus*. These are the poles of reaction to the passage: one euphemistic, the other literal.

The problem centers on the fact that in two passages (Gen. 37:36 and 39:1) the Hebrew text calls Potiphar the "*sārîs* of Pharaoh." These two occurrences are actually but one, since both recount the sale of Joseph to Potiphar. This is due to a not-so-smooth attempt to combine two text traditions, the one identifying the traveling salesmen as Midianites, the other identifying them as Ishmaelites. How, then, are we to understand the word *sārîs*?

It has already been noted above that the Vulgate renders it with Latin *eunuchus*. The Septuagint likewise literally translates with the Greek *spadon*. The rabbinical commentary in the Midrash Rabbah[1] understands the word to mean "eunuch" and without being discomfited by such a translation. On the contrary, this potentially mitigating circumstance for the behavior of Potiphar's wife is used to underscore the fact of God's special interest in Joseph.

[1] Midrash Rabbah II 802 (trans. by R. H. Freedman).

Displaying little regard for the sequence of events, the Midrash takes the "eunuch-hood" of Potiphar as the punishment visited upon the Egyptian for having purchased Joseph allegedly for the purpose of sodomy.

Some scholars have nonetheless been skeptical, offering more or less cogent arguments. It is not persuasive, for example, to argue that Potiphar could not have been a eunuch because he had a wife.[2] Married eunuchs, although not common, are attested.[3] Nor is it sufficient to assume that the seclusion of women or the existence of separate women's quarters necessarily implies the employment of eunuchs; the Athenians of the fifth century B.C. had both without eunuchs. Vergote, in his study of the Joseph material, seems to prefer to look to non-Egyptian sources, notably Assyrian, to explain the word in question, but he does not take it literally.[4] In reviewing Vergote's study, K. A. Kitchen, agreeing that eunuchs are "not commonly attested in Egypt," has taken the view that *sārîs* does not mean "eunuch" in the Pentateuch.[5] On the analogy of the Akkadian cognate *ša-reš-šarri,* which Kitchen holds changed in meaning over a long period of time from the general "official" to the specific "eunuch," he argues that in the Pentateuch *sārîs* means "official." It is evident that the word does mean "eunuch" in the later books of the Old Testament, but beyond this point I am not competent to judge the validity of Kitchen's position. It might be noted, however, that the uncertainty surrounding the date of the final formulation of the Pentateuch might very well affect the strength of his position.

There is, nevertheless, an intriguing fact about *sārîs.* It does not occur in the Pentateuch other than in the story of Joseph and there only once more (Gen. 40:2) in addition to the two instances cited above. The term does not appear in any of those parts of the Pentateuch in which the Egyptian background looms so large. The last-cited occurrence raises some doubt about the meaning of *sārîs,* for it is used there to refer jointly to those two dreaming personages whose fates become intertwined with that of Joseph: the chief butler and the chief baker.[6] These two worthies have something in common with Potiphar, and it may be "eunuch-hood." Admittedly, the appearance of three eunuchs at once is nearly as odd as the fact that *sārîs* occurs in the Pentateuch only in the Joseph story. While it is no doubt dangerous to make too much of such things, it is nonetheless difficult to believe that this singular occurrence in a basically well structured narrative is wholly fortuitous, whether or not the word was intended to signify castrated males.

[2] Adolf Erman and Hermann Ranke, *Aegypten und aegyptisches Leben im Altertum* (Tübingen, 1923) p. 87, n. 10.

[3] Otto Procksch, *Die Genesis übersetzt und erklärt* (Leipzig, 1924) pp. 231 and 391.

[4] Jozef Vergote, *Joseph en Égypte* (Louvain, 1959) pp. 40–42.

[5] See *JEA* XLVII (1961) 159–60.

[6] The epithet occurs here in the plural form.

Several uncertainties must be pointed out. It is not possible to be sure that *sārîs* does not mean something as vague as "official."[7] Nor can we control the possibility that Potiphar and the other two men were rare cases of Egyptian eunuchs. The question of the importation of eunuchs is unanswerable and is not applicable to Potiphar, who is specifically labeled an Egyptian. Is there, then, persuasive evidence that eunuchs were created and regularly employed in Egypt?

Egyptologists have, on the whole, doubted that eunuchs either existed or were to be found in any number in Egypt.[8] The most recent attempt to review the evidence in a systematic fashion was by Dr. Frans Jonckheere.[9] His investigation, which considers the evidence of the Greek authors and both the representational and textual evidence from Egypt, is of special interest because he brings to bear medical knowledge in an attempt to identify and classify eunuchs by physical types.

The Greek authors represent neither uncontaminated nor especially knowledgeable sources. They can often tell us something of what obtained in their own eras or was said to be true of earlier ages. Even Manetho, whose potential reliability exceeds that of the Greek authors, must be regarded with an element of caution. When Manetho tells us that Ammanemes of the 12th dynasty was murdered by his own eunuchs,[10] we can control part of the statement, for it seems not unlikely from earlier evidence that Amenemhat I of the 12th dynasty was indeed assassinated and that his bodyguard may have been responsible. But was the bodyguard composed of eunuchs? Does Manetho have a record or tradition to that effect before him or is he merely assuming it on the basis of circumstances in his own age? It is clear that Manetho is of little use in solving our problem. Likewise one cannot make much of Diodorus Siculus' report that men in Egypt who violated free women were punished by the removal of their genitals.[11] Even if true for the earlier periods of Egyptian history, it would no more constitute evidence for the existence of eunuchs in Egypt than would the sad fate of Peter Abelard demonstrate their existence in medieval France. Jonckheere quite properly dismisses Diodorus' repetition of the account of the Ramesseum reliefs given by Hecataeus of Abdera (3d century B.C.) describing mass castrations; the Greek probably misinterpreted the phallic trophies such as those still visible at Medinet Habu.

Jonckheere's conclusions from representational evidence depend on the identification of physical characteristics which are considered typical of per-

[7] It seems unlikely that *sārîs* is in any way related to the Egyptian word *sr*, "official."

[8] See Vergote, *op. cit.* p. 41, n. 1, for references.

[9] Frans Jonckheere, "L'eunuque dans l'Égypte pharaonique," *Revue d'histoire des sciences et leur applications* VII (1954) 139–55.

[10] Manetho, Frags. 34–36 (trans. by W. G. Waddell); cf. Jonckheere, *op. cit.* p. 148.

[11] Diodorus Siculus i. 78 (trans. by C. H. Oldfather); cf. Jonckheere, *op. cit.* p. 141.

sons who have been castrated before or subsequent to puberty. This kind of evidence is difficult to evaluate in the absence of figures that display these traits and are, at the same time, clearly depicted as *castrati*. For example, we are told that the male servant waiting on the lady Kawit (relief on Kawit's sarcophagus) is a perfect example of a eunuch created prior to puberty.[12] The figure is elongated, has a small head and some mammary development. Those familiar with the art of the 6th through the 11th dynasties will find such characteristics too common to be persuasive on the subject of eunuchs. The treacherousness of such pictorial material is readily apparent in the case of the Nile deities shown on the monument of Sahure, for example, of which Jonckheere says:

> L'ensemble de ces modifications adiposo-mammaires fait que, bien que barbus, les Génies nilotiques ont perdu l'accent viril et revêtu l'allure que l'on s'accorde à qualifier d'intersexuée. Or, ce sont là les transformations somatiques que subissent les individus castrés *après* la puberté.[13]

Earlier he had remarked on the absence of external genitalia and thought it peculiar when so often boatmen and fishermen are shown with genitals exposed.[14] Jonckheere then asks: "Est-il trop hardi, dans ces conditions, de considérer le 'Nil' comme l'expression artistique de cette variété d'eunuque?"[15] These figures were intended to be symbolic of fertility. There is no reason to suppose that eunuchs would occur to the artist as a good fertility symbol. These figures are not "intersexuée"—a most misleading view of the eunuch in any case—but rather bisexual or even hermaphroditic, for they embody both masculine and feminine characteristics. A eunuch is hardly a suitable fertility symbol; he may not be impotent (if castrated after puberty and sexual experience), but he is invariably sterile.

The notion of eunuchs as "intersexual" is misleading in another context. Following a suggestion of Rosellini, Jonckheere sees the use of color in wall paintings as another indicator of eunuchs. In paintings where men are colored red and women yellow, those figures painted a yellowish-brown must be "intersexual," *ergo* eunuchs, since their color is intermediate between the red and yellow of the two standard sexes.[16]

Also somewhat differently represented, in the tomb of Khnumhotep at Beni Hasan, are men in charge of a boat bearing some women and in a workshop

[12] Jonckheere, *op. cit.* p. 143. For the sarcophagus, see G. Bénédite, *Objets de toilette* (Cat. gen. Cairo, 1911) Pl. I.

[13] Jonckheere, *op. cit.* p. 145. The emphasis is his.

[14] *Ibid.* p. 144.

[15] *Ibid.* p. 145. "Cette variété" means a post-puberal eunuch.

[16] See *ibid.* pp. 145–46 with reference to Rosellini. Cf. Vergote, *op. cit.* p. 41, who seems to accept the notion of intersexuality.

which has both male and female workers.[17] The men in charge of the boat have no distinguishing physical characteristics relatable to eunuchs, but two in the workshop are obese. It is not clear why eunuchs would be employed in a place which employs women who do not seem to fit the category normally supervised by eunuchs.

This leads to the question of harems. I remarked above that there is no necessary connection between the existence of harems and the employment of eunuchs. Jonckheere is quick to admit that there is little direct evidence on this subject; the men on duty at the entrance to the women's quarters at Amarna[18] cannot be identified as eunuchs by any of Jonckheere's criteria.

It is necessary to insist that the pictorial evidence offers no unambiguous data on the existence of eunuchs and that all the examples offered by Jonckheere can be readily explained on stylistic grounds or some other conventional artistic considerations.

The evidence from the Egyptian texts is no less ambiguous, nor is it plentiful. Of those words which Jonckheere considers relevant to the eunuch problem,[19] two may be put aside on the grounds that they are either Demotic (*tkr*) or from Ptolemaic texts only (*ḥms*) and have no visible roots in the earlier Pharaonic periods.[20] Two other words do deserve some attention, namely *sẖti* and *ḥm* or *ḥmti.*

The word *ḥm* is attested in Middle Kingdom texts, although most of its occurrences, and the cases of *ḥmti*, are from the late period on.[21] Only the earlier examples need be discussed here. The earliest case is on a stela from Semna[22] on which Senusert III describes as a *ḥm* "one who is driven back from his own frontier." In the context, "coward" is the best translation.[23] In the same manner is the word to be understood in Ramesses II's account of the battle at Kadesh[24] and in a military text of Piankhi.[25] Jonckheere makes much of the fact that *ḥm* is determined by a phallus.[26] If one supposes that the word *ḥm* is related to the word for woman, then the phallus determinative would seem to make the expression analogous to the well known American Indian ex-

[17] Percy E. Newberry, *Beni Hasan* I (London, 1893) Pl. XXIX, 3d and 4th registers from the top on the left.

[18] Norman de G. Davies, *The Rock Tombs of El Amarna* VI (London, 1908) Pl. XXVIII. See Jonckheere, *op. cit.* pp. 146–48, and cf. Vergote, *op. cit.* p. 41.

[19] Jonckheere, *op. cit.* pp. 150–55.

[20] *Ibid.* p. 152. For *ḥms* see *Wb.* III 96.

[21] See *Wb.* III 80.

[22] Kurt Sethe, *Aegyptische Lesestücke* (Leipzig, 1924) p. 84, line 4.

[23] So *Wb.* III 80, 7. Sethe, *Erläuterungen zu den ägyptischen Lesestücken* (Leipzig, 1927) pp. 137–38, suggested "entmannt," "unmännlich" (eig. "weibisch"?).

[24] *Wb.* III 80, 7.

[25] *Wb.* III 80, 8.

[26] Jonckheere, *op. cit.* pp. 150–51, following Lefébure.

pression "squaw-man," that is, a man who behaves like a woman.[27] In military contexts such as those referred to above, the concept "coward" fits and "eunuch" simply does not. The one example of a sexual context which Jonckheere offers seems to depict the *ḥm* as the object of pederasty and contrasted with a man. It is, however, from Edfu and quite late.[28]

The most difficult word to deal with is *sḫti*. The *Wörterbuch* offers only two instances of this word, which it translates "der Verschnittene(?)."[29] It may be related to the word *sḫ*, "to sever."[30] The earlier of the two cases of *sḫti* occurs in *Pyr.* § 1462 *c*, the later in the "Execration Texts."[31] Sethe, in discussing the latter instance, remarks on the obscurity of the former.[32] *Pyr.* § 1462 *c* is to be transliterated *sḫti pf ṯ3y pn sỉn sỉn ỉm.ṯn*. Sethe translates "O jener Verschnittene, o dieser Männliche, es eile, wer da eilen mag von euch beiden."[33] Even if Sethe and Jonckheere were correct in taking the word *sḫti* to mean "castrated one," what would this tell us about eunuchs in ancient Egypt? The answer lies in the context.

The passage comes in a section of the Pyramid Texts which reflects the conflict between Horus and Seth. There is much of sexual import in the story of this struggle, some of it apparently homosexual, and it suggests damage to the testicles of Seth as a parallel to the injury incurred by the eye of Horus. Griffiths[34] and Te Velde[35] have considered these sexual events at some length. Despite the latter's attempts to the contrary, it seems difficult to deny that Seth was thought by some Egyptians to have been castrated, especially when one considers such passages as the following:

> . . . the room in which Isis cried out and the testicles of Seth were cut off.[36]

> If he does not hearken to what I say, I will not give (back) to Horus that eye of his, I will not give (back) to Seth his testicles in this land forever.[37]

[27] Literally, I suppose, "a woman with a phallus." Cf. J. G. Griffiths, *The Conflict of Horus and Seth* (Liverpool, 1960) p. 44.

[28] Jonckheere, *op. cit.* p. 151.

[29] *Wb.* IV 264.

[30] Adriaan de Buck, *The Egyptian Coffin Texts* I (Chicago, 1935) 74 *g*. Cf. R. O. Faulkner, *A Concise Dictionary of Middle Egyptian* (Oxford, 1962) p. 239.

[31] Kurt Sethe, *Die Ächtung feindlicher Fürsten, Völker und Dinge auf altägyptischen Tongefässscherben des Mittleren Reiches* (Berlin, 1926) p. 61, m 5.

[32] *Ibid.* p. 61.

[33] *Ibid.*; Jonckheere merely translates Sethe's German into French.

[34] Griffiths, *op. cit.* pp. 28–53.

[35] H. te Velde, *Seth, God of Confusion* (Leiden, 1967) pp. 53–59 and *passim.*

[36] Pap. London (BM 10059) xiii 3–4; see Griffiths, *op. cit.* p. 36, and Te Velde, *op. cit.* p. 58. The translation is that of Griffiths.

[37] Pap. Leiden I 343 recto xxvii 3–4. The translation is from Griffith, *op. cit.* p. 36. Cf. Te Velde, *op. cit.* p. 57, with almost identical translation.

Pyr. § 1463 *e* also indicates some injury to Seth's testicles, although its exact nature is unclear.[38] If we conclude that at some point in his encounters with Horus Seth was bereft of his testicles, then *Pyr.* § 1462 *c* becomes perhaps more intelligible. The word *ṯꜣy*, which is parallel to *sḫti*, means "a male" in the full sense of sexual potency.[39] In fact, although admittedly in a late text, the term is applied to Horus.[40] Consequently, it seems reasonable to understand *sḫti* in *Pyr.* § 1462 *c* as referring to the castrated Seth.[41] Perhaps totally unrelated, but nonetheless of interest in this connection, is the idea that Seth becomes the prey of fowlers (*sḫti̓w*) in the nether world.[42]

The other instance of *sḫti* occurs in the Execration Texts. The section dealing with Egyptian enemies begins: "All men, all people, all folk, all males, all *eunuchs*, all women, and all officials . . . ."[43] Sethe argued that the word *sḫti̓w*, by virtue of its position in the passage, must mean "eunuch."[44] It must be admitted that this opinion is hard to gainsay. In the light of the case in the Pyramid Texts, it is not unlikely that the phrase means "castrated ones" here. Still it is something of a jump from the context of the other world in the Pyramid Texts to this allegedly genuine list of earthly enemies. In any case, it is apparent that two instances of a word which seems to signify a castrated person are rather slender evidence for the employment of eunuchs in ancient Egypt.

In general, then, we can state that there is no clear evidence for the existence of eunuchs in ancient Egypt, that is to say, men who were deliberately castrated so that they might be employed in circumstances in which fertile men would be deemed dangerous or inappropriate. There does not even appear to be a word meaning "to castrate" which was used with respect to men.[45] If a "Sprachtabu" existed on this subject, it is presently beyond our knowledge. It is interesting to note that the two cases of *sḫti* are earlier than the New Kingdom, a period during which one might suppose that foreign influence might have led to the adoption of the practice of employing eunuchs. The Egyptians knew what castration was, but there is virtually no evidence that they regularly practiced it. There is no evidence of eunuchs as an institution in Egypt.

There remains only the matter of suggesting another explanation of the word *sārîs* in the Joseph narrative. It is by now commonplace for Egyptolo-

[38] Te Velde, *loc. cit.*

[39] *Wb.* V 344.

[40] *Wb.* V 344, 21.

[41] Cf. *Pyr.* § 535: "He (i.e., Horus) loves Teti, he has brought his eye. Seth has brought this: he has brought his testicles." Cf. also *Pyr.* §§ 594 *a*, 679 *d*, 946 *c*.

[42] See J. Zandee, *Death as an Enemy According to Ancient Egyptian Conceptions* (Leiden, 1960) p. 233, with references.

[43] As translated by John A. Wilson in *Ancient Near Eastern Texts Relating to the Old Testament* (2d ed.; Princeton, 1955) p. 329.

[44] Sethe, *Ächtungstexte*, p. 61, a view which Jonckheere, *op. cit.* p. 150, naturally approves.

[45] On *sꜥb*, see *Wb.* IV 43 and Jonckheere, *op. cit.* p. 153. Other words meaning "to cut (off)" do exist: Te Velde, *op. cit.* p. 57, n. 3. Cf. Pap. d'Orbiney vii 9.

gists and biblical scholars to remark on the similarities in the motif of the seduction in the story of Joseph and in the Egyptian tale of the two brothers. It is usual, however, to compare only the gross elements of the two stories: the attempted seduction, the refusal, the false accusation, the exoneration. This is understandable and is traceable to a reluctance to assert that the Hebrew narrative descends from the Egyptian tale. There is, nevertheless, an element of the Egyptian story which has some bearing on the present discussion.

The younger brother in the Egyptian story, in order to lend force to his protestations of innocence to his brother, castrates himself.[46] By its use here it is clearly labeled an extraordinary action. It is intended as a literary device. If one is willing to accept a more intimate connection between the Egyptian and Hebrew narratives, then it is not unreasonable to suppose that *sārîs* in the Hebrew is a reflection of the castration element in the Egyptian story. To have Joseph castrated would be unthinkable to the Hebrew writer. To transfer the castration element to Potiphar, the counterpart of the elder brother, would serve some moral point, such as that inferred by the Midrashic commentator. The castration element in the Egyptian story may even have led later Hebrew writers to think that the Egyptians employed eunuchs and that Potiphar might have been one. If this be so, then the extension of the appellation to the other two officials likewise becomes comprehensible. Aside from the matter of the relationship between the two narratives, there appears to be no fatal objection to my suggestion and it does seem to explain why the term *sārîs* appears only in the Joseph story in the Pentateuch.

[46] Pap. d'Orbiney vii 9; for translation see Wilson, *op. cit.* p. 25.

THREE PHILOLOGICAL NOTES

Miriam Lichtheim

I

A Saying from the Book of Memphis

In *JEA* XLI (1955) 18–29, Faulkner published the definitive text of the "Installation of the Vizier" along with a new translation. On the assumption that, unless new parallel versions are discovered, no further improvements in the reading of the text can be expected, I have grappled with the obscure passage in line 9 which refers to a "saying in the Book of Memphis" and should like to present my rendering of it.

Despite the short lacuna at the end of line 9, it is clear that the "saying" functions as a conclusion to the preceding instructions, for with the word *s3w* at the end of line 9 there begins a new set of instructions. Hence the immediately relevant context is the passage which begins in the middle of line 8 and ends with the end of line 9:

Faulkner translates this passage as follows:

See, the magistrate's safeguard is to act in accordance with regulations, in doing what has been said; a petitioner who has been judged [shall not say: "I have] not [been placed] (9) on my vindication." See, it is a maxim which is in the Book of Memphis, being the word of the Sovereign, the mercy(?) of the vizier and . . . .

In his notes (30–32) Faulkner rejected Davies' rendering of the passage, including his reading of the owl-with-knife group as *dm*, "pronounce."

Now it seems to me that this obscure passage becomes intelligible if one realizes that *m-ḏd* introduces the actual "saying" and that the "saying" thus begins with the word *nb*. I now propose to read the last word of this sentence as *sšmw*, and thus we get a phrase consisting of two parallel sentences: *nb m sfn* and *t̠ʒty m sšm*.

It is true that the *Wörterbuch* does not record such a writing of *sšm*. But among the many variations which it lists (*Wb.* IV 285 ff.) there occur ideographic writings with the knife alone, others in which the pair of walking legs is absent, and some in which the knife is drawn across the letter *s*. Would it then not be plausible that there should also be instances in which, in the absence of the pair of legs, the knife is drawn across the owl?

Next we must consider the meanings of *sfn* and *sšm*. As regards *sfn*, I would agree with Faulkner (his note 31) that in choosing between *zfn*, "be merciful," and *sfn*, "be harsh," the former seems more likely. Hence I suggest that the whole sentence means something like "when the lord is in mercy, the vizier is in action (i.e., on the job)" or more concisely and in the form of a proverb: "Gracious lord, lawful vizier."

It is true that *sfn* and *sšm* could mean something else. But if I have construed the "saying" correctly, its basic meaning is that the mood or character of the king is reflected in the behavior of the vizier—a perfectly sound observation which lends itself to being cast in the form of a "saying" and for which the German proverb "wie der Herr so's Gescherr" affords a parallel (with an irreverent twist). I would then render the whole passage thus:

> See, the magistrate's protection
> is to do things by the rule
> in acting on a pleader's words.
> Then the judged [cannot say]
> "[I was] not [allowed] my right."
> There's a saying in the Book of Memphis
> "Gracious king, lawful vizier."

It must of course be admitted that the short lacuna after *sšmw* makes it impossible to prove beyond doubt that the sentence really ends here and hence that the "saying" is constructed, as I think it is, of two symmetrical alliterating halves. A more serious weakness is that I cannot adduce another instance of the owl-and-knife group which would bear out the reading *sšm*. A Middle Kingdom occurrence of this group, which seemed to offer support, turned out to have the phonetic value *dm* in a writing of the place-name Qedem, as was convincingly shown by H. G. Fischer in his treatment of the text.[1] Despite its infirmities I launch the "saying," to watch it sink or swim.

II

The Expressions *ṯꜣm-ḥr* and *ḥbs-ḥr*

The meaning of *ṯꜣm-ḥr*, "to veil the face," in the sense of being indulgent or forgiving toward someone, has been deduced from passages such as Shipwrecked Sailor, lines 17–19: *ỉw r n s nḥm.f sw ỉw mdw.f dỉ.f ṯꜣm n.f ḥr*, "A man's mouth saves him; his speech makes one veil the face to him." And the nominal form, *ṯꜣmt-ḥr*, occurs in BD 125: *nḥm.k wỉ m-ꜥ nꜣy.k n wpwtyw wddyw ṯms(w) sẖpryw ỉdryt ỉwty ṯꜣmt nt ḥrw.sn*, "Save me from your messengers who inflict wounds, who mete out punishment, who lack face-veiling."[2]

Yet it is curious that the seemingly identical image conveyed by the expression *ḥbs-ḥr* should have the very opposite meaning, that is, "to be inaccessible to pleas."[3] Again, the meaning is well established through passages such as *n ḥbs.ỉ ḥr r nty m bꜣkw*, "I did not cover my face against the enslaved" (Stela of Mentuwosre).[4] The expression occurs in the nominal form also: *ỉnk ḥḏ-ḥr ꜣw-ḏrt nb-ḏfꜣw šw m ḥbs-ḥr*, "I was bright-faced, open-handed, lord of bounty, free of face-covering" (Stela of Inyotef, BM 581).[5] That *ṯꜣm-ḥr* is construed with the preposition *n*, while *ḥbs-ḥr* takes the preposition *r*, is the consequence, and not the cause, of this difference in meaning. This is proved by the existence of the nominal forms, *ṯꜣmt-ḥr* and *ḥbs-ḥr*, quoted above, which convey their meanings without the aid of prepositions.

How then could one account for a development in which the same image, construed with two different verbs, has led to antithetical meanings? The only answer that occurs to me is that the metaphor *ṯꜣm-ḥr* arose in a context in which the "face" was conceived as an angry or threatening one, such as would especially be attributed to the hostile monsters that lurk on the paths of the netherworld. On the other hand, the "face" of *ḥbs-ḥr* is eminently the human face which expresses benevolence by being "bright" (*ḥḏ-ḥr*) and unconcern or even hostility by being "covered." That is to say, *ḥḏ-ḥr* and *ḥbs-ḥr*, paired in the Inyotef stela, are antonyms.

Is there any reason to think that, given the near-identity of *ṯꜣm* and *ḥbs*, the Egyptians ever confused the two metaphors? I think not. For one thing, each

[1] H. G. Fischer, *Inscriptions from the Coptite Nome* ("Analecta Orientalia" XL [Rome, 1964]) pp. 112–17. Fischer's rendering of the passage supersedes that of W. Schenkel in the latter's *Memphis, Herakleopolis, Theben* (Wiesbaden, 1965) p. 216.

[2] See E. A. Wallis Budge, *Book of the Dead* (London, 1910) II 149, lines 17–18.

[3] R. O. Faulkner, *A Concise Dictionary of Middle Egyptian* (Oxford, 1962) p. 167.

[4] Kurt Sethe, *Aegyptische Lesestücke* (2d ed.; Leipzig, 1928) p. 79, lines 13–14.

[5] *Ibid.* p. 80, lines 21–22.

of the two compounds would have been felt as a single unit of expression. Furthermore, it is significant that BD 125, which yielded the example of *ṯ3mt-ḥr*, also has an occurence of *ḥbs-ḥr* in a passage for which I should like to propose a translation somewhat different from that of Barguet. This is in the "Introduction" according to the Papyrus of Ani:[6]

ỉr ᶜḳ.ỉ r st št3t ỉw mdwt.ỉ ḥnᶜ Stš
ḫnm.ỉ tkn ỉm.ỉ ḥbs ḥr.f
ḫrw ḥr ḫt št3wt

Barguet renders:

Si j'entre dans la place secrète, je me disputerai avec Seth, je serai amical avec celui qui viendra à ma recontre et qui voile son visage, étant tombé, à cause des choses secrètes.[7]

I am not sure what *ḫrw ḥr ḫt št3wt* means. But it seems clear that the phrase *ḫnm.ỉ tkn ỉm.ỉ ḥbs ḥr.f* describes an action which parallels the preceding "disputing with Seth" and entails overcoming the opposition of a deity who is evasive or even ill-disposed (*ḥbs-ḥr*). If this is the drift of the sentence, it does not matter much whether *ḫnm* is to be understood as "smelling" or "befriending." Thus we get:

When I enter the secret place
I shall dispute with Seth
I shall smell him who approaches me with covered face
⌈having come upon⌉ the secret things.

In conclusion it may be worth observing that the two distinct concepts expressed by the two metaphors of the veiled, or covered, face—unconcern and forgiveness—are covered in our language by the single metaphor "to shut one's eyes." And this is one of countless instances that point up the concreteness of the Egyptian language which, even as it moved about in the iridescent realm of metaphor, tended to preserve the specific connotation of the original image.

III

The Moods of Ḥapy

The second and third stanzas of the Hymn to the Nile contain a description of the Nile's behavior for which I should like to offer a new translation. Using the Golénischeff Ostracon as the basic text modified by three variants taken from Bacchi's composite text which integrates the Turin Papyrus,[8]

[6] Budge, *op. cit.* Vol. II 119, lines 3–4.

[7] Paul Barguet, *Le livre des morts des anciens Égyptiens* (Paris, 1967) p. 157.

[8] G. Maspero, *Hymne au Nil* (Cairo, 1912) p. 19; E. Bacchi, *L'Inno al Nilo* (Turin, n.d.). The three variants used are *ḫr* at the beginning of lines 2 and 10 and *šsp.n.s* for *šsp.sn* in line 11.

I read the passage as follows:

wsf.f ḫr ḏbb fnḏ
ḫr ḥr nb nmḥw
ḫbꜣ.tw m pꜣwt nṯrw
ḫr s ḥḥ ꜣḳ m rmṯ

ỉr ꜥwn-ỉb nšn tꜣ r ḏr.f
wrw šrỉw ḥr nmỉ
šbb rmṯ ḫft ḫsf.f
ḳd.n sw H̱nmw

wbn.f ḫr tꜣ m ḥꜥꜥwt
ḫr ẖt nbt m ršwt
ṯst nbt šsp.n.s sbyt
ỉbḥ nb kfꜣw

For the understanding of the whole passage, lines 5 (*ỉr ꜥwn-ỉb nšn tꜣ r ḏr.f*) and 7 (*šbb rmṯ ḫft ḫsf.f*) are crucial. Erman-Blackman took *ỉr ꜥwn-ỉb* to refer to the Nile and translated "*If he be niggardly*(?) the whole land is in terror *and* great and small *lament.* – – – –."[9] Roeder started from the same assumption and expanded thus:

> Wenn er grausam ist (*wenig Wasser bringt*), so wird die
> ganze Erde umgestürzt.
> Grosse und Kleine vergehen (*vor Hunger*).
> (Aber) bei seinem Herannahen (*Steigen des Wassers*) vermischen
> sich die Menschen (*werden wieder froh*).[10]

Bacchi took a similar view:

> Praticatore di avidita, il paese intero infuria;
> grandi e piccoli urlano.
> Sono ricompensati[11] gli uomini, quando si avvicina;
> (poichè) Gnum lo ha creato (per ciò).[12]

On the other hand, Wilson took *ỉr ꜥwn-ỉb* to refer to the behavior of the people and to be one of several consequences of the *sluggish* Nile which is described at the beginning of the passage. His translation of the whole passage reads thus:

If he is sluggish, then nostrils are stopped up, and everybody is poor. If there be (thus) a cutting down in the food-offerings of the gods, then a million men perish among mortals, covetousness is practiced, the entire land is in fury, and great and small are

[9] Adolf Erman, *The Literature of the Ancient Egyptians*, trans. Aylward M. Blackman (London, 1927) p. 146.

[10] G. Roeder, *Kulte, Orakel und Naturverehrung im alten Ägypten* (Zürich, 1960) p. 333.

[11] Reading *wšb.tw* with P. Turin and P. Chester Beatty V.

[12] Bacchi, *op. cit.* pp. 6–7.

on the execution block. (But) people are different when he approaches. Khnum constructed him.[13]

Now it seems to me that Erman-Blackman and Roeder were on the right track in sensing that two different approaches of the Nile are described, of which the first is indicated by *wsf.f* and the second by *ỉr ꜥwn-ỉb*. However, if *ỉr ꜥwn-ỉb* is understood to mean "niggardly," that is, deficient, this image would merely be a variation on the theme of sluggishness, and the lines beginning with *ỉr ꜥwn-ỉb* would be mere repetition. I propose to see in *ỉr ꜥwn-ỉb* the plundering, that is, rampaging, Nile, the excessive flood, which is as destructive in its own way as the insufficient inundation.[14] If this is so, then the two stanzas describe the *three* basic moods of Ḥapy and their respective effects upon the people: the sluggish Nile (*wsf*), which brings hunger; the rampaging Nile (*ỉr ꜥwn-ỉb*), which brings turmoil; and the Nile that floods in right abundance (*wbn*), which brings happiness. In each case, the moods and actions of the people are poetically related to that of Ḥapy and seen as a direct reflection of his behavior: his sluggishness is their languor, his rampage their rage, his abundance their joy. And it is this interaction which is summed up in the phrase *šbb rmṯ ḫft ḫsf.f*, which means "people change[15] according to his coming." The whole passage then reads thus:

When he's sluggish, noses clog
  everyone is poor;
As the sacred loaves are pared
  a million perish among men.

When he plunders, the whole land rages
  great and small roar;
People change according to his coming
  he was made by Khnum.

When he floods, earth rejoices
  every belly jubilates;
Every jawbone takes on laughter
  every tooth is bared.

[13] *Ancient Egyptian Texts Relating to the Old Testament*, ed. James B. Pritchard (2d ed.; Princeton, 1955) p. 372.

[14] On records of excessively high Nile see G. Daressy in *Annales du Service des antiquités de l'Égypte* XXIII (1923) 47–48.

[15] For *šbỉ* in the sense of "to change" see T. Eric Peet in *JEA* XII (1926) 71, n. 8. The form *šbb* is a good example of the emphatic *sḏm.f*.

THUTMOSIS III'S BENEFACTIONS TO AMON

Charles F. Nims

In the season of 1953/54 Henri Chevrier, while clearing away the debris on the west face of the north tower of the Second Pylon at Karnak, found lying on the earth at ground level five fragments of granite blocks. These had come from the Sanctuary of the Bark of Amon erected by Thutmosis III, which had been replaced by one built at the time of Philip Arrhidaeus.[1] One of the fragments bears part of an inscription recounting the benefactions of the king to Amon. The lower part of this fragment is eroded by the effects of moisture and salts in the earth. On the drawing (Fig. 7)[2] the eroded areas have been left blank where the signs are not certainly discernible, while in several cases the probable readings are given in the translation and notes. The shaded areas indicate erasures by Amarna zealots. Later restorations in these spots were not always made intelligently, so that evident errors and omissions occur.

The lines of the text are arranged in retrograde, similarly to those in the longer inscription of Thutmosis III on the south wall of the suite begun by Hatshepsut.[3] It is difficult to tell how much of the lines is lost, but I would estimate that the longer lines, 14–17, are not less than three-quarters of the original height, which would make the length of a line 1.35 meters or a little less.

The first and last preserved lines have too little remaining to be translatable. From a study of the text I conjecture that in lines 2–21 there are eleven sections and have divided the translation accordingly.

[1] *Annales du Service des antiquités de l'Égypte* LIII (1956) 27 f. Chevrier gave me permission to publish these fragments, which now lie on the north side of the Bubastite court. The one here given is the only fragment that has special interest. Another, about half the size of this one, seems to bear an additional part of the same inscription, but more than nine-tenths of it is so weathered that it is illegible and the few remaining hieroglyphs are of no import.

[2] The drawing was made by Reginald H. Coleman of the staff of the Epigraphic Survey of the Oriental Institute and checked by the author.

[3] For the various publications of this inscription, see Bertha Porter and Rosalind Moss, *Topographical Bibliography of Ancient Egyptian Hieroglyphic Texts, Reliefs, and Paintings* II (Oxford, 1929) 41 (113).

TRANSLATION AND NOTES

(X + 1) . . . .

I. My majesty erected for him a great gateway of gold,[a] "Amon, Senior in Prestige,"[b] of . . . .

II. . . . (3) a great spacious hall,[c] *ṯꜣ*-pillars[d] of sandstone,[e] inlaid with electrum and costly stone[f] . . . (4) gold and precious costly stone from the choice products of the south countries, brought through the power of my majesty, excellent(?) . . . (5) his likeness following the god.

III. My majesty hewed for him a great [river][g] bark, Amon-user-hat, . . . (6) worked with electrum, its hold plated with silver, the shrine in its midst worked ⟨with⟩[h] gold . . . (7) Upper Retjnu in the first campaign of victory which [my father][i] Amon had commanded.

IV. [My majesty] erected for [him] . . . (8) [which] my majesty [brought][j] with my own hands from the terraces of[k] cedar, worked their extent with gold, with ornaments . . . (9) in valor and victory.

V. My majesty provided for him many offering tables of electrum, *špst*-jars, water jars,[l] . . . (10) necklaces, *ḳrḥt*-vases, broad collars without limit of every costly stone.

VI. My majesty erected for him a resting place(?)[m] . . . (11) in the House of Amon, of sandstone of splendid work, plentiful seals[n] of electrum, red jasper(?)[o] . . . (12) worked with gold and every precious costly stone, the gateways of granite, the door leaves of copper, the images[p] of . . . (13) black bronze[q] and *ỉḥw*-copper.[r]

VII. My majesty erected for him a proper place of hearing, removing the . . . (14) therein which mounted to the town quarter,[s] and I erected the shrine therein from a single (block of) stone, of(?) . . . (15) in accordance with the seal which is in it.

VIII. Lo, my majesty found the Southern Pylon of mud brick, the Southern Gateway . . . (16) stone in the lesser constructions, the double door leaves of cedar, the columns of wood. Then my majesty made it of . . . (17) its [gateway] of granite, its great door leaf of copper, the name of which was made,[t] "Amon, Great of Diadems," made excellent . . . (18) . . . before the image[u] upon it of electrum, the shadow of the god like Amon the likeness(?)[v] . . . (19) . . . [of] granite.

IX. My majesty dug for him the Southern Lake, freshened,[w] extended . . . .

X. (20) . . . the shrine therein made excellent with lustrous alabaster of Hatnub[x] . . . .

XI. (21) . . . in his western sacred place, high . . . (22) . . . .

[a] Here and commonly *sb3* means "gateway," "doorway"; however, in The Epigraphic Survey, *Medinet Habu* VII (Chicago, 1964) Pl. 501, line 9, the word is determined by double door leaves; see also Auguste Mariette, *Karnak* (Leipzig, 1875) Pl. 40, lines 9 and 11. Gateways of gold or electrum are often mentioned. One wonders whether the actual metal was used and, if it was, how it was applied. On the façade of Theban Tomb 189 there is a poorly preserved depiction of a series of gateways or pylons, all in the larger area of Karnak as far as the evidence is extant; see Porter and Moss, *Topographical Bibliography* (2d ed.) I 1 (1960) p. 245, Tomb 189 (2).

[b] I translate the name of this gateway in order to distinguish it from the name of the Fifth Pylon, *wr šft,* for which see Eberhard Otto, *Topographie des thebanischen Gaues* (Berlin, 1952) p. 22.

[c] It is uncertain that *wsḫt* carries any directional significance; see Alan H. Gardiner, *Ancient Egyptian Onomastica* (London, 1947) II 208*.

[d] While *ṯ3* is not known as the name of a column, none of the usual meanings of *ṯ3*, *ṯ3w,* seem to fit here. The columns depicted seem to be papyrus-bud shaped, but this may have little significance.

[e] *ʾInr n rwḏt* here and in line 11 almost certainly is an abbreviation of *ỉnr ḥḏ nfr n rwḏt,* but the term is sometimes used for other stones; see John R. Harris, *Lexicographical Studies in Ancient Egyptian Minerals* (Berlin, 1961) pp. 23 and 72.

[f] *ʿ3t* may have been followed by *špst,* as in line 4, by *nbt,* as in line 10, or by *nbt špst,* as in line 12.

[g] The restorers should have written *n tp ỉtr* before the name of the bark but misunderstood the traces.

[h] The preposition *m* has been omitted after *b3k.*

[i] The restorers have omitted several signs here.

[j] *ʾIn.n,* or similar, must have stood at the end of line 7.

[k] There is no evidence that the neck of the *nw*-jar was ever carved.

[l] The traces suggest *ḳbḥt*-jars.

[m] The traces in the weathered surface suggest *ḫnw.*

[n] *Šnʿt* (for this transliteration, see Étienne Drioton, *Bulletin de la Société française d'Égyptologie,* No. 12 [Feb. 1953] pp. 15 f.) seems a more probable reading than *ḫtmt* both here and in line 15, though I am at a loss to explain the significance in either instance. The "seal," weighing 1/12 *deben,* was a medium of exchange; see Gardiner, *Egyptian Grammar* (3d ed.; London, 1957) § 266, 4.

[o] The traces in the weathered surface fit the reading *ḫnm.*

[p] Plural strokes probably were originally behind the seated figure.

[q] *Ḥsmn km,* certainly the correct reading as against *ḥsmn ḥmty km,* is unknown to Harris, *op. cit.* pp. 57 and 63.

[r] The only other recorded example of this combination is in *Urk.* IV 1668, line 18, on the basis of which *Wb.* I 121, 3, and Wolfgang Helck (*Urkunden der 18. Dynastie, Übersetzung zu den Heften 17–22* [Berlin, 1961] p. 204) take *ỉḥw* to mean "piece," while R. O. Faulkner (*A Concise Dictionary of Middle Egyptian* [Oxford, 1962] p. 29) takes it to be a measure (weight?). The present occurrence suggests that it refers to a type of copper. A passage in the Piankhi Stele, line 112 (Vicomte de Rougé, *Chrestomathie égyptienne* IV [Paris, 1876] 66) which has *ỉḥ* preceded and followed by a *nbw* sign gives no help as to the meaning.

[s] Compare *Urk.* IV 835, lines 3–4: "removing the debris which was on its two sides which mounted to the town quarter." The proposed meaning of *ỉwyt* as "house" in

Wb. I 49, 5, results from erroneous reading of stele Louvre C.15, where the actual word is *rw(y)t*, as J. J. Clère informs me by letter.

[t] The restorers here introduced a superfluous *n*.

[u] As far as I can determine, when *ḥp* is used in connection with door leaves, only here and in The Epigraphic Survey, *Medinet Habu* V (1957) Pl. 253 *B*, line 4, is the word used in the singular. In both instances only a single door leaf is concerned; in the other cases the door leaves are in the plural. Thus it would appear that there was only one image on each door leaf.

[v] The traces suggest the reading *twt*. An inscription of Thutmosis III (*Urk*. IV 183, line 10) and an inscription of Amenhotep III (W. M. Flinders Petrie, *Six Temples at Thebes* [London, 1897] Pl. XII, line 21) contain the phrase *šwt nṯr mỉ šft*.

[w] My colleague Carl DeVries suggests this definition of *ḳbḥy* rather than my proposed "cooled."

[x] "Lustrous alabaster of Hat-nub" was the material of three offering tables dedicated by Thutmosis III; see *Urk*. IV 640, line 10.

THE IDENTITY OF THE ITEMS

For several of the items the identity mentioned is self evident, but others need further consideration. In view of the fragmentary condition of the inscription, some identifications can only be tentative.

I. The Sixth Pylon at Karnak.[4]

II. On the assumption that this "great spacious hall" was closely associated with the preceding item, I would identify it with one or both of the two courts on the north and the south of the vestibule before the Sanctuary of the Bark. The valuables mentioned in line 4 seem more like those in a treasury than ones used in decoration of the structure. A room at the north side of the north court served as a treasury of myrrh.[5] The columns, which are on the west sides and the north and south sides of the respective courts, are papyrus-reed clusters. The capitals are not preserved.

III. The river bark of Amon.

IV. The description best fits the four flagpoles which are noted elsewhere.[6] However, if this identification is correct, it is strange to find this item separated from the mention of the Seventh Pylon, Item VIII, where the flagpoles were placed.

V. Various items of temple furniture.

VI. The granite gateways give the key to this section. These would seem to be those mentioned in inscriptions of Thutmosis III, doorways to the north and south of the vestibule before the Sanctuary of the Bark and the one from the north ambulatory.[7] If the reading of the word at the end of the preserved part

[4] See Otto, *Topographie des thebanischen Gaues*, p. 26.

[5] *Urk*. IV 853, line 9.

[6] *Urk*. IV 643, lines 14–17.

[7] *Urk*. IV 167, lines 6–8, and 850; for the position of the gateways, see *b*, *n*, and *m* on plan *ibid*. p. 625.

of line 10 is correct, Item VI also included the Sanctuary of the Bark itself, where this inscription was carved. The rooms about the sanctuary are built of sandstone.

VII. Certainly the eastern chapel of Karnak, at the "Upper Gateway," which was later called the "Hearing Ear." The alabaster naos with two seated figures carved within it must be the "shrine" referred to here. The figures are a male and a female, which in the time of Herihor were identified as Amon-Re and Amonet.[8]

VIII. The Seventh Pylon at Karnak. The lintel and other parts of the Southern Gateway, built by Amenhotep I, were found by Legrain buried in the court of the cache, to the north of the east tower of the Seventh Pylon.[9] When I identified the Southern Pylon as the Eighth Pylon,[10] I did not realize that the present inscription continues through line 19 with the description of the Southern Pylon, which it now seems certain that Thutmosis III replaced.[11] Even if one should suppose that the name of this pylon was incorrectly restored, it is the Seventh and not the Eighth Pylon which has a gateway of granite. The pillars of wood mentioned in connection with the Southern Pylon may have been part of a porch before it. The last word of this section, "granite," probably referred to the material of either the colossal statues or the obelisks which stood on either side of the dromos, but more likely to the latter.

IX. That this was the Sacred Lake to the south of the Thutmosid structures of Karnak is shown by a reference elsewhere to the rebuilding of the house of the High Priests of Amon on the Southern Lake by the High Priest Amenhotep.[12]

X. Almost certainly the way station of Thutmosis III, with the inner shrine of alabaster, to the southeast of the Seventh Pylon, near the Sacred Lake.

XI. The 18th-dynasty temple within the inclosure wall at Medinet Habu is described as "his (i.e., Amon's) sacred place"[13] and may be the item referred to here, but the description of it as being "high" suggests that it may rather be the newly discovered temple of Thutmosis III above and behind the Hathor

[8] I have drawn attention to this chapel in *Proceedings of the Twenty-third International Congress of Orientalists* (London, 1955) pp. 79 f. and in *Thebes of the Pharaohs* (London and New York, 1965) pp. 101 f., but a more extensive examination of the building and its antecedents is needed. For the inscription of Herihor, see *JNES* XIV (1955) 116 f.

[9] See *Annales du Service des antiquités de l'Égypte* IV (1903) 14 ff.

[10] See *Thebes of the Pharaohs*, p. 102, and *ZAS* XCIII (1966) 99, n. 22.

[11] See Otto, *op. cit.* p. 27.

[12] Mariette, *Karnak*, Pl. 40, line 7.

[13] *Urk.* IV 882, line 11.

Chapel at Deir el-Bahri.[14] This temple was under construction in year 45,[15] and it is possible that the Sanctuary of the Bark was built no earlier.[16]

The fragmentary inscription here published and discussed adds a few facts to our knowledge of the history of ancient Egypt. I am happy to be able to present it to my teacher, colleague, and friend, John A. Wilson, who has gathered and digested many such fragments to give us an interpretation of Egyptian culture.

[14] See *JEA* LIII (1967) 25 ff.

[15] See *JEA* XLVI (1950) 44 ff.

[16] William C. Hayes (*Cambridge Ancient History,* rev. ed. of Vols. I & II, fasc. 10 [1962] part 2, p. 32) puts it in year 46 or later.

ONCE AGAIN THE COREGENCY OF THUTMOSE III AND AMENHOTEP II

Richard A. Parker

This subject might seem to have been exhausted after the spate of recent work on it, and if I return to it as the topic for a tribute to my old friend and teacher it is not only because it is a problem to which he once offered a tentative solution but also because I believe the last word has still to be said.

In 1964 Erik Hornung, in his excellent monograph *Untersuchungen zur Chronologie und Geschichte des Neuen Reiches* ("Ägyptologische Abhandlungen" XI), using the results of Helck's investigation of Manetho,[1] proposed (p. 34) a coregency of about a year and a half for Thutmose III and Amenhotep II. Three years later, on the basis of a lunar date in Year 19 of Amenhotep II, Hornung concluded that a coregency of that length was now astronomically established.[2]

In the interim, Redford published an exhaustive analysis of the problem of the coregency and allied matters.[3] He rejected any coregency longer than a few years on compelling grounds and offered as a plausible solution to the "first victorious campaign" problem a coregency of two and one-third years, with Amenhotep II setting out for Takhsy while Thutmose III was still alive and returning from the campaign with the latter dead. This "first victorious campaign" of Year 3 (Amada stela) then yielded precedence to the "first victorious campaign" of Year 7 (Memphis stela) since that was his first while sole ruler.[4]

With knowledge of Redford's article but not of Hornung's, Cyril Aldred finished off a discussion of the jubilees of Amenophis II with a brief consideration of the coregency possibility between Thutmose III and his successor. He wrote:

> . . . in the present writer's view too little consideration has been given to the architectural features of the Amada temple in discussing this problem. A close study of the reliefs of this temple will show that the building was not erected by one king and finished by his successor, but was designed integrally from the start as a monument con-

[1] W. Helck, *Untersuchungen zu Manethō und den ägyptischen Königslisten* ("Untersuchungen zur Geschichte und Altertumskunde Ägyptens" XVIII [Berlin, 1956]) p. 66.

[2] E. Hornung, "Neue Materialien zur ägyptischen Chronologie," *ZDMG* CXVII (1967) 11–16.

[3] D. B. Redford, "The Coregency of Tuthmosis III and Amenophis II," *JEA* LI (1965) 107–22.

[4] *Ibid.* p. 121.

secrated by both kings, and the design is carefully balanced like a left and a right-hand throughout the entire decoration of the monument. In no place is Tuthmosis III described as *mꜥꜣ ḫrw* and in the south side-chapel both kings assist at the foundation ceremonies. The only feature that is off balance is the "Station of the King" dated to year 3 of Amenophis II, but this may be taken to confirm that at this time Amenophis II was the more dynamic member of the partnership.[5]

The "Station of the King" is the location of the Amada stela itself in the rear wall of the sanctuary, with Amenhotep II offering wine to Reᶜ-Harakhti and Amon-Reᶜ, all in a bark, in the register above the stela. Thutmose III is nowhere present on this wall.

The key to Hornung's determination of a coregency of a year less than two and one-third is a lunar date equating III *šmw* 6 with lunar day 7 in the 19th year of Amenhotep II. This comes from the verso (actually the recto) of P. Leningrad (Petersburg) 1116A[6] and was taken by Hornung from Helck's recent publication[7] of that text. If III *šmw* 6 is lunar day 7 (*dnît*), then *psḏntyw* would fall on II *šmw* 30 and a lunar month should begin on or very close to that date when calculated. And indeed Hornung found that on June 8, 1419 B.C., a lunar month by calculation did begin on II *šmw* 30. Since this was Amenhotep's 19th year, his first had to fall in 1438/37 B.C. and so a coregency of one and one-third years was proved.

Unfortunately, I do not believe that the equation so necessary for the establishment of this result will hold up under scrutiny. But before we turn to the particular passage whose rendering by Helck I propose to dispute, some preliminary remarks are advisable. The verso of P. Leningrad 1116A was once the lower half of a large papyrus dealing with accounts of grain. Consequently between columns there are lacunae of approximately the same number of lines as the average preserved, or about fourteen. The preserved lines were numbered consecutively, however, in the publication. The earliest date preserved is II *šmw* 10 (+ x) in line 18 (line 43 has II *šmw* 17) and the latest is III *šmw* 10 in line 205. The last line is 222. That the papyrus dates from the reign of Amenhotep II seems clearly proven.[8] That it is from his Year 19 is a reasonable conclusion from the fact that line 19 mentions an allotment "from the grain of Year 18." In 1419 B.C., we know from Hornung's calculation, II *šmw* 30 was June 8. Even allowing for the subtraction of thirteen days to convert the Julian to a Gregorian date, II *šmw* 10 (+ x) would still have been in May, well after

[5] C. Aldred, "The Second Jubilee of Amenophis II," *ZAS* XCIV (1967) 6.

[6] W. Golénischeff, *Les papyrus hiératiques Nos. 1115, 1116A et 1116B de l'Ermitage Impérial à St. Pétersbourg* (1913) Pls. 15–22, esp. Pl. 22, lines 192 and 200.

[7] W. Helck, "Materialien zur Wirtschaftsgeschichte des Neuen Reiches," Teil IV (Akademie der Wissenshaften und der Literatur in Mainz, *Abhandlungen der geistes- und sozialwissenschaftlichen Klasse*, Jahrgang 1963, Nr. 3 [Wiesbaden, 1963]) 620–33, esp. p. 629.

[8] Redford in *JEA* LI 107–10.

the harvest. Since grain would presumably have been apportioned from the current year's income, the specific mention of Year 18 indicates an older supply, most plausibly from the immediately preceding harvest.

Beginning with line 56 there are a number of allotments of grain for the month of III *šmw* (lines 59, 60, 63, 64, 65, 80, 85, 90). Line 123, after an intercolumnar lacuna, mentions "the offerings ( ) for (*prt*, lunar day 26)," and line 126 has "the offerings (*wdnw*) for (*snt*, day 6)." Note that both these days have the determinatives . In lines 130–31 and again in 135–36 Helck finds other lunar days mentioned which I cannot accept. In lines 130 and 135 we have "given to him for the (*tꜣ*) ," which Helck[9] takes to be the fifth (lunar) day, normally written (*iḫt ḥr ḫꜣwt*, day of offerings on the altar).[10] Whatever *ḫꜣyti* may mean here,[11] it can hardly be taken as *ḫꜣwt*, since Coptic ϣⲏⲩⲉ evidences no *t*.

Lines 131 and 136 have "given to him for the (*tꜣ*) ," which Helck[12] would take as the seventh lunar day, first quarter, normally written .[13] Lacking the proper determinatives for a lunar day and having the article, the word in question is the usual writing for *dnit*, "basket," and I would so take it here while granting that its meaning is obscure. But then lines 133 and 138 have "given to him for the (*pꜣ*) of *Nb-pḥty-Rꜥ* (Ahmose I)," and this *nw* is untranslatable and even more puzzling.

We may now turn to the section that is most important and which it is advisable to present in full.[14]

192. III *šmw* 6, from [the] lower north[ern granary] of the House of the Adorer (the Queen):
193. *ꜣImn-msw* of [the gran]ary for the offerings (*wdnw*) of . . . , 30+ sacks
194. The baker . . . to the excess in this place.
195. The date-worker *Mn-nḫt* . . . to the dates of (*snt*, sixth lunar day) from the upper granary, 13 sacks

(Lacuna of about fourteen lines)

[9] *Op. cit.* pp. 626–67.

[10] Parker, *The Calendars of Ancient Egypt* (*SAOC* No. 26 [1950]) p. 11.

[11] It may be the same word as *ḫꜣty* (*Wb.* III 222, 5), apparently related to *ḫꜣ*, "office." A better reference, for which I am indebted to Professor Klaus Baer, is P. British Museum 10052, page 1, line 3, discussed by T. Eric Peet, *The Great Tomb-Robberies of the Twentieth Dynasty* (Oxford, 1930) I 158, note 1.

[12] *Loc. cit.*

[13] Parker, *loc. cit.*

[14] Golénischeff, *op. cit.* Pl. 22.

196. . . . for the offerings . . . *ḥḳꜣt* . . .

197. [G]iven to him for the offerings (*wdnw*) of 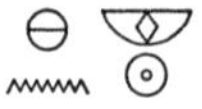 (*psḏntyw*, first lunar day),[15] 1/4 sack 2/3 oipe

198. [Gi]ven to him for the drink-supply of *psḏntyw*

199. [Giv]en to him for the servants from the granary of the House of the Adorer

200. [*Mn*]-*ḫ*ᶜ*w* for the offerings (*wdnw*) of the (*tꜣ*) 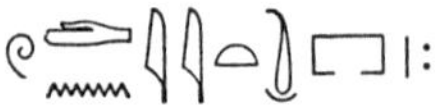

201. [Give]n to him for the offerings (*wdnw*) of *psḏntyw* of . . .

202. [Given to] him for the drink-supply of *psḏntyw*

203. [Given] to him for the [servants from the] granary of the House [of the Adorer] . . .

204. . . . in exchange for barley . . . .

205. [III *š*]*mw* 10, the 60 storehouses of the House . . .

206. . . . for the good bread . . . sacks

207. Good [bread] (for)  (*snt*, sixth lunar day) of . . . sacks

(The following lines to 222, the last, contribute nothing.)

The writing of *psḏntyw* is identical in lines 197, 198, 201, and 202. Such a writing, without the *tyw*-bird, is not uncommon and is found, for example, on the Ahmose stela in a listing of lunar month feasts beginning with 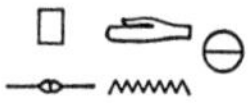 and continuing with the second, fourth, fifth, and sixth lunar days.[16] Helck's rendering of 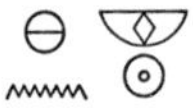 as the "9th day feast"[17] is clearly an oversight on his part and cannot be accepted. The same verdict must be given to his interpretation of *wdnyt* in line 200 as *dnỉt*, the seventh lunar day, first quarter. We have already discussed the misinterpretation of *dnỉt*, "basket," as the seventh lunar day in lines 131 and 136. *Wdnyt*, with initial *w* and the house determinative and without the feast and day determinatives, is no better candidate than the former for the seventh lunar day. In *Wb*. I 392, 12, *wdnyt* is taken as "offering hall,"[18] and I see no reason to reject that rendering here.

It was on lines 192 and 200, however, with the misinterpretation of *wdnyt*, that Hornung based his lunar-civil day equation. Granted that we must reject it, can anything of worth for chronology be won nevertheless from lines 192–207? Let us look more closely at what is given us. There are two dates, III *šmw* 6 (line 192) and III *šmw* 10 (line 205). Between them there are four issues of grain for the offerings and drinks for *psḏntyw* and one issue of dates

[15] Parker, *loc cit.* [16] *Urk*. IV 27, lines 4–5. [17] Helck, *op. cit.* p. 629.

[18] There are three references given, the last of which is the present passage. The Medinet Habu example is now to be found in *Medinet Habu* VII (*OIP* XCIII [1964]) Pl. 582 *B*, where Amon-Reᶜ is called *nb wdnyt* () *ḥry-ỉb Ḥt-kꜣ-Ptḥ*, "lord of the offering hall in Memphis."

for *snt*. Two lines after III *šmw* 10 is a further entry for grain, for "good bread" for *snt*.

At Medinet Habu the Feasts of the Sky, that is, the lunar feasts of the month, were eight in number. In the calendar they began with day 29 (*ꜥḥꜥ . . .*) and continued with day 30 (*prt Mn*), day 1 (*psḏntyw*), day 2 (*ꜣbd*), day 4 (*prt sm*), day 6 (*snt*), day 10 (*sw 10 ꜣbd*), and day 15 (*smdt*, full-moon day).[19] In passing, we may note that neither day 5 nor day 7 was celebrated, a fact which may speak against finding either in the Leningrad papyrus. Of these eight feasts, the most important by far, to judge from the quantity of offerings presented to Amon, were *psḏntyw* and *snt*.[20] These would necessarily have required more extensive preparation.

Now it is a reasonable conclusion that grain was issued in advance of a feast in order that it could be milled and baked into loaves. The preparation of beer would take longer than baking bread but could well be done in three or four days.[21] On either III *šmw* 6, then, or just possibly, because of the lacuna, on a day following III *šmw* 6 but before III *šmw* 10, grain was issued for the feast of *psḏntyw*, and the expectation would be that the feast would occur rather soon but no earlier than the time required to make beer.

To assist the discussion from now on it will be found useful to have a framework of possible dates for *psḏntyw* in the civil months of II and III *šmw*, based on the twenty-five year cycle scheme of the Late Period.[22] We recall that Hornung found that in 1419 B.C. a lunar month began on II *šmw* 30. With this as a starting point in the 9th year of the cycle we can construct the table given below. It indicates a lunar month beginning on III *šmw* 11 in 1420 B.C., cycle year 8. Calculation, however, shows that it actually began on June 18, or III *šmw* 10. Since, again by calculation, the preceding lunar month began on II *šmw* 11 it is possible that through poor visibility, or conceivably because a lunar cycle was indeed in use,[23] the following month's beginning may have been delayed a day to the 11th.

[19] *Medinet Habu* III (*OIP* XXIII [1934[) Lists 7–14 on Pls. 148 and 150.

[20] For bread and beer alone, five sacks were required for each of these two feasts. For the six minor feasts, one sack for each was the allotment.

[21] J. L. Burckhardt, in his *Travels in Nubia* (2d ed.; London, 1922) p. 201, describes the making of *bouza*, which is surely the counterpart of ancient *ḥnḳt*, as follows: "Strongly leavened bread made from Dhourra is broken into crumbs, and mixed with water, and the mixture is kept for several hours over a slow fire. Being then removed, water is poured over it, and it is left for two nights to ferment. This liquor, according to its greater or smaller degree of fermentation, takes the name of Merin, Bouza, or Om Belbel . . . . Unlike the other two, which, being fermented with the crumbs of bread, are never free from them, the Om Belbel is drained through a cloth, and is consequently pure and liquid."

[22] Parker, *Calendars*, p. 25.

[23] I am not as sanguine as Hornung (*ZDMG* CXVII 14–15) that a lunar cycle was already in use by the 18th dynasty. The possibility of it cannot be denied, but there is no proof whatever of its existence.

In any event, whether *psḏntyw* was III *šmw* 10 or 11, either day would be ideal with respect to the issuance of grain on III *šmw* 6; and the same would be true for the issue of grain on III *šmw* 10 for *snt* on III *šmw* 15/16. But if 1420 B.C. was the 19th year of Amenhotep II, then his first year was 1439/38 B.C. and the length of his coregency was two years and four months The attractiveness of this theory is that it conforms exactly to Redford's plausible solution of the "first campaign" problem and that it explains the "Station of the King" in the Amada temple on a better basis than Aldred's assumption that Amenhotep II was merely the more dynamic of the ruling partners. The situation may be best illustrated by the accompanying diagram, which shows the

25-Year Cycle Dates for II and III *šmw*

Cycle Year	Day	Years B.C.	Cycle Year	Day	Years B.C.	Cycle Year	Day	Years B.C.
1	27	1452/1427	10	20	1443/1418	18	23	1435/1410
2	16	1451/1426	11	9	1442/1417	19	12	1434/1409
3	5	1450/1425	12	28	1441/1416	20	2	1433/1408
4	24	1449/1424	13	17	1440/1415	21	21	1432/1407
5	14	1448/1423	14	6	1439/1414	22	10	1431/1406
6	3	1447/1422	15	26	1438/1413	23	29	1430/1405
7	22	1446/1421	16	15	1437/1412	24	18	1429/1404
8	11	1445/1420	17	4	1436/1411	25	8	1428/1403
9	30	1444/1419						

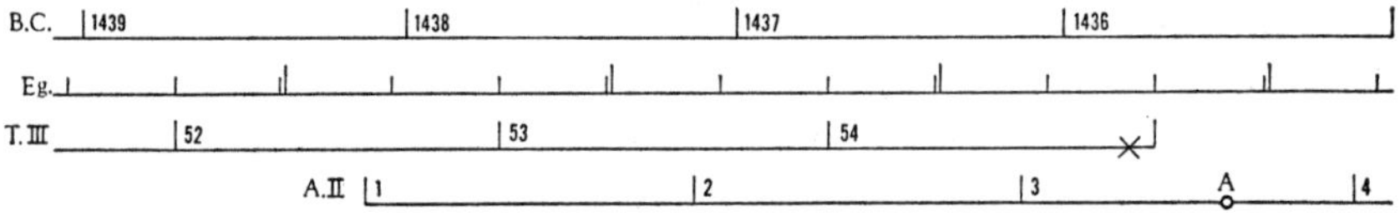

approximate relationship to one another of four years: the Julian, the Egyptian beginning with I ꜣḫt 1, the regnal year of Thutmose III beginning I *šmw* 4 (with his death on III *prt* 30 marked by "X"), and the regnal year of Amenhotep II beginning IIII ꜣḫt 1 (with "A" marking the date of the Amada stela, III *šmw* 15, in Year 3). In his third year, while still coregent, Amenhotep would have embarked on his "first" campaign. During it Thutmose III would have died, and Amenhotep would have returned as sole ruler. Later, in Year 7, his true "first" campaign would have been embarked upon.

By means of our table of lunar dates, one can easily check on other *psḏntyw* dates in relation to III *šmw* 6, but the results are unsatisfactory. III *šmw* 30 in 1419 B.C. and III *šmw* 20 in 1418 are not good and we cannot, of course, go farther down since Amenhotep II cannot be thought of as numbering his years from the IIII ꜣḫt 1 which came eight months *after* the death of Thutmose III.

Going back from 1420 B.C. we have III *šmw* 22 in 1421, III *šmw* 3 in 1422, and III *šmw* 14 in 1423. This date, in relation to III *šmw* 6, would be at least a possible one but would mean a coregency of five and a fraction years, and this would put us again in the necessity of adequately explaining the "first campaign" years of 3 and 7. Advocates, if any, of a still longer coregency may check their proposals against the lunar dates preceding 1423 in our table.

Something remains to be said about the two lunar days mentioned earlier, *prt* in line 123 and *snt* in line 126. In the Medinet Habu calendar, as we have seen, there was no festival for lunar day *prt* (the 26th of the month). There were, however, festivals for the 30th day (*prt Mn*) and the 4th day (*prt sm*). It occurs to me as possible that either one of these two was the actual festival intended by the entry in line 123. However, if we assume that the 26th is correct it would have fallen on III *šmw* 6, since we have calculated that II *šmw* 11 was *psḏntyw*. The entry in the journal would then presumably have been a day or two before III *šmw* 6. The same date would apply to line 126, mentioning offerings for *snt* (day 6). What these "offerings" would be is not clear, but the two preceding lines mention a brew-house and a brewer. *Snt*, as we have noted, would fall on III *šmw* 15/16. An entry ten days or so before may seem too far in advance, but the preparation for and the celebration of *psḏntyw* would intervene and in any case we are ignorant of the exact purpose of the grain issue. Dates were issued on III *šmw* 6 (line 195) for *snt*. Probably they required longer preparation for whatever use they were put to, since grain for "good bread" was not issued till III *šmw* 10.

To sum up: Redford has argued cogently and convincingly for a coregency of Amenhotep II with Thutmose III, most plausibly for two and one-third years, which would account satisfactorily for the "Station of the King" at Amada. The evidence of the dates in P. Leningrad 1116A is entirely in favor of a coregency of the same length, as opposed to a shorter or a slightly longer one. This strong additional support to Redford's position seems to me to make it well-nigh certain.

ADDENDUM

It was after my manuscript was in the hands of the printer that my friend Jürgen von Beckerath sent me an offprint of his own article criticizing Hornung's lunar equation on grounds identical with mine and suggesting that Amenhotep's Year 19 could well be 1420 B.C. with a coregency of two years and four months.[24] Were this all, my own paper would be unnecessary though von Beckerath's three pages and a half do not go into details nor discuss the historical background of the problem. However, he has introduced an element of doubt in suggesting that 1417 B.C. would also fit the lunar situation of the papyrus entries if it were taken as Year 20 of Amenhotep, and he would regard

[24] "Ein neues Monddatum der ägyptischen Geschichte," *ZDMG* CXVIII (1968) 18–21. Some incorrect dates therein may confuse the reader. Thus (p. 19) Hornung's equation should be given as II *šmw* 30 = *psḏntyw* = June 8, 1419 B.C., and (p. 21) the correct year to go with June 16 is 1417 B.C.

both alternatives as equally probable. The possibility of 1417 being Year 20, however, I would reject on what seem to me compelling grounds.

(1) The dates of the papyrus entries fall in May, and that is well after harvest. If the year were 20 then the mention of "grain of Year 18" in line 19 would imply that all the harvest of Year 19 as well as that of the current Year 20 was available, for surely the normal way of disbursing grain would be to exhaust the older supply first and not, for example, use up all for Year 19 while still keeping on hand some from Year 18, to be allotted at the same time as the current harvest of Year 20. That the papyrus dates are for Year 19 seems to me the only likely conclusion.

(2) A glance at the 25-year cycle given above shows indeed that in 1417 B.C. *psḏntyw* should fall on III *šmw* 9, a date which seems to fit appropriately with disbursements for that feast on III *šmw* 6. However, that the 25-year cycle was in use in the 18th dynasty is an unprovable assumption and calculation of a lunar date should always be preferred to a cyclical one. Now calculation shows that a lunar month began not on III *šmw* 9 but rather on III *šmw* 8. The preceding month began, again by calculation, on II *šmw* 8, negating the possibility that through poor observation *psḏntyw* was delayed until III *šmw* 9. Unless a cycle was in use, then, and that would be pure supposition, the feast fell on III *šmw* 8 in 1417 B.C. But grain allotments for the feast were made no earlier than III *šmw* 6 and included in these was grain for the drink-supply. I submit that this is really too little time for the total beer-making process.

(3) Von Beckerath dismisses,[25] rather too casually in my opinion, the historical background which led Redford to suggest two and one-third years as the logical coregency. The difficulty of two "first campaigns" and now also that of the "Station of the King" are satisfactorily explained by the longer coregency and remain unsolved by the shorter.

In the light of these considerations, I see no reason to alter the conclusion expressed above that a coregency of two years and four months is the only possible choice.

[25] *Ibid.* p. 21, n. 9.

HATHOR AT THE JUBILEE

Edward F. Wente

Professor John A. Wilson in his "Illuminating the Thrones at the Egyptian Jubilee"[1] discussed certain preparatory rites of Amenhotep III's initial sed-festival that are depicted on the pylon of the temple of Soleb. This ceremonial, which lasted from the fourth month of the second season, day 26, to the first month of the third season, day 1, began at "daybreak of the sed-festivals."[2] Also at daybreak of the king's third jubilee in Year 37 occurred the erection of the djed-pillar that is portrayed on the rear wall of the northern portico of Kheruef's tomb chapel. In officiating at these preliminary rituals Amenhotep III wore the blue crown and had not yet donned the jubilee garb. In Kheruef's southern portico the king is thrice represented outfitted with the jubilee regalia, and it is thus strange to find Hartwig Altenmüller[3] suggesting that the southern wall is to be read before the northern one. In his attempt to correlate Kheruef's jubilee scenes with episodes of the Ramesseum Dramatic Papyrus, he has made several misinterpretations of what is represented in Kheruef's chapel and has ignored the relatively late month and day dates given for the ceremonies in the southern portico. It is hoped that these lines, penned in honor of Professor Wilson's seventieth birthday, may shed some illumination on aspects of the final episodes of the jubilee following the example of my preceptor and friend.

The scenes in Kheruef's southern portico that relate to the first jubilee[4] illustrate three major episodes, in each of which Kheruef was probably de-

[1] *JAOS* LVI (1936) 293–96.

[2] For the translation of *ḥḏ-tꜣ* as "daybreak" (in terms of the natural day) rather than "day before," see Richard A. Parker, *The Calendars of Ancient Egypt* (*SAOC* No. 26 [1950]) p. 62, and Böker in *Paulys Realencyclopädie der classischen Altertumswissenschaft* IX A_2 (1967) 2371–72. In terms of the astronomical day the expression would, strictly speaking, denote part of the preceding day (cf. Parker, *op. cit.* p. 81, n. 17). The plural *ḥbw-sd*, also used in Kheruef's inscriptions (*Urk.* IV 1860, line 13, 1869, line 16, 1871, line 7), perhaps refers to the multiplicity of rites comprised in a jubilee, whether on a single day as in "I was prophet of Anubis on the day of the jubilee festivals (*ḥbw-sd*) in the first jubilee (*ḥb-sd tpy*) of His Majesty" (*Urk.* IV 1851, line 10) or during the entire jubilee as in *m ḥbw-sd 3-nw n ḥm.f*, "in the third jubilee festivals of His Majesty" (*Urk.* IV 1860, line 4, though Wolfgang Helck's copy omits the plural strokes before *3-nw*), to be compared with the parallel statement in *Urk.* IV 1860, line 2, where plural strokes are absent.

[3] *Jaarbericht ex Oriente Lux*, No. 19 (1965-66) pp. 421–42.

[4] See Ahmed Fakhry in *Annales du Service des antiquités de l'Égypte* XLII (1943) Pl. XL and pp. 488–500; *Urk.* IV 1865–71.

picted as a participant. According to a long inscription in the upper register, just to the left of the throne scene, the high officials were on day 27 of the second month of the third season rewarded by the king, and immediately beneath this text an intentionally damaged scene shows Kheruef being decorated with golden necklaces at the foot of the dais. The next episode, which took place on the same day, was the royal procession from the Malqata palace, "The Palace of the House of Rejoicing," and is illustrated in the upper register to the left of the long inscription. Two registers of priests and officiants precede the royal couple as they emerge from the palace gateway. Although the last two figures of the lower register are badly damaged and their titles are lost, enough of their feet is preserved to enable one to state that the penultimate figure is the only unshod member of the entire procession. It is significant that wherever Kheruef is depicted on the walls of his chapel he is barefooted, even when he is in the company of others who may be shod, and it therefore seems likely that the penultimate figure is Kheruef in his role of castellan.

Occupying the left portion of the upper half of this wall, the final episode, which occurred on the first or second day of the third month of the third season,[5] comprised the towing of the evening solar bark bearing the king, the queen, the chief lector priest, two viziers, and the castellan Kheruef at the prow. The tow-rope is drawn by high officials on land; in a register above them princesses shake sistra, and court ladies, several of whom carry gazelle-headed wands[6] and menat-necklaces, await the bark's arrival. These three episodes thus comprise the throne scene, the entire upper half of the wall, and a section of the bottom half just to the left of the dais.

The remainder of the lower panel contains first a scene of four pairs of girls bearing flasks of libation water.[7] Since it is stated that they were made to stand at the foot of the throne in the king's presence, this scene is associated with the throne scene of the first episode. Eric Uphill[8] suggests that a scene on the façade of Osorkon II's Bubastite Festival Hall, showing certain women holding jars,[9] "recalls the princesses shown in the tomb of Kheruef." In fact, their equation is assured through a textual parallel: the horizontal line of inscription bordering the top of the Kheruef scene reappears in Osorkon II's reliefs as

[5] See Helck in *Mitteilungen des Instituts für Orientforschung* II (1954) 194.

[6] See Hermann Kees, *Studien zur aegyptischen Provinzialkunst* (Leipzig, 1921) p. 29, n. 4; Jacques Vandier, *Manuel d'archéologie égyptienne* IV (Paris, 1964) 401, with n. 2. Women with such wands appear also in Osorkon II's Bubastite Festival Hall; see Eduard Naville, *The Festival-Hall of Osorkon II. in the Great Temple of Bubastis* (London, 1892) Pls. I, XIV, and XXV (block VI).

[7] See Kurt Lange and Max Hirmer, *Ägypten: Architektur, Plastik, Malerei in drei Jahrtausenden* (4th ed.; München, 1967) Pls. 166–67.

[8] *JNES* XXIV (1965) 381.

[9] Naville, *op. cit.* Pls. XIV (block 3) and XV (block 4).

a text (apparently poorly copied) on the upper part of blocks 4 and 5 of Naville's Plate XV.

In the Bubastite version these girls are distributed over two registers, and in both occurrences men carrying circular or hoop-shaped objects (probably poorly drawn vessels) occupy the register above them. These men were the "Great Ones of Upper and Lower Egypt,"[10] and it is obvious that blocks 4 and 5 of Naville's Plate XV contain the logical continuation of registers on blocks 2 and 3 of his Plate XIV. Although only seven girls with flasks are depicted at Bubastis, it is possible that one has been lost or omitted at the left edge of block 4 on Naville's Plate XV.

Several authors[11] have referred to the Kheruef girls as princesses of Amenhotep III, whose daughters do appear elsewhere in Kheruef's jubilee reliefs, where they are referred to as *msw nswt*, "king's children,"[12] at the erection of the djed-pillar or individually as *sꜣt-nswt*, "king's daughter," in the scene of the towing of the evening bark. However, the four pairs of girls with flasks are *msw wrw*, an expression which designates children of either Egyptian officials or foreign chieftains.[13] That these girls are of foreign origin is suggested both by the horizontal text at the top of the Kheruef panel, where reference is made to the "daughter of the Mentiu" giving cool water to the sovereign, and by the text below two similar girls on block 3 of Naville's Plate XIV: "All foreign lands bring their best, bearing ewers of ⟨gold⟩[14] and flasks of electrum."

To the left of the girls in the Kheruef panel, the remainder of the bottom half of the wall is occupied by two registers of female acrobatic dancers and musicians who are said to be introduced before the baldachin. That their performance is also connected with the initial episode is indicated by the hymn to

10 See Kees in F. W. von Bissing, *Das Re-Heiligtum des Königs Ne-Woser-Re (Rathures)*. III. *Die grosse Festdarstellung* (Leipzig, 1928) pp. 58–59, and Helck, *Untersuchungen zu den Beamtentiteln des ägyptischen Alten Reiches* (Ägyptologische Forschungen" XVIII [1954]) p. 18. Vladimir Vikentiev's notion, presented in *Bulletin de l'Institut d'Égypte* XXXVII (1956) 301–3, that the expression *wrw šmꜥw mḥw* reflects the Libyan background of certain aspects of the jubilee deserves some consideration.

11 E.g. William Hayes in *Bulletin of the Metropolitan Museum of Art* N.S. VI (1948) 277; Lange and Hirmer, *Ägypten* (4th ed.) p. 97; W. Stevenson Smith, *The Art and Architecture of Ancient Egypt* ("Pelican History of Art" Z14 [Harmondsworth and Baltimore, 1965]) pp. 150–51; Christiane Desroches-Noblecourt, *Tutankhamen* (New York, 1963) p. 122.

12 For the expression in reference to princesses see Kurt Sethe, *Dramatische Texte zu altaegyptischen Mysterienspielen* ("Untersuchungen zur Geschichte und Altertumskunde Aegyptens" X [Leipzig, 1928]) p. 178 (69b), and Hermann Grapow, *Untersuchungen zur ägyptischen Stilistik*. I. *Der stilistische Bau der Geschichte des Sinuhe* (Berlin, 1952) p. 98.

13 See *Wb.* II 139, 8–9. In addition *msw wrw* may be used to designate "students"; see Georges Posener, *Littérature et politique dans l'Égypte de la XIIe Dynastie* (Paris, 1956) p. 6, and Hellmut Brunner, *Altägyptische Erziehung* (Wiesbaden, 1957) p. 41.

14 Emended on the basis of the vertical text before the Kheruef girls, where *nmswt n nbw s(n)bwt n ḏꜥmw* is now to be read.

Hathor extending above the musicians,[15] Hathor being enthroned directly behind the king in the baldachin.

Vikentiev[16] recognized the existence of parallels to these performers in reliefs on Osorkon II's monument. The first half of the horizontal text above the dancers[17] reappears with certain deviations at Bubastis,[18] and while there is no direct parallel at Bubastis to Kheruef's female acrobatic dancers, their activity is perhaps mirrored in the pose of two male dancers on blocks 4 and 5 of Naville's Plate XV. Closer parallels exist at Bubastis for several of the performers in Kheruef's lower register.

Since it is claimed that Amenhotep III's first jubilee was celebrated in accordance with writings of old,[19] antecedents to the Kheruef material might be expected as well. Both Helck[20] and Altenmüller[21] have shown that the ceremonies associated with the erection of the djed-pillar in Kheruef's northern portico find their complement in texts and illustrations in the Middle Kingdom Ramesseum Dramatic Papyrus.

For the three figures with lion masks at the very left end of the lowest panel in Kheruef's southern portico Henri Wild[22] has cited two parallels from the Old Kingdom. On a fragment in the British Museum[23] a figure with a lion-type headdress holds a wand in the shape of a human arm and is accompanied by youths whose activity is described as dancing. To their left are two dancing women whose headdresses and upraised right arms possibly relate them to the three women preceding the lion-masked figures in Kheruef's chapel. In a scene in the tomb of Mereruka[24] a similar group of youths escorts a bound prisoner. The lion-mask is absent there, but one of the youths carries the armlike wand before the prisoner's face. Smith's suggestion[25] that these two representations and related ones "perhaps represent the games and dances of a festival such as we find celebrated at the feast of Hathor of Cusae in the Middle Kingdom at Meir" seems substantiated by the scene just below the Mereruka youths[26] in

[15] See Fakhry in *Annales du Service des antiquités de l'Égypte* XLII 498.

[16] *Bulletin de l'Institut d'Égypte* XXXVII 306–8.

[17] See Lange and Hirmer, *Ägypten* (4th ed.) Pl. 168.

[18] Naville, *op. cit.* Pls. XV (block 5) and XIV (block 1, at bottom).

[19] See *Urk.* IV 1867, line 15.

[20] *Orientalia* N. S. XXIII (1954) 383-411.

[21] *Jaarbericht ex Oriente Lux* No. 19, pp. 421–22.

[22] See *Sources orientales. VI. Les danses sacrées* (Paris, 1963) pp. 76–77 and 100.

[23] Published in T. G. H. James (ed.), *Hieroglyphic Texts from Egyptian Stelae*, Part I (2d ed.; 1961) Pl. XXV 3; cf. Vandier, *Manuel d'archéologie égyptienne* IV 402–3.

[24] The Sakkarah Expedition, *The Mastaba of Mereruka* II (*OIP* XXXIX [1938]) Pl. 162.

[25] W. Stevenson Smith, *A History of Egyptian Sculpture and Painting in the Old Kingdom* (2d ed.; London, 1949) p. 210.

[26] The Sakkarah Expedition, *The Mastaba of Mereruka* II, Pl. 164; cf. Vandier, *Manuel d'archéologie égyptienne* IV 410–12.

which girls, three of whom hold arm-shaped wands, perform for Hathor. This type of wand, held also by the first lion-masked figure in Kheruef's chapel, appears to be related to bone, ivory, and wooden instruments of similar form which Hans Hickmann[27] has associated with the cult of Hathor.

The other Old Kingdom lion-masked figure referred to by Wild occurs on a fragment discovered in the forehall of Sahure's mortuary temple[28] and is nearly identical with the lion-masked personage facing left in the Kheruef panel. Borchardt[29] did not specify whether the fragment originally formed part of the decoration of this hall, and perhaps his silence is indicative that he had reservations. It has been suggested[30] that the lion-masked figure is the prototype of Bes, whose association with Hathor is well known.[31]

Not far from the spot where the Sahure fragment was found Borchardt uncovered four fragments of dancers[32] in the northern passage of the ambulatory that surrounded the columned court. He believed that these pieces, which formed part of the decoration of the east half of the southern wall of this passage, depicted dancers similar to ones in certain private tombs of the Old Kingdom. Actually the Sahure fragments derive from a scene comparable to that of the acrobatic dancers and musicians in Kheruef's chapel, and to this scene must also have belonged the piece with the lion-masked figure.

The left-most of Borchardt's fragments contains parts of two figures corresponding to the man with folded shoulder, who carries a staff and scepter and leads a procession of female musicians, and to the girl performer preceding him in Kheruef's lower register. Borchardt's upper middle fragment and his right-hand one bear portions of two girls in a dance posture similar to that of the two pairs of girls to the left of the kneeling clappers in Kheruef's chapel. Borchardt mistook his middle bottom fragment as depicting a girl with extended legs;[33] he should have positioned it at a quarter of a revolution to the right, for the girl is actually bending deeply in a pose similar to that of the first three dancers to the left of a shrine in the register above Kheruef's musicians.[34]

[27] In *Bulletin de l'Institut d'Égypte* XXXVII 102. This type of wand is to be differentiated from a similar stick carried by dwarfs tending baboons; see Vandier d'Abbadie in *Revue d'Égyptologie* XVI (1964) 159.

[28] Ludwig Borchardt, *Das Grabdenkmal des Königs Śaꜣḥu-reᶜ* II (*WVDOG* XXVI [1913]) Pl. 22 top right and pp. 38–39.

[29] *Ibid.* Vols. I (*WVDOG* XIV [1910]) 12 and 40 and II 38–39.

[30] See Hans Bonnet, *Reallexikon der ägyptischen Religionsgeschichte* (Berlin, 1952) p. 109; Wild in *Sources orientales* VI 100; Vandier, *Manuel d'archéologie égyptienne* IV 402.

[31] According to Brunner, *Die Geburt des Gottkönigs* ("Ägyptologische Abhandlungen" X [Wiesbaden, 1964]) p. 106, Bes is not attested in the Old Kingdom, but this, he admits, may be due to the one-sided nature of extant source material.

[32] Borchardt, *op. cit.* Vols. I 15 and II, Pl. 54 and pp. 64–65.

[33] Cf. Norman de Garis Davis, *The Mastaba of Ptahhetep and Akhethetep at Saqqareh* I (London, 1901) Pl. XXI; The Sakkarah Expedition, *The Mastaba of Mereruka* II, Pl. 162.

[34] See Lange and Hirmer, *Ägypten* (4th ed.) Pl. 168.

There are slight variations in the Old and New Kingdom renditions, both in posture and in costume. In general, the dress of the Sahure girls is rendered in greater detail; for example, in Kheruef's chapel a simple broad collar is substituted for the elaborate knotted cord about the neck. The dress of these performing artists suggests that they were Libyans,[35] and the variegated striped pattern of the skirts of similar dancers on unpublished jubilee *talatat* of Amenhotep IV at Karnak confirms their foreign origin.

From the Middle Kingdom there are also textual and iconographic parallels to the Kheruef material. In the Theban tomb chapel of the vizier Antefoker's wife Senet, to the right of scenes relating to the funeral, there is a section of wall on which are depicted Hathoric performances in the presence of the deceased couple.[36] Above the clapping hands[37] of three girls in the upper register occurs the phrase "opened are the doors of heaven so that the god may go forth,"[38] a text that appears above Kheruef's choir directors in the form "opened are the doors so that the god may go forth pure." It is possible that the two groups of three clapping women in Senet's tomb are to be linked with the six clapping women arranged in two groups around the tambourine-player in Kheruef's lower panel, while the two dancing girls at the left in Senet's scene bear some resemblance in hairdress and gesture to the three dancing girls to the left of these Kheruef musicians. In Senet's mural the text above a flutist and a singer says: "Come, Sobek,[39] to Antefoker and do what he desires." This address is repeated above two similar artists in Kheruef's

[35] See Elisabeth Staehelin, *Untersuchungen zur ägyptischen Tracht im Alten Reich* ("Münchner ägyptologische Studien" VIII [Berlin, 1966]) pp. 130–32, and Vikentiev in *Bulletin de l'Institut d'Égypte* XXXVII 306–7.

[36] Norman de Garis Davies and Alan H. Gardiner, *The Tomb of Antefoḳer, Vizier of Sesostris I, and of His Wife, Senet (No. 60)* (London, 1920) Pls. XXIII–XXV; cf. Wild in *Sources orientales* VI 65–66 and Vandier, *Manuel d'archéologie égyptienne* IV 431–35.

[37] See Hickmann in *Bulletin de l'Institut d'Égypte* XXXVII 67–76 as opposed to the interpretation of Adolphe Gutbub in *Mélanges Maspero. I. Orient ancien* ("Mémoires publiés par les membres de l'Institut français d'archéologie orientale du Caire" LXVI) 4me fasc. (1961) p. 59.

[38] The text also appears in the tomb of Amenemhat at Beni Hassan (Percy E. Newberry, *Beni Hasan* I [London, 1893] Pl. XXIX), in connection with the hauling of the deceased's statue to the temple (cf. Gutbub, *loc. cit*). Here the doors of the shrine are open revealing the statue, and the expression "doors of heaven" clearly refers to the doors of the shrine (see Jaroslav Černý in *JEA* XXXIV [1948] 120).

[39] The address to Sobek within a Hathoric context remains obscure in its significance, but perhaps it has to do with the crocodile's association with the concept of rebirth; see László Kákosy in *Mitteilungen des Deutschen archäologischen Instituts*, Abteilung Kairo, XX (1965) 116–20 and Paul Barguet, *Le temple d'Amon-Rê à Karnak* (L'Institut français d'archéologie orientale du Caire, "Recherches d'archéologie, de philologie et d'histoire" XXI [Le Caire, 1962]) p. 185, n. 5. Note the identification of Re, Sobek, and Hathor as the western bas in the Coffin Texts; see Adriaan de Buck, *The Egyptian Coffin Texts* II (*OIP* XLIX [1938]) 386*d*–387*a*.

chapel: "Come, pray, Sobek, to the Son of Re, Amenhotep III, given life, and do what he desires."

In Senbi's mortuary chapel at Meir a series of Hathoric ceremonies is executed in the deceased's presence.[40] They also adjoin the depiction of the funeral cortege, a fact suggesting that they are of mortuary significance. Although Senbi's musicians and dancers are not directly paralleled in Kheruef's chapel, the clause *ỉw.s ḳꜣ.t(ỉ) m šn(w) Rꜥ* in the song of the harper reappears in the second person as *ỉw.t ḳꜣ.tỉ m šny Rꜥ m šny Rꜥ* in Kheruef's hymn to Hathor[41] and should be rendered "she is (var. 'you are') exalted in the hair of Re."[42]

Inasmuch as the southern arm of Sahure's ambulatory contained remnants of a jubilee scene,[43] it is plausible that the five fragments found in or near the northern arm also belonged to a jubilee scene resembling Kheruef's. The iconography of these Hathoric performances in a royal context would thus predate their appearance in private tomb chapels of the Middle Kingdom. Since one aspect of the jubilee seems to have been the symbolic death and revitalization of the king, it is not unreasonable to posit a borrowing of essentially royal Hathoric iconography by commoners to enhance their prospects for a potent existence after death. Both the Senet and Senbi Hathoric rites adjoin scenes of the funeral, whose symbolic efficacy Jürgen Settgast[44] has demonstrated. Evidence for a democratization of Hathoric jubilee symbolism is provided in Senbi's chapel by the text before a dancer who says in addressing Senbi: "May you repeat a million sed-festivals while Hathor gladdens you therein."[45]

[40] Aylward M. Blackman, *The Rock Tombs of Meir* I (London, 1914) Pls. II–III; cf. Vandier, *Manuel d'archéologie égyptienne* IV 427–28, and Wild in *Sources orientales* VI 68.

[41] See Fakhry in *Annales du Service des antiquités de l'Égypte* XLII 498 (with omissions).

[42] Both Blackman, *The Rock Tombs of Meir* I 23, and Alfred Hermann, *Altägyptische Liebesdichtung* (Wiesbaden, 1959) p. 24, unaware of the Kheruef text, misunderstood the clause.

[43] See Borchardt, *Das Grabdenkmal des Königs Śaꜣḥu-reꜥ* II 69. In addition to the jubilee scenes in Sahure's mortuary temple indicated by Borchardt (*ibid.* pp. 54–56), see the identification by Gardiner in *JEA* XXX (1944) 28. On the later survival of another genre of scene that appears in Sahure's funerary temple, the Libyan family, see J. J. Clère in *Mitteilungen des Deutschen archäologischen Instituts,* Abteilung Kairo, XVI (1958) 43.

[44] *Untersuchungen zu altägyptischen Bestattungsdarstellungen* ("Abhandlungen des Deutschen archäologischen Instituts Kairo," Ägyptologische Reihe III [Glückstadt etc., 1963]).

[45] Blackman, *The Rock Tombs of Meir* I 26, translates: "Smell thou Hathor therein!" However, the particle *r.f* seems to be used only after the plural imperative; cf. Gardiner, *Egyptian Grammar* (3d ed.; London, 1957) § 252, 3 (a), and Gustave Lefebvre, *Grammaire de l'égyptien classique* (Institut français d'archéologie orientale "Bibliothèque d'étude" XII [2d ed.; Le Caire, 1955]) § 587 (a). For *r.f* used in a temporal clause see Lefebvre, *op. cit.* § 587 (c). Our interpretation of *ḫnm* is supported by *ḫnm ṯw Nbw m mrt.n.k,* "the Gold (i.e., Hathor) gladdens you with what you have desired," in Louvre C 15, cited in Gardiner, *Notes on the Story of Sinuhe* (Paris, 1916) p. 97.

Given the pre-eminence accorded to Hathor in the Kheruef throne scene, where she occupies the seat that would normally be the queen's,[46] the prominence of the Hathoric performances in the lower register, and the king's voyage in the solar bark, it would appear that the theme of the entire wall was the sacred marriage of Hathor to the king, identified with the sun god.[47] This ritual enactment of the cosmological union of the sun god with his mother insured the king's symbolic rebirth at the end of the jubilee, just as the erection of the djed-pillar of Ptah-Sokar-Osiris at the beginning of the jubilee guaranteed the permanence of the Egyptian kingship through the application of chthonian myth and symbolism. Since Hathor is absent from the mythological background of the Ramesseum Dramatic Papyrus and the episodes in Kheruef's southern portico occurred considerably later than the djed-pillar rites, it is difficult to envisage a close relationship between the southern wall and the papyrus ritual. The two walls of Kheruef's chapel, depicting two rituals of different mythological backgrounds, converge in asserting Amenhotep III's endurance as holder of the divine kingship.

This kingship, maintained by an individual standing at the apex of his society, reflected "a corporate personality which embodied his subjects,"[48] and in a sense the king's triumph in the jubilee expressed the collective aspirations of the society. Although the Kheruef jubilee walls possess the element of biography in the sense that Kheruef participated in certain historic jubilees, their import transcends the temporal and mundane. In a tomb context the significance of these scenes is projected into eternity, and as a member of the corporate society both now and in the hereafter Kheruef shared in the guarantees acquired by the king in the jubilee rituals.

The atemporal quality of these jubilee scenes is suggested in two passages from the funerary wishes inscribed in Kheruef's mortuary chapel. One is an invocation to Ptah-Sokar-Osiris that "he may grant a coming-forth from the earth in the following of His Majesty on that day of circumambulating the walls,"[49] a wish inspired by a rite performed in connection with the djed-

[46] Queen Tiye stands behind Hathor in the throne scene, and her status in relation to the king is stated in the inscription before her: "It is like Maat following Re that she is in the following of Your Majesty" (*Urk.* IV 1866, line 10). Through the use of the emphatic *wnn.s* her position is likened unto that of of Re's daughter Maat.

[47] On the union of the king with his mother Hathor see Wolfhart Westendorf in *ZAS* XCIV (1967) 144–45 and on Hathor as mother and wife of the sun god see Bonnet, *Reallexikon der ägyptischen Religionsgeschichte*, pp. 280–81; see also Schafik Allam, *Beiträge zum Hathorkult (bis zum Ende des Mittleren Reiches)* ("Münchner ägyptologische Studien" IV [Berlin, 1963]) pp. 113–16.

[48] J. Gwyn Griffiths, *The Origins of Osiris* ("Münchner ägyptologische Studien" IX [Berlin, 1966]) p. 161.

[49] Fakhry in *Annales du Service des antiquités de l'Égypte* XLII 501 (Inscription 3).

pillar. The other probable allusion to an episode in the jubilee is contained in an invocation to "Khepri, who is in the evening bark (*sic*)" that he might grant "the grasping of the tow-rope of the god's boat in the presence of the great god."[50] Although it is possible that "His Majesty" and the "great god" in these wishes refer not to the king but to the gods invoked, the transfer of reference from king to deity becomes a moot point in view of the king's peculiar relationship to these divinities in the jubilee. At the erection of the djed-pillar the king shares in the triumphant resurrection of his father Ptah-Sokar-Osiris, while as occupant of the solar bark he is assimilated to the sun god after his symbolic marriage to Hathor.

[50] *Ibid.* p. 503 (line 3 of inscription). The phrase *šsp wꜣrt* is possibly borrowed from the horizontal text above the princesses in the upper register of the southern wall of the portico, poorly rendered in *Urk.* IV 1870, line 6.

SOME EGYPTIANISMS IN THE OLD TESTAMENT

Ronald J. Williams

Almost a score of years ago, the eminent scholar whom we seek to honor in this volume wrote: "When Hebrew religion had reached a point where it needed a certain mode of expression it could find in another literature phrases and thoughts which would meet the need."[1] Its geographical location and the fortunes of history combined to draw Israel into the cultural orbit of Egypt. When Palestine was incorporated into the Egyptian Empire during the New Kingdom, the conditions for cultural interchange were ideal, although the borrowing was for the most part on the side of the Hebrews. Elsewhere[2] I have attempted briefly to sketch Israel's debt to Egypt, but the exigencies of space there prevented, among other things, a complete listing of the idiomatic phrases which found their way from the Egyptian language into the Hebrew of the Old Testament. In the following pages a few more clear instances of such linguistic borrowings are discussed.

On reading the Book of Lamentations recently, I was struck by the expression רוּחַ אַפֵּינוּ , "breath of our nostrils" (Lam. 4:20), in a context which clearly refers to King Zedekiah, as may be inferred from II Chron. 35:25. This epithet, unique in Hebrew literature, immediately called to mind the similar address in the Abydus inscription of Ramses II: *pr-ꜥꜣ ꜥ.w.s. pꜣ ṯꜣw n fnd·n*, "Pharaoh, l.p.h., the breath of our nostrils" (*Inscr. dédic.* line 40). Subsequently I discovered that this similarity had already been noted almost forty years earlier by the indefatigable Gressmann,[3] who also called attention to an Akkadian parallel in some of the Amarna letters of the fourteenth century B.C. In the latter, the salutation to the Egyptian king includes the words *ša-ri balāṭi*(TI.LA)*-ia*, "breath of my life" (*EA*, Nos. 141:2, 142:1, 143:1 f., 144:2). Hieroglyphic texts describe the ruler in similar terms. At Medinet Habu Ramses III is called *ṯꜣw n ꜥnḫ n ḥnmmt*, "breath of life for the sun-folk" (*Medinet Habu* V, Pl. 353, line 4). In texts contained in two Amarna tombs Akhnaten is spoken of as *ṯꜣw n fndw nb ssn·tw ꞽm·f*, "the breath of all nostrils, by whom men breathe" ("Bibliotheca Aegyptiaca" VIII 24, line 7), and *ṯꜣw·ꞽ ꜥnḫ·ꞽ ꞽm·f tꜣy(·ꞽ) mḥyt*, "my breath, by which I live, my north wind" (*ibid.*

[1] J. A. Wilson, *The Burden of Egypt* (Chicago, 1951) p. 229.

[2] In the forthcoming second edition of *The Legacy of Egypt*, ed. J. R. Harris (Oxford, 1969).

[3] H. Gressmann, *Der Messias* (Göttingen, 1929) p. 28. Cf. also J. de Savignac in *Vetus Testamentum* VII (1957) 82 f.

p. 92, lines 3 f.). The *ku* of Akhnaten is also said to be *ṯȝw n ᶜnḫ sḏm* [*ḫr*]*w* . . . , "the breath of life who hears the voice of . . ." (*ibid.* p. 28, line 15).

All such passages, of course, reflect the divine nature of the king in ancient Egypt, who was the source of life and well-being for his people. Thus, in another Amarna letter, Abimilki of Tyre writes to his Egyptian suzerain as follows: *ma-an-nu ba-la-aṭ* LÚ.GÌR *e-nu-ma la-a it-ta-ṣí ša-a-ru iš-tu* UZU*pí šarri*(LUGAL) *be-li-šu*, "what is the life of a person when no breath comes forth from the mouth of his lord the king?" (*EA*, No. 149:21–23).[4] In still another letter, Abimilki includes a hymn, purely in the Egyptian style, in which the pharaoh is portrayed as the sun-god *ša i-ba-li-iṭ i-na še-ḫi-šu ṭābi*(DÙG[!].GA), "who gives life by his sweet breath" (*EA*, No. 147:9).[5]

In the same way Ramses II receives the designation *dd ṯȝw r fnd nb*, "he who gives breath to the nostrils of all" (*Inscr. dédic.* line 37), just as the god Ptah is called *ṯȝw n ᶜnḫ n ḥr-nb*, "breath of life for all people" (Pap. Harris I xliv 7). Of the sun-god Rēᶜ it is said in the Instruction for Merikarēᶜ (lines 131 f.), from the First Intermediate Period, *ỉr·n·f ṯȝw n-ỉb ᶜnḫ fndw·sn*, "it was in order that their nostrils might live that he made the air,"[6] and a hymn to the evening sun affirms *dỉ·k ṯȝw r fndw·sn*, "thou givest breath to their nostrils" (BD XV; see Budge, *BD* [1898] p. 50). Likewise Yahweh, on creating man, "breathed into his nostrils the breath of life" (Gen. 2:7), and Job is depicted as saying וְרוּחַ אֱלוֹהַּ בְּאַפִּי, "the breath/spirit of God is in my nostrils" (Job 27:3).

A second idiom reminiscent of Egyptian sources may be found in the Book of Lamentations: שִׁבְתָּם וְקִימָתָם הַבִּיטָה, "look at their sitting and rising/standing" (Lam. 3:63). The only other occurrence of this expression appears in the Psalter: אַתָּה יָדַעְתָּ שִׁבְתִּי וְקוּמִי, "thou knowest my sitting and my rising/standing" (Ps. 139:2). This collocation of two verbs in the sense of "to conduct oneself," referring to one's manner of life, is normally expressed in Hebrew by the verbs צֵאת וָבֹא, "to go out and in" (e.g. I Kings 3:7, Ps. 121:8, I Sam. 18:13 and 16, II Chron. 1:10, Num. 27:17).[7] The verbs *ᶜḥᶜ* and *ḥmsỉ*, "to stand and sit," are frequently employed in Egyptian with the same nuance.[8]

[4] Albright has shown convincingly that the scribe who wrote the correspondence from Abimilki was an Egyptian; cf. *JEA* XXIII (1937) 190–203.

[5] Here *i-ba-li-iṭ* appears to be a scribal aberration for the D-theme *uballaṭ*.

[6] The scribe has mistakenly omitted the *n* before *ỉb* and written an *s* after *ᶜnḫ* in Pap. Leningrad 1116A.

[7] Cf. the similar use in Egyptian of *prỉ* and *hȝỉ*, "to go up and down" (Sinuhe B 49; *Urk.* IV 116, line 4; Louvre C 286, line 26; Hammamat No. 191, line 5), or of *prỉ* and *ᶜḳ*, "to go out and in" (*Urk.* IV 433, lines 11 f.; 498, line 7; 1105, lines 8 f.).

[8] Cf. Wilhelm Spiegelberg, "Varia," *Receuil de travaux* XXIV (1902) 182 f., No. LVII: *ᶜḥᶜ ḥmsj*, "leben."

The earliest examples occur in the Pyramid Texts: *h3* NN *pw ꜥḥꜥ ḥms ḫnti ib·k ꜣInpw is*, "O NN, live before your heart like Anubis" (*Pyr.* § 2198 *a–b*), and *h3* NN *ꜥḥꜥ ḥms r ḫ3 m t ḫ3 m ḥnḳt*, "O NN, live on a thousand loaves and a thousand (jars of) beer" (*Pyr.* § 214 *b;* so also §§ 2026 *b*–2027 *a*). In the Old Kingdom Teaching for Kagemni we read *wn·in ꜥḥꜥ·sn ḥms·sn ḫft(w)*, "so they proceeded to live accordingly" (Pap. Prisse 2, 7). There are two instances in the Teaching of Ptaḥḥotpe: *ḳsn ꜥḥꜥ ḥmst*, "standing and sitting (i.e., any activity) are painful," in a description of old age (Ptaḥḥotpe 23 [L. II]), and *ꜥḥꜥ ḥms r nmtt·k*, "conduct yourself according to your position" (Ptaḥḥotpe 221). In a tomb of the Middle Kingdom the occupant is described as *ꜥḥꜥw ḥmsw ẖr sḫr·f*, "living under his governance" (Newberry, *El Bersheh* II, Pl. XXI top, lines 9 f.), and the Coffin Texts express the pious wish *ꜥḥꜥ·f ḥms·f iw·k ḫft-ḥr·f*, "may he live whilst thou art in front of him!" (*CT* II 99 *a–b* = 94 *e*). Later examples may also be cited, such as two passages from the tomb of Rekhmirēꜥ, the vizier of Thutmose III: *ꜥḥꜥ·i ḥms·i ḥ3ty·i ẖr ḥ3tt pḥwyt*, "I spend my life, my mind being occupied with the prow and stern ropes" (Rekhmirēꜥ Biography, line 17), and *ꜥḥꜥ·i ḥms·i ḫt·i ḥr psd*, "I live with my rod on the back" *ibid.* line 30).

We turn next to the writings of Deutero-Isaiah and to a verse which has troubled commentators to such a degree that some have sought to emend the text, even though it is linguistically sound: אָכֵן אַתָּה אֵל מִסְתַּתֵּר, "truly thou art a God who hides himself" (Isa. 45:15).[9] The difficulty arises from the fact that this is a concept unique in the Old Testment. It is fundamentally different from the metaphorical statements that Yahweh has hidden himself, in the sense that he has apparently withdrawn from giving aid when called upon (cf. Pss. 10:1, 89:47 [Eng. 46]). The latter are more akin to the common complaint that the Deity has hidden his face from his petitioner (cf. Pss. 13:2 [Eng. 1], 30:8 [Eng. 7], 44:25 [Eng. 24], 88:15 [Eng. 14], 104:29, Job 13:24).

For parallels we must look to Egyptian literature, where the doctrine of the mysterious, hidden god is all-pervasive. The Instruction for Merikarēꜥ (line 124) says of Rēꜥ: *imn·n sw nṯr rḫw ḳdw*, "the god who knows characters has hidden himself." Such descriptions are especially frequent in the case of the solar deity Amūn, whose very name means "hidden,"[10] as we read in the Cairo Hymn to Amūn: *imn rn·f r msw·f m rn·f pw n ꜣImn*, "whose name is hidden from his children in this name Amūn of his" (Pap. Boulaq No. 17 v 3 f.). A papyrus of the mid-thirteenth century B.C. praises Amūn as an invisible force pervading all things: *wꜥ ꜣImn imn sw r-r·sn sḥ3p sw r nṯrw bw rḫ·tw iwn·f w3 sw r ḥrt mḏ sw r dw3t*, "Amūn is unique who hides himself from the gods. No

[9] Klostermann, Duhm, and other scholars would read אִתְּךָ for אַתָּה !

[10] Cf. K. Sethe, *Amun und die acht Urgötter von Hermopolis* (Berlin, 1929) pp. 87–90; J. Zandee, *De hymnen aan Amon van Papyrus Leiden I 350* (Leyden, 1948) pp. 82–85.

man knows his nature; he is more remote than the sky and deeper than the underworld" (Pap. Leyden I 350 iv 17 f.; cf. Ps. 139:8). As late as the first century after Christ, the Greek writer Plutarch quoted Manetho on the name of the god Amūn to the following effect: τὸ κεκρυμμένον οἴεται καὶ τὴν κρύψιν ὑπὸ ταύτης δηλοῦσθαι τῆς φωνῆς "he thinks this expression to mean 'what is concealed' and 'concealment,' " and then goes on to remark that the Egyptians gave the name Amūn to him whom they worshipped ὡς ἀφανῆ καὶ κεκρυμμένον ὄντα, "as being invisible and concealed" (Plutarch *Isis and Osiris* 9 D).

The fourth turn of phrase to which we now direct our attention also occurs in the writings of Deutero-Isaiah, where Israel is exhorted הַרְחִיבִי מְקוֹם אָהֳלֵךְ, "enlarge the place of your tent" (Isa. 54:2). This is the only instance of the idiom, but the same writer states the opposite a few chapters earlier: צַר-לִי הַמָּקוֹם, "the place is too narrow for me" (Isa. 49:20). The concept of wideness of place in the sense of freedom of access is well known to Egyptian sources. In the Old Kingdom, the Instruction for Kagemni states *wsḫ st nt hr*, "the contented man has free access" (Pap. Prisse 1, 2), and the sage Ptaḥḥotpe declares *wsḫ st nt ỉꜣš n·f*, "the one who has been summoned has free access" (Ptaḥḥotpe 225).[11] The exiled Sinuhe, in the Middle Kingdom, speaking of his new life in Asia, wrote: *wsḫ st·ỉ*, "I have complete freedom" (Sinuhe B 155). In the 18th dynasty, a minor functionary of Queen Hatshepsut by the name of Senemyaʿḥ lists among his titles *wsḫ st m pr-ʿnḫ*, "having free access in the House of Life" (*Urk.* IV 513, line 10). Thutmose III, in his coronation inscription at Karnak, affirms that Amūn had granted him sovereignty *dỉ·ỉ wsḫ swt ỉr wỉ*, "that I might make spacious the places of him who made me" (*Urk.* IV 163, line 6).

Closely associated with this idiom is the expression *wsḫ nmtt*, "wide of stride," implying untrammelled freedom of movement. In the case of a king it is vividly portrayed in the reliefs which depict the monarch striding forth victorious as he smites the heads of his foes. The earliest examples of the expression come from the Pyramid Texts where, for instance, a son is described as *wsḫ nmtt·f*, "with his stride broad" (*Pyr.* § 886 *c;* cf. §§ 2123 *c*, 917 *c*). At Abydus Ramses II, addressing Sety I, declares *nmtt·k wsḫ·tỉ m ẖnw dwꜣt*, "your stride is broad in the netherworld" (*Inscr. dédic.* line 91). A New Kingdom papyrus speaks of *wsḫ nmtt*[12] *m st štꜣ·tỉ*, "one wide of stride in the secret place" (Pap. Anastasi III i 2), and a stela from the beginning of the Ptolemaic period states *wsḫ n·k nmtt(·ỉ) n pr-nsw*, "my stride was wide for you in the palace" (*Urk.* II 3, line 12).

[11] The British Museum papyrus (L. II) has the variant *w[s]ḫ st nt stꜣ wḥmw*, "the one whom the herald has brought in has free access."

[12] On the corrupt writing see Gardiner, *Late-Egyptian Miscellanies* ("Bibliotheca Aegyptiaca" VII [Bruxelles, 1937]) p. 20*a*, n. 11.

This cliché too finds its echo in biblical literature. A psalm which occurs twice in the Old Testament says תַּרְחִיב צַעֲדִי תַחְתָּי , "thou dost make my steps wide" (Ps. 18:37 [Eng. 36]).[13] A second psalmist writes הֶעֱמַדְתָּ בַמֶּרְחָב רַגְלָי , "thou hast established my feet in a broad place" (Ps. 31:9 [Eng. 8]). The opposite is stated in two passages: לֹא־יֵצַר צַעֲדֶךָ , "your steps will not be constricted" (Prov. 4:12), and יֵצְרוּ צַעֲדֵי אוֹנוֹ , "his mighty steps are constricted" (Job 18:7).

Our final example comes from a book which exhibits many Egyptian influences, as scholars have long observed. The verse in question (Prov. 17:27) reads:

> He who has knowledge is sparing of his words;
> The man of understanding is of a calm spirit.

The Hebrew expression קַר־רוּחַ , which means literally "cool of spirit," is unknown elsewhere in biblical literature. For this reason it seems to have been a source of perplexity to readers, for even the Massoretes preserved a variant reading of the first element in the form of the *Qᵉrē* יְקַר for וְקַר . This would mean something like "excellent of spirit," which is hardly an improvement. The more recent attempt by L. Kopf to elucidate the word by means of an Arabic root[14] appears to me less than convincing. It would seem to be far more profitable to interpret this figure of speech in the light of its Egyptian analogues.

From very early times the Egyptians employed the words *tꜣ*, "hot," and *ḳb*, "cold," to express the concepts "passionate" and "calm" respectively. In the celebrated Affirmation of Innocence, the deceased says *ỉ šd-ḫrw pr m Wryt n tꜣ·ỉ*, "O Disturber, who came forth from Weryt, I have not been passionate/hot-tempered" (BD CXXV; see Budge, *BD* [1898] p. 256, lines 1 f.). The sage Ipuwer declared *ỉw ms tꜣw ḥr ḏd*, "indeed, the hot-tempered man says" (*Admonitions* v 3; cf. Pap. Ramesseum I B iii 7). On the other hand, Ptaḥḥotpe asserted *nn ḳb n ntt m ḫt·f*, "what is in his body will not become cool/calm" (Ptaḥḥotpe 459; cf. 462), and the lector-priest Neferti prophesied that "the desert animals shall drink at the streams of Egypt, *ḳbb·sn ḥr wḏbw·sn n gꜣw strỉ st*, and through lack of anyone to frighten(?) them away shall be calm" (Neferti, lines 35–37; cf. Merikarēʿ, line 68). An example from the New Kingdom runs *pr·n(·ỉ) mỉn ḥr gr ḳbb*, "it was in silence and calmness that I departed today" (Theban Tomb 110, North Stela, line 15).

These terms are frequently expanded by the addition of parts of the body. Thus we find *ỉb*, "heart/mind," in *ỉw nswt nt tꜣ-ỉb* ⟨*ḥr*⟩ *sḫr·f*, "the flame of a

[13] The variant in II Sam. 22:37 gives the last word as תַּחְתֵּנִי .

[14] *Vetus Testamentum* VIII (1958) 200 f.

quick-tempered man sweeps over him" (Ptaḥḥotpe 378), and *ỉn wnn ỉb·k ḳb r·s,* "will you remain calm about it?" (*Egyptian Letters to the Dead,* Pl. 1, line 8). In the same way *ẖt,* "body/belly," is used in *prw pw n tꜣ-ẖt,* "it is the talk[15] of the passionate man" (Ptaḥḥotpe 352), and *sẖpr šnty m ḳb-ẖt,* "to make a quarrelsome man into an amicable one" (Ptaḥḥotpe 323), or *ỉnk sš n ḥrt-ỉb ḳb-ẖt dꜣr srf,* "I was a scribe of favor, amicable, controlling passion" (Hatnub Graffito No. 10, 3 f.). Similarly *r,* "mouth," is combined in *m ỉr nḥb ṯṯ r-m pꜣ tꜣ-r,* "do not join in quarrelling with a man of unbridled mouth" (Amenemope v 10; cf. xii 16), and *grw wꜣḥ-ỉb ḳb-r ꜣỉ(r) srf,* "silent, patient, calm of speech, subduing passion" (Theban Tomb 65; cited in *Belegstellen* to *Wb.* V 23, 12).

The Hebrew phrase קַר־רוּחַ finds its antithesis in אִישׁ חֵמוֹת (Prov. 22:24). The latter was coined to render the Late Egyptian *pꜣ šmm,* "the passionate man," which appears in the passage (Amenemope xi 13) which inspired the verse in Proverbs. The only other occurrence of the expression, this time in the form אִישׁ חֵמָה (Prov. 15:18), is in antithetic parallelism with the normal Hebrew idiom אֶרֶךְ אַפַּיִם (cf. Prov. 14:29, 16:32), which has as its opposite counterpart קְצַר אַפַּיִם (Prov. 14:17). A variant of this is אֶרֶךְ־רוּחַ (Eccles. 7:8) with its opposite קְצַר־רוּחַ (Prov. 14:29; cf. Exod. 6:9).

15 For the meaning of *prw* cf. *prw n r* in Ptaḥḥotpe 627.

Egyptian god Amon represents an exceptional pronunciation of this name; the form to be expected would be Ἀμμούνιος.

The epithet ἄωρος frequently occurs in Greek epitaphs and particularly on Greco-Egyptian stelae. It is very often used in reference to children who are said to have "died prematurely," but sometimes it is associated with adults who died in their twenties and thirties[11] and perhaps even at older ages. Χαῖρε is one of the two most frequently occurring words of farewell in Greek epitaphs, the other being εὐψύχει.[12] Ὡς ἐτῶν, "about (so-and-so many) years," may seem strange to the modern mind and calls for comment. It was not unusual for the common people of Greco-Roman Egypt, just as it is not in some places today, to state the age of a person in approximate terms, which often show a considerable discrepancy in years. From papyri which confirm this observation we choose two examples from Tebtunis, from A.D. 42. In some of the abstracts of contracts of that year a certain Ptolemaios, son of Chairemon, acted as signatory on eight documents. In three of these he is said to be about 75 years old, in four others he is said to be about 72 years old, and in one document he is said to be about 74 years old. In all eight contracts he is identified as a man "with a scar above the left elbow."[13] Another individual, Eutychos, son of Eutychos, may have acted as signatory on five contracts. In two of these he is said to be about 32 years old, but in the first instance he is identified as a man "with a scar on the right knee" and in the other he is said to have "a scar on the ankle bone of the right foot." In the third contract he is said to be about 30 years old "with a scar on the middle of his nose." As the signatory in the fourth contract he is said to be about 41 years old "with a scar on the right calf." In the fifth contract he is said to be about 52 years old "with a scar on the ankle bone of the right foot."[14] While one can question the identity of this man especially in the cases in which different kinds of scars are attributed to the signatory, the two instances in which he is described "with a scar on the ankle bone of the right foot" can very likely be understood as referring to the same person, although he is said in

---

forms of this name see Charles Kuentz in Société royale égyptienne de papyrologie, *Études de papyrologie* II (Le Caire, 1934) 49, and Preisigke, *Namenbuch*, p. 26; see also W. Dittenberger, *Orientis Graeci Inscriptiones Selectae* I (Leipzig, 1903) 210, No. 130; U. Wilcken, *Urkunden der Ptolemäerzeit* II (Berlin, 1957) 107; F. Dunand in *Chronique d'Égypte* XXXVIII (1963) 134 f.

11 See Hooper, *Funerary Stelae*, p. 29; Zaki Aly in *SAAB* XL 110–11, stele IV (uncertain) and stele V, and p. 132, stele XIX.

12 See Marcus N. Tod, "Laudatory Epithets in Greek Epitaphs," *Annual of the British School at Athens*, 1951, pp. 182–90.

13 Arthur E. R. Boak, *Papyri from Tebtunis* I ("Michigan Papyri" II [Ann Arbor, 1933]) 40 f., 45 f., 46 f., 55, 56 f., 57 f., 60 f., 61 f.

14 *Ibid.* pp. 24, 39, 63 f., 76 f., 77 f.; see also V. B. Schuman in *Classical Weekly* XXVIII (1934–35) 95 f. and Hooper, *Funerary Stelae*, p. 29.

one of these to be about 32 years old and in the other about 52 years old. No wonder, then, that the young Isarous is said to be "about" 13 years old.

The year, month, and day of Isarous' death are given in the inscription, but the name of the emperor is not mentioned. Thus it is impossible to establish the exact date of the stela from the inscription alone. The relatively long reign (at least 13 years) seemingly narrows the choice of emperors to whose reigns the stela can be attributed. However, the year 13 can refer to a number of imperial reigns, from certain Julio-Claudian emperors to Diocletian, that is, from the first to the end of the third or the beginning of the fourth century. Thus unless through the archeological evidence of the grave and the stylistic characteristics of the stela the period can be more closely limited, a wide choice still remains.

As far as the archeological evidence is concerned, no information was available to this writer except that the stela was found in the western desert of northern Egypt. It is well known, however, that stelae of this and similar types have been found at several sites in northern Egypt, in the Delta region and especially at Terenuthis (Kom Abou Billou) on the edge of the western desert about forty miles northwest of Cairo.[15]

As to the stylistic characteristics of the stela, the rounded pediment certainly indicates that it cannot antedate the Roman period in Egypt, but no closer dating can be established from that fact since rounded pediments as well as triangular ones occur on funerary stelae from the first to the fourth centuries.[16] Sculptural details such as the position of the feet shown in profile to the right can hardly give us any chronological clue, for the feet are shown in various positions on Greco-Roman stelae as well as on Christian-Coptic ones.[17] This unnatural position of the feet may sometimes have resulted from carelessness on the part of the provincial stonecutter but probably is due more frequently to the difficulty of executing the feet in front view. It seems, however, that in some instances the stonecutter, or the designer, intentionally followed the traditional Egyptian way of representing the feet in profile, since he was able to execute more difficult features, such as the face of the figure on our stela, in a quite naturalistic way.

[15] See C. C. Edgar, *Greek Sculpture* (Le Caire, 1903) pp. 36–37, 40–49, 52; J. G. Milne, *Greek Inscriptions* (Oxford, 1905) pp. 52, 56–57, 59; Henri Gauthier in *ASAE* XXI (1921) 203–11; C. C. Edgar in *ASAE* XV (1915) 108–12; Zaki Aly in *SAAB* XXXVIII and XL. For a more detailed bibliography (some references, however, being inaccurate) see Hooper, *Funerary Stelae from Kom Abou Billou,* where also reference is made to collections of similar stelae in various museums.

[16] See Milne, *Greek Inscriptions*, Pl. IX, No. 9212; Edgar, *Greek Sculpture,* p. xi, Pls. XIX, Nos. 27534–35, XXI, Nos. 27542 and 27546, XXII, No. 27620; Hooper, *Funerary Stelae,* Pls. VII *a*, VIII *a–b*, XIII *d*, XVI *d;* Gauthier in *ASAE* XXI 203 f. and plate (unnumbered).

[17] See W. E. Crum, *Coptic Monuments* (Le Caire, 1902) Pls. LI, Nos. 8690 and 8689, and LIII, No. 8697.

Neither the garments (chiton and himation, which were worn by both males and females and by young and old) nor the position of the arms help us to determine the period to which the stela belongs. Nor does the hair, marked by incised lines on the head and ending in long hanging tresses which clearly indicate a young female, provide any clue for dating. Such hair styles, with more or less elaborate locks and tresses, can be assigned to the period from the first to the fourth century. It is true that on stelae of this class various hair styles can be observed: Greek, Julio-Claudian, Antonine, and Severan. But such hair fashions were not confined to their particular period, and earlier styles were imitated in popular art of later times.[18] The very fact that sometimes two different types of hairdress are represented on two female figures on the same stela[19] shows how unfeasible it is to use hair style as a criterion for dating.

While Isarous' stela may be a work of no pretension, it exhibits some unusual characteristics. The figure, with the exception of the feet, is treated naturalistically. This is especially true of the face which, although slightly worn, still preserves sensitively modeled features which may possibly represent an attempt to reproduce the likeness of the deceased girl. The stela is carved not in sunken-relief, as are more ordinary, similar gravestones, but in bas-relief, which, at least in some instances,[20] can be seen in works of higher quality and greater detail. It is also to be observed that, instead of two couchant jackals, on our stela appears a rarer combination, a jackal and a falcon. Another feature occurring but rarely on stelae of this class can be seen in the palms of the hands, which are turned outward but sideward.[21] The inscription in even and regular characters is incised on the architrave rather than below the figure as is usually the case. The stela is somewhat freer in style than the more ordinary types and therefore could belong to a relatively early period, perhaps the last part of the first or the first part of the second century, but it must be admitted that the naturalistic treatment of the face and other variations from the more ordinary types supply no criteria for more exact dating, and understandably so. In the field of art to which this stela belongs, an art practiced for the general public, better works occur alongside those of inferior quality at any period for a variety of reasons, as is well exemplified by the collection of funerary stelae from Terenuthis, where the coins found in the graves made it clear that stelae

[18] See Edgar, *Greek Sculpture*, p. XIV; see also Zaki Aly in *SAAB* XXXVIII 64 f., 67 f., 82, 87, and cf. Hooper, *Funerary Stelae*, p. 33, n. 9.

[19] E.g. Edgar, *Greek Sculpture*, Pl. XXIII, No. 27548, from Kom Abou Billou.

[20] Hooper, *Funerary Stelae*, pp. 10 ff.

[21] This feature can also be seen on stelae published by Zaki Aly in *SAAB* XL 114–15, Figs. 7–8; for another example see Hooper, *Funerary Stelae*, Pl. VI *d*, No. 20.

of superior and inferior quality as well as those of varying styles were produced throughout the long period from the first to the fourth century.[22]

Nor can any exact dating be derived from a study of the occurrences of the name Isarous. It seems that this name was not seldom used in the papyrological documents of the second century of our era. However, it occurs, apparently less frequently, in the papyri of the first and third centuries as well.[23]

Our small stela is an example of Greco-Egyptian syncretistic art, and we wish briefly to discuss some of the features which point to its syncretistic character.

The pedestals, on which a falcon and a jackal rest, are not likely to represent "a reminiscence of the old Egyptian standard" as suggested by Edgar.[24] It seems to us that they represent, on a small scale, a doorway crowned with a cavetto cornice. Doorways crowned with cavetto cornices are common in

[22] Cf. Hooper, *Funerary Stelae*, pp. 3 f. and 32, n. 8. Hooper dates the Terenuthis burials to the late third and early fourth centuries because the majority of the coins found in them are from that period. The coins from the first and second centuries testify, according to Hooper, "to the saving habits of the people." Since he nowhere states that early coins and later coins were found together in the same graves, we assume that they were found separately. The main shortcoming of Hooper's otherwise very useful book is its lack of archeological details, which either were not available to him or not evaluated by him. It is important to know exactly what coins were found in what tombs. Hooper's statements that "the majority of the stelae were undoubtedly completed about the same time" (p. 35, n. 30) and "may be dated within a limited period of time" (p. 17) and that one stela (Pl. IX *a*) because of its unusual characteristics "may belong to the Ptolemaic period" and another (Pl. IX *b*) "may also belong to an earlier period" (p. 11) call for more detailed discussion. Hooper appropriately refers (p. 35, n. 32) to a stela from Kom Abou Billou published by Zaki Aly (*SAAB* XXXVIII, Pl. XVI and p. 86) the style of which, because of its peculiar pharaonic features, he considers "analogous" to the two (Hooper's Pl. IX *a–b*) mentioned above. To these observations we should like to add that Edgar dated eight inscribed stelae from Kom Abou Billou as well as a Greek metrical epitaph found with them to late Ptolemaic or early Roman times (*ASAE* XV 108–12 and XI [1911] 1–2) and that Milne (*Greek Inscriptions*, pp. 52, 56–57, 59) dated the stelae which he published from Kom Abou Billou to the first and second centuries. Thus, it seems that the cemetery of Kom Abou Billou was used over a longer period of time and that the coins of the first and second centuries, far from "testifying to the saving habits of the people," may properly belong to the burials of these two centuries. Klaus Wessel (*Koptische Kunst* [Recklinghausen, 1963] p. 96) has recently but, unfortunately, superficially discussed the dating of the stelae from Kom Abou Billou. What he says about the Egyptian names of the months is of no consequence for determining the ethnic group for which the stelae were made. What seems to transpire from the study of these stelae is that they represent a mixed population of Egyptians and Greeks. Moreover, Egyptian month names were used in Greek documents throughout the Roman period.

[23] See pp. 99 f., n. 1.

[24] Edgar, *Greek Sculpture*, p. XIII, repeated by Gauthier in *ASAE* XXI 204. There are instances in which one or two jackals of Anubis (or of Wepwawet) are represented on a standard (e.g. H. D. Lange and H. Schäfer, *Grab- und Denksteine des Mittleren Reichs* IV [Berlin, 1902] Pls. X, No. 20104, XIII, No. 20144, XIX, No. 20255, XLIV, No. 20557; G. Maspero and H. Gauthier, *Sarcophages des époques persane et ptolémaïque* [Le Caire, 1939] Pls. V 2 and XII), but these representations are quite distinct from those we are discussing and there is no developmental link between them.

Egyptian architecture of pre-Ptolemaic and especially Ptolemaic and Roman times.[25] The setting of the stela is that of an aedicula, and the two pedestals represent its doorway. There are stelae on which only one such pedestal is shown,[26] but even in many such cases the shape of the pedestal is reminiscent of part of a temple doorway and suggests architectural origin. Certainly, the two parts of the doorway have been used by the lapicide of our stela as supports for two symbolic animals (the falcon and the jackal), but their relationship to a temple doorway can be clearly perceived when this stela, or one published by Hooper,[27] is compared with stelae on which two true pedestals are seen. Some stelae with true pedestals are made in the shape of a *naiskos* (small shrine) in which the figure of the deceased is carved fully *en face*.[28] The two true pedestals, with a jackal on each side of the figure of the deceased, are shown in true proportion to the figure and are shaped differently from the pedestals on our stela. They are true copies of an older Egyptian sculptural tradition, as can be seen from their representation on Middle and New Kingdom stelae and on coffins of the New Kingdom and the late period.[29]

It is also to be observed that the floral capitals of the two columns on our stela are of Egyptian origin and inspiration, representing an architectural tradition which can be traced as far back as the Ramesside period.[30]

[25] For example at Philae in the porch of Nectanebos (Berlin Photo 26), the temple of Hathor (Berlin Photos 95–96), and Trajan's "kiosk" (Berlin Photo 635); in the temple of Ptah at Karnak (see Jean Capart, *Egyptian Art* [London, 1923] Pl. XLIX); in the Edfu temple (see K. Lange and M. Hirmer, *Ägypten* [4th ed.; München, 1967] Pl. 264).

[26] See e.g. *A General Introductory Guide to the Egyptian Collections in the British Museum* (1964) p. 231, Fig. 83; Zaki Aly in *SAAB* XL 145, Fig. 30; Edgar, *Greek Sculpture,* Pls. XX, No. 27538, XXI, Nos. 27542 and 27544, XXIV, No. 27532; Milne, *Greek Inscriptions,* Pls. VIII, Nos. 9207 and 9258, IX, Nos. 9251 and 9256; Otto Koefoed-Petersen, *Les stèles égyptiennes* ("Publications de la Glyptothèque Ny Carlsberg," No. 1 [Copenhague, 1948]) Pl. 90. Such an arrangement, with only one pedestal which is sometimes seen standing free, is often the result of the lapicide's composition and design, especially in cases where a reclining figure is shown; since the upper part of the reclining figure fills the upper right part of the stela, the only space available for a pedestal is the upper left part (see e.g. Hooper, *Funerary Stelae,* Pls. IX *c*, XII *c*, XVI *d*).

[27] Hooper, *Funerary Stelae,* Pl. VII *d*.

[28] See Ernst Pfuhl in *Mitteilungen des Kaiserlich Deutschen Archaeologischen Instituts, Athenische Abteilung* XXVI (1901) 294, No. 38; see also p. 293, No. 37. According to Pfuhl these stelae are from the late Hellenistic or early Roman period.

[29] See e.g. Lange and Schäfer, *Grab- und Denksteine des Mittleren Reichs* IV, Pls. IX, No. 20093, X, No. 20100, XXI, No. 20282, XVIII, No. 20392; Pierre Lacau, *Stèles du Nouvel Empire* (Le Caire, 1909–1957) Pls. XXXII, No. 34.054, XLIV, No. 34.093; Ahmad Badawi in *ASAE* XLIV (1944) Pls. XVIII–XIX; Maspero and Gauthier, *Sarcophages des époques persane et ptolémaïque,* Pls. XXI and XLII.

[30] See e.g. Uvo Hölscher, *The Excavation of Medinet Habu* IV ("Oriental Institute Publications" LV [Chicago, 1951]) 10 and Pl. 4, where the uppermost member of a multiple capital shows a remarkable resemblance to the capitals on our stela.

The two symbolic animals on our stela, the falcon and the jackal, represent a rarer combination than the two jackals most frequently shown.[31] Both animals are familiar figures in Egyptian mortuary art. A pair of jackals (or recumbent dogs)[32] facing each other appears as a decorative motif on stelae as early as the Middle Kingdom[33] and from then on throughout the New Kingdom, the late period,[34] and the very last phase of Egyptian funerary art.[35] The "two-jackal"[36] motif is then carried over into the Greco-Egyptian funerary monuments[37] and makes its final appearance on late Greco-Egyptian and Roman coffins and masks.[38] Anubis, invoked in the formulas of funerary offerings inscribed in the oldest mastabas, the god of embalming and guide of the dead, was worshiped under many titles and was predominant among the funerary gods before Osiris attained prominence; he was embodied in the jackal (or wild dog). No wonder, then, that this animal appears in Egyptian funerary art in the round, in relief and painting, and in Book of the Dead papyri.

[31] See Edgar, *Greek Sculpture*, p. xiii and Pls. XXII, No. 27623, XXIII, No. 27621; *SAAB* XXXVIII, Pls. II (opp. p. 68) and IX (opp. p. 80) and p. 88, where Zaki Aly speaks of a falcon with the sun disk on its head although such a figure is not visible on Pl. XIX; Hooper, *Funerary Stelae*, pp. 7 and 22 f., Pls. VII *d* and VIII *d*.

[32] On "recumbent dog," "jackal," and "wolf" see Sir Alan Gardiner, *Egyptian Grammar* (3d ed.; London, 1957) pp. 459 f. (E 15–18); G. Posener, S. Sauneron, and J. Yoyotte, *Dictionary of Egyptian Civilization* (New York, 1959) p. 139 (jackal).

[33] E.g. Lange and Schäfer, *Grab- und Denksteine des Mittleren Reichs* IV, Pls. III, No. 20027, IX, No. 20093, X, No. 20100. On Middle Kingdom stelae, as stated in their inscriptions, the recumbent dog or jackal represents Wepwawet more frequently than Anubis; see J. Vandier, *Manuel d'archéologie égyptienne* II (Paris, 1954) 488. There is an interesting stela on which the stonecutter produced two identical animals facing each other but named one Anubis and the other Wepwawet, while in the accompanying inscription Osiris, Anubis, and Ptah-Sokar are mentioned (Lacau, *Stèles du Nouvel Empire*, Pl. LIII, No. 34.117). On stelae of the late period, however, it seems that the recumbent dog or jackal more frequently signifies Anubis.

[34] E.g. Lacau, *Stèles du Nouvel Empire*, Pls. XXXII, No. 34.054, XXXV, No. 34.060, XLIV, No. 34.093, XLVIII, No. 34.099; Maspero and Gauthier, *Sarcophages des époques persane et ptolémaïque*, Pls. II, IX, X, XXI, XLII.

[35] E.g. Ahmed Bey Kamal, *Stèles ptolémaiques et romaines* II (Le Caire, 1904) Pls. II, No. 22003, VI, No. 22014, VII, No. 22018, VIII, No. 22022; Milne, *Greek Inscriptions*, Pl. XI.

[36] Not seldom only one jackal appears on a stela; see e.g. Lange and Schäfer, *Grab- und Denksteine* IV, Pls. VIII, Nos. 20085 and 20089 (on which see Vandier, *Manuel d'archéologie égyptienne* II 488), XVI, Nos. 20194 and 20192; Kamal, *Stèles ptolémaiques et romaines* II, Pl. XIII, No. 22040; Edgar, *Greek Sculpture*, Pls. XXI, Nos. 27542 and 27544, XXII, No. 27620, XXIII, No. 27622, XXIV, No. 27532; Milne, *Greek Inscriptions*, Pls. VIII, Nos. 9258 and 9207, IX, No. 9256.

[37] E.g. W. Spiegelberg, *Die demotischen Denkmäler* III (Berlin, 1932) Pls. III, No. 50029, V, No. 50033, VIII, No. 50038; Milne, *Greek Inscriptions*, Pls. VIII, No. 9226, IX, No. 9212, XI (six stelae).

[38] E.g. C. C. Edgar, *Graeco-Egyptian Coffins, Masks, Portraits* (Le Caire, 1905) Pls. V, XIV, XVI, XLVI; W. S. Smith, *Ancient Egypt* (4th ed.; Boston, 1960) p. 190, Fig. 131 (cf. P. D. Scott-Moncrieff, *Paganism and Christianity in Egypt* [Cambridge, 1913] pp. 126 f.).

It is true that the combination of a jackal and a falcon as a decorative motif does not appear on ancient Egyptian funerary monuments and that it appears but rarely on funerary stela of the Greco-Roman period, as rarely as a combination of a falcon and any other animal.[39] But there are New Kingdom coffins on which a "two-falcon" motif occurs along with the "two-jackal" motif.[40] It is probable that on our stela as well as on the monuments referred to above, the falcon, sacred to Horus, appears in the capacity of a funerary deity, that is, as a member of the Osirian triad (Osiris, Isis, Horus). These deities as well as Anubis are among the most frequently represented figures to which the deceased is introduced and before whom he appears.[41] The role of the falcon in Egyptian funerary religion is well known,[42] and the appearance of the falcon and the jackal on our stela need not be explained as a variation on the funerary theme of "two jackals," for it conveys a meaning well attested in Egyptian funerary religion and art.

Another symbolic feature of the stela is the so-called *orans* attitude indicated by the elevated arms of the deceased.

All those who have discussed the stelae of the Greco-Roman period, as well as historians of Coptic and early Christian art, have commented upon this gesture, which is often seen on funerary monuments of the early centuries of our era. Edgar noted that on Greco-Egyptian stelae "it is almost entirely confined to children, the young woman of twenty-one . . . being the oldest person whom we find thus represented."[43] It has been observed, however, that on stelae from subsequent excavations in the Delta region this attitude ap-

[39] For a mummified falcon and a recumbent cow (Hathor?) see Spiegelberg, *Die demotischen Denkmäler* III, Pl. III, No. 50028. Cf. Henri Gauthier, *Cercueils anthropoïdes des prêtres de Montou* (Le Caire, 1913) p. 373 and Pl. XXVII, where a bull and a falcon are shown facing each other in a vignette for the first chapter of the Book of the Dead. See also Maspero and Gauthier, *Sarcophages des époques persane et ptolémaïque*, p. 86 and Pl. XXVII, where a Hathor-cow and a falcon, both couchant on a shrinelike pedestal, are shown facing each other; the accompanying text is the first part of chapter 71 of the Book of the Dead.

See Spiegelberg, *op. cit.* Pl. IV, No. 50031, for a falcon which may, however, be part of the symbolism represented by the two wings and sun disk shown above it. The same can be said of the representation of a falcon on an uninscribed stela attributed to the late period (Lange and Schäfer, *Grab- und Denksteine* I 289 and IV, Pl. XX, No. 20272). Edgar, *Greek Sculpture*, Pl. XX, No. 27539, illustrates a funerary stela showing a reclining woman with three falcons wearing wigs and double crowns standing against the background of an Egyptian propylon.

[40] E.g. *ASAE* XLIV, Pls. XVIII–XIX.

[41] See e.g. Spiegelberg, *Die demotischen Denkmäler* III, Pls. III, IV, V, VI, VIII, X; Milne, *Greek Inscriptions*, Pl. XI.

[42] See Spiegelberg in *ZAS* LXII (1926) 27–32; L. V. Žabkar, *A Study of the Ba Concept in Ancient Egyptian Texts* (Chicago, 1968) pp. 84 f.

[43] Edgar, *Greek Sculpture*, p. XIII.

pears in connection with individuals in their later twenties and thirties as well.[44] Zaki Aly suggests that the *orans* attitude may refer "to the state of being unmarried,"[45] and J. Schwartz seems to share this opinion when he states that the *orantes* represent those who died prematurely before being married.[46] It is true that children and young people are very frequently represented in the *orans* attitude, but the stela of Sarapous, who "died prematurely, childless, devoted to her husband,"[47] and is represented in the *orans* attitude, shows that the interpretation of Schwartz and Zaki Aly cannot be accepted.

As to the meaning of the gesture itself, most scholars agree that on Greco-Egyptian stelae it expresses an act of devotion, worship, adoration, blessedness, or even mourning.[48] They also point out that the difference between the *orantes* figures of Greco-Egyptian pagan stelae and Christian ones is that on the former the arms are raised higher and the forearms are held up more vertically while on the Christian stelae the arms are only slightly raised.[49] Since, however, both ways of holding the arms are seen on both Christian and pagan stelae, we agree with Hooper[50] that the angle of elevation of the arms cannot be considered a determining factor in distinguishing pagan stelae from Christian ones, at least not, we would like to add, in distinguishing pagan stelae from early Coptic ones. It is certain that our stela of Isarous is a Greco-Egyptian pagan stela; the similarity of the position of her arms to that of several figures in the collection from Terenuthis and other sites in the Delta region is unquestionable;[51] however, some early Coptic stelae show the arms in a position that closely resembles that of Isarous and figures on other Greco-Egyptian pagan stelae.[52] The similarity of the *orans* attitude on pagan and

[44] See Zaki Aly in *SAAB* XXXVIII 62, where, however, he cites an uncertain example; for a good example see *SAAB* XL 115, Fig. 8 (the young man having died at the age of 27), and for further examples see Hooper, *Funerary Stelae*, p. 20.

[45] *SAAB* XL 115 f.

[46] *Chronique d'Égypte* XXX (1955) 124.

[47] See Hooper, *Funerary Stelae* Pl. VII *c*, No. 58. Sarapous' forearms are shown at a wider angle very similar to the typical Christian *orans* gesture (see *ibid.* p. 13, n. 3).

[48] See *ibid.* pp. 20, 29, 39, n. 65; Zaki Aly in *SAAB* XXXVIII 63 and 88 and XL 107. C. Bonner in *Proceedings of the American Philosophical Society* LXXXV (1941) 89 questions the interpretation of the *orans* gesture as a sign of mourning.

[49] See Zaki Aly in *SAAB* XXXVIII 63; Hooper, *Funerary Stelae*, p. 20; H. Leclercq in *Dictionnaire d'archéologie chrétienne et de liturgie* XII (1936) 2297; W. E. Crum in *Proceedings of the Society of Biblical Archaeology* XXI (1899) 251.

[50] *Funerary Stelae*, p. 20.

[51] See e.g. Zaki Aly in *SAAB* XL 114, Fig. 7; Hooper, *Funerary Stelae*, Pl. VI *d*. Cf. further *SAAB* XXXVIII, Pls. VII, XIII, XV; *SAAB* XL 105–6, Figs. 2–3, p. 112, Fig. 6; Hooper, *Funerary Stelae*, Pls. V *a* and *c*, VI *b–c*, VII *a;* Edgar, *Greek Sculpture*, Pl. XXI, No. 27547 (from Tell Basta).

[52] See e.g. Crum, *Coptic Monuments*, p. 143 and Pl. LIII, No. 8697 (reproduced also by Leclercq in *Dictionnaire d'archéologie chrétienne et de liturgie* XII 2318, Fig. 9097), and cf.

Christian funerary monuments brings us to the final point of the discussion of the symbolism of our stela, that is, to the question of the origin of the *orans* gesture.

Some scholars have simply stated that the *orans* attitude was borrowed from classical art.[53]

Crum pointed to "an undeniable resemblance" of some Egyptian representations to the Christian *orans* figures but argued that since "the rare Egyptian monuments wherein such a gesture is represented all belong to Graeco-Roman times, there is no need to seek an Egyptian genealogy" for them; he therefore regarded them as "directly borrowed from European models."[54]

According to Edgar, "although not foreign to purely Greek art, the gesture is yet so characteristic of Egyptian ceremonial that the popularity of the type may be partly ascribed to native influence."[55]

Bonner, Zaki Aly, and Hooper discuss the possibility of a connection between the *orans* gesture and the Egyptian hieroglyphic sign for Ka, itself consisting of two upraised arms. Bonner refers to Ebers, stating that the latter "conjectured that the frequent occurrence of these orantes on Coptic grave monuments was partly to be explained by the influence of the old hieroglyph for the Ka, the double or personality-soul . . . ."[56] Zaki Aly repeats the same statement and calls this explanation "ingenious and plausible."[57] Hooper[58] thinks that "a connection between outstretched arms and the hieroglyphic symbol of the *Ka* . . . is appealing, but the relationship between the two may

Milne, *Greek Inscriptions*, Pl. VIII, No. 9207, and p. 55 (standing figure), and Hooper, *Funerary Stelae*, Pls. V *d*, XII *b* and *d* (small figures), and esp. Pl. IX *a–b;* cf. further Crum, *Coptic Monuments*, Pl. LII, No. 8693 (reproduced also by Leclercq, *op. cit.* p. 2318, Fig. 9098), with Hooper, *Funerary Stelae*, Pl. VII *c*, No. 58, and *SAAB* XL 115, Fig 8.

[53] See Zaki Aly in *SAAB* XXXVIII 62; cf. Leclercq, *op. cit.* pp. 2291–2322, where classical, Egyptian, and Christian *orans* gestures are discussed, but the question of origin is not treated.

[54] Crum in *Proceedings of the Society of Biblical Archaeology* XXI 251 f.; cf. Zaki Aly in *SAAB* XXXVIII 63 f., where he repeats Crum's argument, but without proper reference.

[55] Edgar, *Greek Sculpture*, pp. xii f. Edgar's statement is repeated by Zaki Aly in *SAAB* XXXVIII 62, again without proper reference.

[56] Bonner in *Proceedings of the American Philosophical Society* LXXXV 89.

[57] *SAAB* XXXVIII 64. Neither Bonner nor Zaki Aly correctly understood Ebers' suggestion. In his study of Coptic art, Ebers referred not to the *kꜣ* sign as such but to the hieroglyphic figure of a man with raised arms, that is, *ḳꜣỉ*, meaning "tall," "high," "exalted," etc. It is the latter sign which Ebers thought influenced Coptic representation of figures with upraised arms: "Das alte 𓂓, das an der hieroglyphischen Figur 𓀠 das Hohe und auch die Erhebung des Gemüthes sammt den mit ihr zusammenhängenden Handlungen wie Freude, Dank, Gebet symbolisirt, finden wir sicher an mehreren menschlichen Gestalten . . . " (G. Ebers, *Sinnbildliches: Die Koptische Kunst* [Leipzig, 1892] p. 22).

[58] See *Funerary Stelae*, pp. 19 f.

only be coincidental." He goes on to say that "the use of the human figure with arms held upward appears to have been general throughout the ancient world," from Mesopotamia to Crete[59] and from predynastic to Ptolemaic and Roman times.

It is certainly true that representations of figures with upraised arms occur throughout the ancient world from prehistoric times to the latest period[60] and that they frequently occur on Egyptian coffins from the Middle Kingdom to Ptolemaic and Roman times. This gesture is often associated with the goddesses Isis, Nephthys, Nut, and Amentet, who, together with other deities, are often painted or engraved on coffins. Their pictures are accompanied by texts which promise special protection to the dead, who are often identified with Osiris. These pictures show the arms raised in two different positions: extended straight out from the shoulders and bent upward at the elbows[61] or less extended and bent upward at the elbows.[62] Variation in the position of the arms is found on Greco-Egyptian as well as Coptic stelae. The resemblance between the figures with upraised arms on Greco-Egyptian and Coptic stelae and those of Egyptian goddesses painted or engraved on coffins seems to point to an artistic tradition which developed during the Middle Kingdom, continued until the syncretistic Greco-Egyptian period, and was carried over into Christian Coptic art. Therefore, the *orans* gesture seen on Egyptian funerary monuments of the syncretistic period may be said to have a certain "Egyptian genealogy" and may be "ascribed to native influence." We think, however, that this influence may have been of a purely external nature, carried on by artists who were long exposed to the visual stimulation of a variety of similar motifs. It was especially the popular artist who in the late period, led by the external similarity of funerary motifs, kept reproducing them, often without understanding their inner meaning and their distinctive characteristics. The position of the arms of the Egyptian goddesses represented on coffins is associated with the idea of "protecting" and "encircling" the deceased resting in

[59] See summary of Mary H. Swindler's paper entitled "The Goddess with Upraised Arms" in *AJA* XLV (1941) 87 and cf. Hooper, *Funerary Stelae*, p. 39, n. 63.

[60] To examples previously known from various collections add Wessel, *Koptische Kunst*, p. 95, Fig. IV.

[61] See e.g. the representation of a goddess on a 12th-dynasty coffin in William C. Hayes, *Royal Sarcophagi of the XVIII Dynasty* (Princeton, 1935) Fig. 20; see also *ibid.* Pl. XV (Isis) and frontispiece (Nephthys). For Isis and Nephthys see also British Museum, *Hieroglyphic Texts from Egyptian Stelae*, Part VIII, by I. E. S. Edwards (London, 1939) Pls. XVI and XVIII, and *ASAE* XLIV, Pls. XVIII–XIX. For Nut see E. A. W. Budge, *The Mummy* (Cambridge, 1925) Pl. XXXII.

[62] See e.g. P. Lacau, *Sarcophages antérieurs au Nouvel Empire* (Le Caire, 1903–4) Pl. XVIII, No. 28072; for representations of Nut see Gauthier, *Cercueils anthropoïdes*, Pls. II, VI, XX, XXXIV, XXXVI, and for Amentet see Maspero and Gauthier, *Sarcophages des époques persane et ptolémaïque*, Pl. IV.

the coffin, as the accompanying texts mention,[63] and not with the idea of adoration, prayer, or worship, which seems to be most generally accepted as the significance of the *orans* gesture.

Whether the "Egyptian genealogy" of the *orans* gesture can be pressed even further and associated with the hieroglyphic sign *ḳ3ỉ* representing a man with arms raised above his head, as Ebers thought, is highly questionable. The word *ḳ3ỉ* means "(be) high," "(be) exalted," etc.; the sign is also used as a determinative with words meaning "joy," "rejoice," "extol," "mourn," and, as Gardiner pointed out,[64] with "dancing" at a funeral. But this seems a tenuous and vague association, and a relationship between the hieroglyph of a man with upraised arms and the figures on Greco-Egyptian and Coptic stelae must be said to be highly questionable in the least, if not altogether unacceptable. It should be recalled that this hieroglyphic sign is not used to indicate a gesture of prayer, adoration, or worship. The latter, as can be seen on numerous stelae and Book of the Dead papyri, is usually denoted by a quite different position of the arms: extended in front, bent at the elbows, with the palms of the hands turned outward.

The same can be said in regard to a relationship between the figures on Greco-Egyptian stelae and the hieroglyphic sign for *k3*. The word *k3*, represented by two raised arms, has many meanings: alter ego, personality, fortune, kingship, etc. But there is no relationship, in either meaning or representation, between the sign for *k3* and the *orans* figures on Greco-Egyptian and Coptic stelae.

Still, although we must reject the possibility of any derivation of the *orans* gesture from the Egyptian *ḳ3ỉ* and *k3* signs, we wish to point to some Egyptian representations of figures with upraised arms which may be considered the first occurrences of *orantes* and might have served as models for the stonecutters and designers of the Greco-Egyptian stelae.

One such representation, published by Heinrich Schäfer,[65] shows the figure of a man with both arms extended out from the shoulders, bent at the elbows, and the forearms raised in a vertical position. It is painted on a small wooden coffin of a mummified serpent which is now in the Berlin Museum. On either side of the man with upraised arms is a brief hieratic inscription which reads *ḥtpw ḥtpw*, "peace, peace,"[66] and which the man addresses to the serpent god called *p3-nb-ʿnḫ*, "the lord of life,"[67] represented on the two longer sides of

[63] See Hayes, *Royal Sarcophagi*, pp. 188 and 89 (text 15), pp. 188 and 120 (text 16); Badawi in *ASAE* XLIV 193 and 197, Pls. XVIII–XIX.

[64] In *JEA* XLI (1955) 10 f.

[65] *ZAS* LXII (1927) 40 f. and Fig. 2.

[66] Schäfer translates it "Gnade, Gnade" (*ibid.* p. 41, n. 3).

[67] See Spiegelberg in *ZAS* LXII 38.

the coffin. This coffin is certainly pre-Ptolemaic and very probably belongs to the Persian period in Egypt.[68] Unlike the figures of Egyptian goddesses painted or carved on coffins, this is a human figure shown in an attitude of adoration or prayer and is therefore to be considered the oldest example of the *orans* gesture found in Egypt thus far.

A funerary stela in the British Museum[69] shows three figures, a child between two adults, with arms raised in the same position as those of the man adoring the serpent god on the Berlin coffin; they are being escorted by Anubis to Osiris seated on a throne. A demotic inscription carved below the scene contains the names of the three individuals adoring Osiris. The stela is dated by Spiegelberg to the Roman period.[70]

At this point we wish to call attention to an uninscribed stela[71] showing a figure clad in the Egyptian manner which bears striking resemblance to the figure painted on the Berlin serpent coffin, especially in the posture and the position of the arms. In our opinion, these two monuments and the British Museum stela described above are to be considered the models after which the Greco-Egyptian and Roman stelae were produced. On all three monuments human, not divine, figures are represented with arms upraised in an attitude of adoration or prayer, in the presence of deities on two of the monuments; the faces of the adoring figures are all shown in profile. From these figures the line of stylistic development leads to the first *orantes* shown *en face*[72] and then to the well developed figures of the later Greco-Egyptian stelae which are exemplified by the stela of Isarous.

When younger peoples came to Egypt to learn, "she had only memories left," as John A. Wilson puts it. And, yet, the younger peoples did learn from her; if not that best she once could offer, at least they learned what they felt they needed. Thus the "slumbering colossus," as Wilson calls Egypt, deserved that "mysterious air of majesty" which in her late days she wore.

The small monument dedicated to a young girl, Isarous, is an example of that fascination which ancient Egypt exerted upon the younger Greeks when they came in contact with her, settled amidst her people, and intermingled

[68] See *ZAS* LXII 38 and 41; see also J. Leibovitch in *ASAE* XLIV 252.

[69] See Schäfer in *ZAS* LXII 41 f. and Fig. 4; the picture is also shown in A. Erman, *A Handbook of Egyptian Religion*, trans. by A. S. Griffith (London, 1907) p. 231, Fig. 119. See also S. Sharpe, *Egyptian Inscriptions from the British Museum* II (London, 1855) 64. Hooper, *Funerary Stelae*, p. 39, n. 62, refers to this stela and states that it "may be a prototype of the Kom Abou Billou stelae" but fails to discuss this point.

[70] See *ZAS* LXII 41, n. 6.

[71] *SAAB* XXXVIII, Pl. XVI and p. 86; see also n. 22 on p. 104 above.

[72] See Hooper, *Funerary Stelae*, p. 11 and Pl. IX *a–b*.

with them. They copied her ancient symbols and assimilated some of the ideas which these symbols expressed, while at the same time they preserved the freshness of their younger culture, their language, and their not-so-serious outlook on the life beyond.

We are happy to dedicate these lines to John A. Wilson, who taught us so well what Egypt meant to the ancient world.

BIBLIOGRAPHY OF JOHN A. WILSON

Elizabeth B. Hauser

BOOKS

The Burden of Egypt: An Interpretation of Ancient Egyptian Culture ("Oriental Institute Essay"). Chicago: University of Chicago Press, 1951.

La cultura Egipcia. Traducción de Florentino M. Torner. México: Fondo de Cultura Económica, 1953. (Spanish translation of *The Burden of Egypt* [Chicago, 1951].)

The Culture of Ancient Egypt ("Phoenix Books" P11). Chicago: University of Chicago Press, 1956. (First published as *The Burden of Egypt* [Chicago, 1951].)

Al-ḥaḍārah al-Miṣrīyyah. Translation by Aḥmad Fakhrī. Cairo: Renaissance Book Shop, 1957. (Arabic translation of *The Burden of Egypt* [Chicago, 1951].)

L'Égypte: Vie et mort d'une civilisation. Traduction par Élisabeth Julia. Grenoble-Paris: Arthaud, 1961. (French translation of *The Burden of Egypt* [Chicago, 1951] with preface by Georges Posener.)

Signs & Wonders upon Pharaoh: A History of American Egyptology. Chicago: University of Chicago Press, 1964.

La civiltà dell'antico Egitto. Traduzione di Mariangela Vandoni. Milano: Arnoldo Mondadori, 1965. (Italian translation of *The Burden of Egypt* [Chicago, 1951].)

JOINT PUBLICATIONS AND CONTRIBUTIONS

The Language of the Historical Texts Commemorating Ramses III. Part II of *Medinet Habu Studies, 1928/29* ("Oriental Institute Communications," No. 7). Chicago: University of Chicago Press, 1930.

Medinet Habu. Vol. I: *Earlier Historical Records of Ramses III* ("Oriental Institute Publications," Vol. VIII). By the Epigraphic Survey. Chicago: University of Chicago Press, 1930.

Medinet Habu. Vol. II: *Later Historical Records of Ramses III* ("Oriental Institute Publications," Vol. IX). By the Epigraphic Survey. Chicago: University of Chicago Press, 1932.

Medinet Habu. Vol. III: *The Calendar, the "Slaughterhouse," and Minor Records of Ramses III* ("Oriental Institute Publications," Vol. XXIII). By the Epigraphic Survey. Chicago: University of Chicago Press, 1934.

"The Ferment of Progressive Ideals within Organized Religion among the Hebrews." Chapter in "The Reconstructive Forces of the Christian Religion," Study VII. American Institute of Sacred Literature, *The Institute* XVIII, No. 7 (Chicago, 1934).

"School Writings of the Middle Kingdom and Empire," pp. 901–5 in *Mélanges Maspero*, Vol. I, 2d fasc. ("Mémoires de l'Institut français," Vol. LXVI). Le Caire: L'Institut français d'archéologie orientale, 1935–38.

Historical Records of Ramses III: The Texts in Medinet Habu Volumes I and II Translated with Explanatory Notes ("Studies in Ancient Oriental Civilization," No. 12). With WILLIAM F. EDGERTON. Chicago: University of Chicago Press, 1936.

"Hieroglyphic Inscriptions," pp. 11–13 in GORDON LOUD, *The Megiddo Ivories* ("Oriental Institute Publications," Vol. LII). Chicago: University of Chicago Press, 1939.

Medinet Habu. Vol. IV: *Festival Scenes of Ramses III* ("Oriental Institute Publications," Vol. LI). By the Epigraphic Survey. Chicago: University of Chicago Press, 1940.

The Intellectual Adventure of Ancient Man: An Essay on Speculative Thought in the Ancient Near East ("Oriental Institute Essay"). With H. and H. A. FRANKFORT, THORKILD JACOBSEN, and WILLIAM A. IRWIN. Chicago: University of Chicago Press, 1946.

Before Philosophy. The Intellectual Adventure of Ancient Man: An Essay on Speculative Thought in the Ancient Near East ("Pelican Books" A198). With H. and H. A. FRANKFORT and TH. JACOBSEN. Harmondsworth, Middlesex: Penguin Books, 1949.

Ancient Near Eastern Texts Relating to the Old Testament. Edited by JAMES B. PRITCHARD, Egyptian texts translated by JOHN A. WILSON. Princeton, New Jersey: Princeton University Press, 1950; 2d ed., corrected and enlarged, 1955.

Frühlicht des Geistes: Wandlungen des Weltbildes im alten Orient ("Urban-Bücher," Nr. 9). With HENRI and H. A. FRANKFORT and THORKILD JACOBSEN. Stuttgart: W. Kohlhammer Verlag, 1954. (German translation of *The Intellectual Adventure of Ancient Man* [Chicago, 1946] without chapters VII–IX and plates.)

Medinet Habu. Vol. V: *The Temple Proper.* Part I ("Oriental Institute Publications," Vol. LXXXIII). By the Epigraphic Survey. Chicago: University of Chicago Press, 1957.

El pensamiento prefilosófico. Traducción de ELI DE GORTARI. 2d ed. México: Fondo de Cultura Económica, 1958. (Spanish translation of *The Intellectual Adventure of Ancient Man* [Chicago, 1946].)

"Introduction" to JAMES HENRY BREASTED, *Development of Religion and Thought in Ancient Egypt* ("Harper Torchbooks," No. 57). New York: Harper, 1959.

"Ägypten." Chapter in *Propyläen Weltgeschichte.* Vol. I. Berlin etc.: Propyläen Vorlag, 1961.

"Egyptian Culture and Religion." Chapter in *The Bible and the Ancient Near*

East: Essays in Honor of William Foxwell Albright. Edited by G. ERNEST WRIGHT. Garden City, New York: Doubleday, 1961.

Medinet Habu. Vol. VI: *The Temple Proper*. Part II ("Oriental Institute Publications," Vol. LXXXIV). By the Epigraphic Survey. Chicago: University of Chicago Press, 1963.

Most Ancient Verse. Selected and translated by THORKILD JACOBSEN and JOHN A. WILSON, with an introduction by DAVID GRENE. Chicago: The Oriental Institute of the University of Chicago, 1963.

"Egypt—The Kingdom of the 'Two Lands.'" Chapter in *At the Dawn of Biblical History*. E. A. SPEISER, Editor ("The World History of the Jewish People." First Series: "Ancient Times." Vol. I). London: W. H. Allen, 1964.

Medinet Habu. Vol. VII: *The Temple Proper*. Part III ("Oriental Institute Publications," Vol. XCIII). By the Epigraphic Survey. Chicago: University of Chicago Press, 1964.

"A Century of Near Eastern Archaeology and the Future," pp. 113–22 in *The Role of the Phoenicians in the Interaction of Mediterranean Civilizations*. Edited by WILLIAM WARD. Beirut: American University Centennial Publications, 1968.

"Egitto." Traduzione di FERNANDO SOLINAS. Bibliographical details unknown. (Italian translation of "Ägypten" [Berlin, 1961].)

ARTICLES

"The Texts of the Battle of Kadesh," *American Journal of Semitic Languages and Literatures* XLIII (1926/27) 266–87.

"On Papyrus Harris 78:8—10; 79:3," *Zeitschrift für ägyptische Sprache und Altertumskunde* LXV (1930) 60–61.

"Ceremonial Games of the New Kingdom," *Journal of Egyptian Archaeology* XVII (1931) 211–20.

"Ancient Text Corrections in Medinet Habu," *Zeitschrift für ägyptische Sprache und Altertumskunde* LXVIII (1932) 48–56.

"The Descendants of *ḥwny-r-ḥr*," *ibid.* pp. 56-67.

"The ᶜ*EPERU* of the Egyptian Inscriptions," *American Journal of Semitic Languages and Literatures* XLIX (1932/33) 275–80.

"The Kindly God," *ibid.* pp. 150–53.

"Life Eternal in Old Egypt," *Asia* XXXIII (1933) 236–42.

"The Libyans and the End of the Egyptian Empire," *American Journal of Semitic Languages and Literatures* LI (1934/35) 73–82.

"Illuminating the Thrones at the Egyptian Jubilee," *Journal of the American Oriental Society* LVI (1936) 293–96.

"What Was Civilization?" *Presbyterian Tribune* LII, No. 12 (New York, 1937) pp. 7–8.

"Arnold Walther, May 31, 1880–May 18, 1938," *American Journal of Semitic Languages and Literatures* LV (1938) between pp. 224 and 225.

"The Megiddo Ivories," *American Journal of Archaeology* XLII (1938) 333–36.

"Between Wars: The First Twenty Years of the Oriental Institute," *University of Chicago Magazine*, November 1939, pp. 4–9.

"Shouts in the Temple," Chicago Drama League, *The Curtain Rises* II, No. 2 (November 1939) pp. 8 and 22.

"The Egyptian Middle Kingdom at Megiddo," *American Journal of Semitic Languages and Literatures* LVIII (1941) 225–36.

"Funeral Services of the Egyptian Old Kingdom," *Journal of Near Eastern Studies* III (1944) 201–18.

"Possibilities of World Understanding," International House, *The International Quarterly* VIII, No. 1 (New York, 1944) pp. 14–16 and 44–46.

"The Assembly of a Phoenician City," *Journal of Near Eastern Studies* IV (1945) 245.

"Albert Ten Eyck Olmstead, 1880–1945," *Journal of Near Eastern Studies* V (1946) 1–6.

"The Near East in 1946," *The Biblical Archaeologist* IX (1946) 70–73.

"The Artist of the Egyptian Old Kingdom," *Journal of Near Eastern Studies* VI (1947) 231–49.

"The Oath in Ancient Egypt," *Journal of Near Eastern Studies* VII (1948) 129–56.

"The Oriental Institute: Thirty Years and the Present," with THORKILD JACOBSEN, *Journal of Near Eastern Studies* VIII (1949) 236–47.

"Three Decades of the Breasted Vision," *University of Chicago Magazine*, May 1949, pp. 8–9 and 20.

"Ancestral Voices Prophesying," American Library Association, *ALA Bulletin* XLV (1951) 316–23.

"A Note on the Edwin Smith Surgical Papyrus," *Journal of Near Eastern Studies* XI (1952) 76–80.

"A Group of Sixth Dynasty Inscriptions," *Journal of Near Eastern Studies* XIII (1954) 243–64.

"Harold Hayden Nelson, 1878–1954," *ibid.* p. 118.

"Three Comments on Orthogenetic and Heterogenetic Urban Environments: Cities in Ancient Egypt," *Economic Development and Cultural Change* III, No. 1 (October 1954) p. 74.

"The New Discoveries in Egypt," *The Near East*, December 1954, pp. 7–15.

"Egyptian Technology, Science, and Lore," *Journal of World History* II (1954/55) 209–13.

"Buto and Hierakonpolis in the Geography of Egypt," *Journal of Near Eastern Studies* XIV (1955) 209–36.

"Henri Frankfort (1897–1954)," *Year Book of the American Philosophical Society*, 1955, pp. 439–42.

"Nasser Wins by Defeat," *University of Chicago Magazine*, February 1957, pp. 11–13 and 28.

"Egypt's Positive Neutralism," *The Delphian Quarterly* XLIII, No. 3 (Summer 1960) pp. 1–5 and 17.

"A Late Egyptian Book of the Dead," Oberlin College, *Bulletin of the Allen Memorial Art Museum* XIX (1961/62) 91–96.

"Water and Ancient Egypt," Ermitazh, Leningrad, *Travaux du Département oriental* (*Trudy Otdela Vostoka*), 1963(?), pp. 125–28.

"Would You Believe . . . ," University of Chicago, *Chicago Today* IV, No. 1 (Winter 1967) pp. 30–36.

"Crackpots and Forgeries," University of Chicago, *Chicago Today* V, No. 1 (Winter 1968) pp. 50–54.

"The Joseph Smith Egyptian Papyri: Translations and Interpretations," *Dialogue: A Journal of Mormon Thought* III (1968) 67–85.

VARIA

The Texts of the Battle of Kadesh. Typewritten thesis (Ph.D.). University of Chicago, 1926.

"Introduction" to the film *Human Adventure* for colleges. Same for high schools. Mimeographed. Chicago, n.d.

"Biographical Memoir of James Henry Breasted, 1865–1935." Presented to the National Academy of Sciences, 1936. Published, with Breasted bibliography, in the Academy's *Biographical Memoirs* XVIII (1937) 94–121.

"Exploring Civilization." Convocation address, 1937. Published in *University of Chicago Magazine*, April 1937, pp. 9–11.

"An Archeologist Looks at Civilization." Published in *Hyde Park Baptist News* I, No. 3 (Chicago, 1937).

"The New Past in Archeology." Radio address. Published in *Talk: A Quarterly Digest of Addresses . . . Broadcast over the Columbia Network* II, No. 3 (New York, 1937) pp. 21–26.

"The New Past." Radio series: "Archaeology—What Is It?" "Diggers' Luck." "Detective Work on Dead Languages." Mimeographed. Chicago, 1937.

"The Present State of Egyptian Studies." Published in *The Haverford Symposium on Archaeology and the Bible*. Edited by ELIHU GRANT. New Haven, Connecticut: The American Schools of Oriental Research, 1938.

"The Other End of the Telescope." Published in *Hyde Park Baptist News* III, No. 5 (Chicago, 1938).

"The Progress of Man." Radio discussion by JOHN WILSON, RICHARD McKEON, and LOUIS WIRTH. *The University of Chicago Round Table*, December 25, 1938.

"Archeology and the Higher Life." Published in *Hyde Park Baptist News* IV, No. 7 (Chicago, 1939).

"Ira Maurice Price, Scholar and Teacher." Memorial address, 1939. Published in *American Journal of Semitic Languages and Literatures* LVII (1940) 115–19.

A Radio Discussion of the Jews by MALCOLM WILLEY, LOUIS WIRTH, and JOHN WILSON. *The University of Chicago Round Table*, January 28, 1940.

"Archaeology As a Tool in Humanistic and Social Studies." Remarks addressed to archaeologists at the University of Chicago's 50th anniversary celebration, 1941. Published in *Journal of Near Eastern Studies* I (1942) 3–9.

"New Frontiers for the University." Convocation address, 1943. Published in *University of Chicago Magazine*, October 1943, pp. 8–10 and 14.

"The Near East." Lecture, 1946. Published in *A Foreign Policy for the United States*. Edited by QUINCY WRIGHT. Chicago: University of Chicago Press, 1947.

"Should a United Nations Army Enforce Partition of Palestine?" Radio discussion by *Sir* ARTHUR CREECH-JONES, BARTLEY CRUM, REINHOLD NIEBUHR, JOHN WILSON, and WALTER WRIGHT. *The University of Chicago Round Table*, February 22, 1948.

"The Case of the Two Coptic Patriarchs." Story published in *The Baker Street Journal: An Irregular Quarterly of Sherlockiana* IV, No. 1 (New York, 1949) pp. 74–85.

"Five Thousand Years of Modern Egypt." Lecture, 1951. Condensation published in *Bulletin of the Near East Society* IV, No. 7 (September 1951) pp. 3 and 10–11.

"What Does the American Heritage Mean?" Radio discussion by RALPH E. ELLSWORTH, CLARENCE R. DECKER, and JOHN A. WILSON. *Northwestern University Reviewing Stand* XVI, No. 24 (July 15, 1951).

"The Constitution of Ancient Egypt." Two lectures, 1952. Condensation published in Alexandria University, *Bulletin of the Faculty of Arts* X (1956) 3–35.

"Oriental History: Past and Present." American Oriental Society presidential address, 1952. Published in *Journal of the American Oriental Society* LXXII (1952) 49–55.

"Islamic Culture and Archaeology." Paper for Colloquium on Islamic Culture at Princeton University, 1953. Published in *Middle East Journal* VIII (1954) 1–9.

"Authority and Law in Ancient Egypt." Paper for Symposium on Authority and Law in the Ancient Orient, 1954. Published in *Journal of the American Oriental Society*, Supplement No. 17 (1954) pp. 1–7.

"The Idea of a University." Radio discussion by LAWRENCE A. KIMPTON, CHARLES H. PERCY, and JOHN A. WILSON. *The University of Chicago Round Table*, June 5, 1955.

"The Royal Myth in Ancient Egypt." Paper, 1956. Published in *Proceedings of the American Philosophical Society* C (1956) 439–42.

"Tensions in the Near East." Lecture, 1956. Printed and distributed by the Citizens' Board of the University of Chicago.

"Civilization without Cities." Paper for Symposium on Urbanization and Cultural Development in the Ancient Near East, 1958. Published in *City Invincible*. Edited by CARL H. KRAELING and ROBERT M. ADAMS. Chicago: University of Chicago Press, 1960.

"Temples on the River Nile." Address, 1960. Printed and distributed by the Citizens' Board of the University of Chicago.

"Rescue on the Nile." Lecture, 1961. Condensation published in *Context: A University of Chicago Magazine* I, No. 1 (Spring 1961) pp. 1–3.

"La révolution d'Amarna." Extracted from *L'Égypte: Vie et mort d'une civilisation* (Traduction par Élisabeth Julia [Paris, 1961]). *La table rond,* No. 162 (Juin 1961) pp. 27–53.

"Medicine in Ancient Egypt." Paper for Symposium on Medical Lore and Practice in the Ancient Near East, 1961. Published in *Bulletin of the History of Medicine* XXXVI (1962) 114–23.

"Ancient Egyptian Medicine." Editorial in *Journal of the International College of Surgeons,* Section I, Vol. XLI, No. 6 (June 1964) pp. 665–73.

"Triumph and Failure in Ancient Egypt." University of Chicago Monday Lectures, 1966/67. Published in *Changing Perspectives on Man.* Edited by Ben Rothblatt. Chicago and London: University of Chicago Press, 1968.

BOOK REVIEWS

Badre, Albert Y., and Siksek, Simon G. *Manpower and Oil in the Arab Countries* (American University of Beirut, Faculty of Arts and Sciences, "Social Science," No. 16). Beirut, n.d. *Middle East Journal* XV (1961) 476.

Beckerath, Juergen von. *Tanis und Theban: Historische Grundlagen der Ramessidenzeit in Aegypten* ("Aegyptologische Forschungen," Vol. XVI). Glückstadt: J. J. Augustin, 1951. *Journal of Near Eastern Studies* XIII (1954) 126–29.

The Cambridge Ancient History. Revised Edition of Volumes I & II (as issued in fascicles). Cambridge, England: The University Press. *Journal of the American Oriental Society* LXXXIII (1963) 116–18.

Vol. I, Chap. XIV. W. Stevenson Smith, *The Old Kingdom in Egypt and the Beginning of the First Intermediate Period.* 1962.

Vol. I, Chap. XX. William C. Hayes, *The Middle Kingdom in Egypt: Internal History from the Rise of the Heracleopolitans to the Death of Ammenemes III.* 1961.

Vol. II, Chap. II. William C. Hayes, *Egypt: From the Death of Ammenemes III to Seqenenre II.* 1962.

Vol. II, Chap. IX. William C. Hayes, *Egypt: Internal Affairs from Tuthmosis I to the Death of Amenophis III.* Parts 1 and 2. 1962.

Chapman, Suzanne, and Dunham, Dows. *The Royal Cemeteries of Kush.* Vol. III. Boston: Museum of Fine Arts, 1952. *Journal of Near Eastern Studies* XIII (1954) 132–33.

Davies, Norman de Garis. *The Temple of Hibis in el Khargeh Oasis.* Part III: *The Decoration* ("Publications of the Metropolitan Museum of Art, Egyptian Expedition," Vol. XVII). New York, 1953. *American Journal of Archaeology* LX (1960) 70.

Dunham, Dows. *The Royal Cemeteries of Kush.* Vols. II and IV. Boston: Museum of Fine Arts, 1955 and 1957. *Journal of Near Eastern Studies* XVII (1958) 152–55 and XVIII (1959) 286–87.

EDEL, ELMAR. *Altägyptische Grammatik*. Vol. I. Roma: Pontificium Institutum Biblicum. *Journal of Near Eastern Studies* XVI (1957) 134–35.

EDWARDS, I. E. S. *The Pyramids of Egypt*. London: Penguin Books, 1947. *Journal of Near Eastern Studies* VII (1948) 128.

FERRÉ, NELS F. S. *Pillars of Faith*. New York: Harper & Bros., 1948. *Journal of Religion* XXVIII (1948) 229.

GARDINER, *Sir* ALAN. *Egypt of the Pharaohs: An Introduction*. Oxford: Clarendon Press, 1961. *Journal of Near Eastern Studies* XXI (1962) 67–72.

GARDINER, ALAN H. *The Royal Canon of Turin*. Oxford University Press, 1959. *Journal of Near Eastern Studies* XIX (1960) 297–99.

GARNOT, JEAN SAINTE FARE. *L'Hommage aux dieux sous l'ancien empire égyptien d'après les textes des pyramides*. Paris: Presses Universitaires de France, 1954. *Journal of Near Eastern Studies* XV (1956) 127–28.

GORDON, CYRUS H. *Lands of the Cross and Crescent*. Ventnor, New Jersey: Ventnor Publishers, Inc., 1948. *Journal of Near Eastern Studies* VII (1948) 128.

GREEN, MOSHE. *The Ḫab/piru* ("American Oriental Series," Vol. XXXIX). New Haven, Connecticut: American Oriental Society, 1955. *Journal of Near Eastern Studies* XVI (1955) 139–41.

GRINSELL, L. V. *Egyptian Pyramids*. Gloucester, England: John Bellows, Ltd., 1947. *Journal of Near Eastern Studies* XII (1953) 223.

Grosser historischer Weltatlas. Teil I: *Vorgeschichte und Altertum. Kartenwerk*. Erläuterungen von HERMANN BENGSTON und VLADIMIR MILOJČIČ. München: Bayerischer Schulbuch-Verlag, 1953. *Journal of Near Eastern Studies* XIV (1955) 186.

HAYES, WILLIAM C. *Egypt: From the Death of Ammenemes III to Seqenenre II*, *Egypt: Internal Affairs from Tuthmosis I to the Death of Amenophis III*, and *The Middle Kingdom in Egypt*. See the *Cambridge Ancient History*.

HAYES, WILLIAM C. *A Papyrus of the Late Middle Kingdom in the Brooklyn Museum*. Brooklyn: Brooklyn Museum, 1955. *American Journal of Archaeology* LX (1960) 68–70.

HAYES, WILLIAM C. *The Scepter of Egypt. A Background for the Study of Egyptian Antiquities in the Metropolitan Museum of Art*. Part I: *From the Earliest Times to the End of the Middle Kingdom*. New York: Harper in co-operation with the Metropolitan Museum of Art, 1953. *Journal of Near Eastern Studies* XIV (1955) 203–5.

Same. Part II: *The Hyksos Period and the New Kingdom (1675–1080 B.C.)*. Cambridge, Massachusetts: Harvard University Press, 1959. *Journal of Near Eastern Studies* XIX (1960) 296–97.

HELCK, WOLFGANG. *Untersuchungen zu den Beamtentiteln des ägyptischen Alten Reiches* ("Aegyptologische Forschungen," Vol. XVIII). Glückstadt: J. J. Augustin, 1954. *Journal of Near Eastern Studies* XV (1956) 263–65.

HINTZE, FRITZ. *Untersuchungen zu Stil und Sprache neuägyptischer Erzählungen* (Deutsche Akademie der Wissenschaften, Institut für Orientforschung, "Veröffentlichungen," Nr. 2). Berlin: Akademie Verlag, 1950. *Journal of Near Eastern Studies* XI (1952) 227–30.

JONCKHEERE, FRANS. *Le papyrus médical Chester Beatty* ("La médicine égyptienne," No. 2). Bruxelles: Fondation égyptologique Reine Élisabeth, 1947. *Journal of Near Eastern Studies* VII (1948) 128.

JOUGUET, PIERRE, and others. *Les premières civilisations*, nouvelle rédaction du volume paru sous le même titre en 1926 (*Peuples et civilisations: Histoire générale*, Vol. I). Paris: Presses Universitaires de France, 1950. *Journal of Near Eastern Studies* X (1951) 290.

KANTOROWICZ, ERNST H. *The King's Two Bodies: A Study in Mediaeval Political Theology*. Princeton, New Jersey: Princeton University Press, 1957. *Comparative Studies in Society and History* I (The Hague, 1959) 394–96.

Karnak-Nord IV (1949-1951) ("Fouilles de l'Institut français du Caire," Vol. XXV). Fouilles conduit par CL. ROBICHON, rapport de P. BARGUET et J. LECLANT. Le Caire: Institut français d'archéologie orientale, 1954. *Journal of Near Eastern Studies* XVI (1957) 63–64.

KOEFOED-PETERSEN, OTTO. *Les stèles égyptiennes* ("Publications de la Glyptothèque Ny Carlsberg," No.1). Copenhagen, 1948. *Journal of Near Eastern Studies* IX (1951) 115.

Kush. Vol. I. Khartoum: Sudan Antiquities Service, 1954. *Journal of Near Eastern Studies* XIV (1955) 275–76.

Land of Enchanters: Egyptian Short Stories from the Earliest Times to the Present Day. Edited by BERNARD LEWIS. London: Harvill Press, 1948. *Journal of Near Eastern Studies* IX (1950) 114–15.

MACADAM, M. F. LAMING. *The Temples of Kawa*. Vols. I and II. London: Oxford University Press, 1949 and 1955. *Journal of Near Eastern Studies* XII (1953) 63–65 and XVI (1957) 141–42.

MURRAY, MARGARET A. *The Splendour That Was Egypt: A General Survey of Egyptian Culture and Civilization*. New York: Philosophical Library, 1949. *Journal of Religion* XXX (1950) 278–79.

Never To Die: The Egyptians in Their Own Words, selected and arranged, with a commentary, by JOSEPHINE MAYER and TOM PRIDEAUX. New York: Viking Press, 1938. *The New Republic* XCVII (1938/39) 108–9.

OTTO, EBERHARD. *Ägypten: Der Weg des Pharaonenreiches*. Stuttgart: W. Kohlhammer Verlag, 1953. *Journal of Near Eastern Studies* XIV (1955) 276.

PORTER, BERTHA, and MOSS, ROSALIND L. B. *Topographical Bibliography of Ancient Egyptian Hieroglyphic Texts, Reliefs, and Paintings*. Vol. VII. Oxford: Clarendon Press, 1951. *Journal of Near Eastern Studies* XIII (1954) 126.

POSENER, GEORGES. *Littérature et politique dans l'Égypte de la XIIe Dynastie*. Paris: Honoré Champion, 1956. *Journal of Near Eastern Studies* XVI (1957) 275–77.

RANKE, HERMANN. *Die ägyptischen Personennamen*. Band II. Glückstadt: J. J.

Augustin, 1952. *Journal of the American Oriental Society* LXXIII (1953) 99–104.

RAPHAEL, MAX. *Prehistoric Pottery and Civilization in Egypt* ("The Bollingen Series," Vol. VIII). Translated by NORBERT GUTERMAN. Washington, D.C.: Pantheon Books, 1947. *Journal of Near Eastern Studies* IX (1950) 64.

SCHOTT, SIEGFRIED. *Altägyptische Liebeslieder, mit Märchen und Liebesgeschichten.* Zürich: Artemis-Verlag, 1950. *Journal of Near Eastern Studies* XII (1953) 220–21.

SMITH, JOSEPH LINDON. *Tombs, Temples & Ancient Art.* Norman, Oklahoma: University of Oklahoma Press, 1956. *Natural History* LXV (1956) 390–91.

SMITH, W. STEVENSON. *The Old Kingdom in Egypt and the Beginning of the First Intermediate Period.* See the *Cambridge Ancient History.*

SPARROW, GERALD. *The Sphinx Awakes.* New York: Pitman, 1956. *Journal of Modern History* XXIX (1957) 167–68.

STOCK, HANNS. *Der erste Zwischenheit Aegyptens* ("Analecta Orientalia," No. 31; "Studia Aegyptiaca," Vol. II). Roma: Pontificium Institutum Biblicum, 1949. *Journal of Near Eastern Studies* X (1951) 132.

SWAIN, JOSEPH WARD. *The Ancient World.* 2 vols. New York: Harper, 1950. *Journal of Near Eastern Studies* XI (1952) 87–88.

THOMPSON, *Sir* HERBERT. *The Coptic Version of the Acts of the Apostles, and the Pauline Epistles in the Sahidic Dialect.* Cambridge, England: Cambridge University Press, 1932. *American Journal of Semitic Languages and Literatures* L (1933/34) 110–12.

TILL, WALTER. *Koptische Dialektgrammatik mit Lesestücken und Wörterbuch.* München: C. H. Beck, 1931. *American Journal of Semitic Languages and Literatures* XLVIII (1931/32) 133.

VERCOUTTER, JEAN. *Essai sur relations entre Égyptiens et Préhèlenes* ("L'Orient ancien illustré," No. 6). Paris: Maisonneuve, 1954. *Journal of Near Eastern Studies* XIV (1955) 276.

WEILL, RAYMOND. *XIIe Dynastie, royauté de Haute-Égypte et domination Hyksos dans le Nord* (Institut français d'archéologie orientale, "Bibliothèque d'étude," Vol. XXVI). Le Caire, 1953. *Journal of Near Eastern Studies* XIV (1955) 131–33.

WERBROUCK, MARCELLE. *Le temple de Hatshepsout à Deir el Bahari.* Bruxelles: Fondation égyptologique Reine Élisabeth, 1949. *Journal of Near Eastern Studies* XI (1952) 296–98.

WINLOCK, H. E. *The Rise and Fall of the Middle Kingdom in Thebes.* New York: Macmillan Company, 1947. *Archaeology* II (1949) 109–10.